PRAISE FOR *Love by the Glass*

"A sophisticated and elegant book about love, marriage—
and the drink that made everything that much sweeter."
—*Rocky Mountain News*

"A memoir, a love story and a wine tutorial."
—*Chicago Tribune*

"Charming."
—*The Miami Herald*

"Candidly romantic . . . a timely taste of lives lived
happily and well with wineglass in hand."
—*The Seattle Times*

"I am deeply inspired by this heartwarming story of how
two people found love and—even better—a way to
get paid for drinking wine."
—DAVE BARRY

"Even for those of us who don't know Mondavi from Mateus,
Love by the Glass is a treat. Wine columnists Dottie Gaiter
and John Brecher have one of the best marriages
you'll ever see, and a delightful story to tell."
—CARL HIAASEN

"My weekly anticipation of the next John and Dottie column pales in comparison to my eagerness to pore over each page, each word of this brilliant autobiography of two phenomenal journalists. *Love by the Glass* exquisitely describes the lives and wines of this passionate duo who have so eloquently made wine accessible and compelled collectors of all varieties to 'open that bottle' and share the love that is wine."

—CHARLIE TROTTER

"This book is a warm and personal gift to all of us, a needed reminder that while wine is indeed for special occasions, every day you get to spend with those you love is a special occasion worth celebrating with wine."

—ANDREA IMMER

"*Love by the Glass* is a moving love story, a fascinating wine guide, and a compelling social history. How far we've all come from the innocence of Mateus rosé, and we couldn't hope for better guides to the ensuing decades than Dottie Gaiter and John Brecher. The story of their lives together has all the warmth and richness of the great wines they write about."

—JAMES B. STEWART

Photo: Mary Lou Foy

DOROTHY J. GAITER and JOHN BRECHER are the authors of "Tastings," the weekly wine column of *The Wall Street Journal*. John was Page One editor of the paper from 1992 to 2000, and Dorothy was a national reporter and editor covering issues of race. John previously worked at *The Miami Herald* and *Newsweek,* and Dorothy at *The Miami Herald* and *The New York Times*. They are known to television viewers from their appearances on *Martha Stewart Living, Today,* and CNBC, and are the authors of *The Wall Street Journal Guide to Wine*.

LOVE BY THE GLASS

Love by the Glass

Tasting Notes from a Marriage

Dorothy J. Gaiter
AND John Brecher

RANDOM HOUSE TRADE PAPERBACKS

NEW YORK

Library of Congress Cataloging-in-Publication Data

Gaiter, Dorothy J.
   Love by the glass : tasting notes from a marriage / Dorothy J. Gaiter and John Brecher.
       p.   cm.
   ISBN 0-8129-6686-4
   1. Gaiter, Dorothy J. 2. Brecher, John. 3. Wine writers—United States—Biography. I. Brecher, John. II. Title.

TP547.G28 A3   2002
641.2'2'092273—dc21
[B]   2001043100

Book design by Barbara M. Bachman

To Zoë and Media

Contents

Boone's Farm Apple Wine and Mateus

. . .

*W*E WERE TAPING A SHOW CALLED *The Splendid Table* for Minnesota Public Radio, and host Lynne Rossetto Kasper got right to the point. "All right, you two," she asked, "how do we get your jobs?" Sooner or later, people always ask us that. We review wine for a living.

Only a few people in the United States get paid to write full-time about wine for general-interest publications, and we're among those few. What's more, we write about it for one of America's biggest and most respected newspapers, *The Wall Street Journal*. Our column, which is called "Tastings," is popular and influential. We get fan mail every day. "I particularly enjoy the way you let millions of people into your lives for a vicarious experience of a personal pleasure," wrote one reader, Peter Daane, a lawyer from Newnan, Georgia. Or as John and Mimi Lonergan of

San Francisco put it simply: "We appreciate your informal, lifestyle-oriented view of wine."

People stop us on the street to say they saw us on Martha Stewart's television show or tasting Champagne with Katie and Matt on *Today.* They tell us we've had a positive impact on their lives. We get to taste great wines from all over the world and the *Journal* pays for it. While we don't take advantage of any other perks of the job—we don't accept any free wine, free meals, or free trips and we don't attend private events or press-only functions—we're those rare journalists who have nothing to complain about. In fact, we may be the only journalists in the world who have nothing to complain about. *Nada.*

Well, that's not entirely true. We did have a complaint, once. We were telling Dottie's cousin Jon Smith that our work on the column keeps us from drinking our own wine. We taste six or eight bottles of wine every night, which means we don't have the time or the inclination, after all of those, to open bottles from our own collection. We have about five hundred bottles now, sitting in a cleverly designed wine "cellar" that used to be a closet in our Manhattan apartment. Generally, these aren't great, expensive, rare wines. They're more special than that. They're wines we've collected over the years because they mean something to us. They're from our trips to wine regions in California, France, and Italy, signed bottles from winemakers, bottles that remind us of rowing in Central Park as the sun set or of snuggling on a cold night in front of a fireplace, bottles from the birth years of our daughters, Media (from the fine 1989 vintage) and Zoë (from the equally fine 1990 vintage). We long to drink some of these wines, and some of them need drinking, but there's no time anymore.

When we told Jon our dilemma, he paused for a second, tried to look empathetic, swiveled in his chair while holding his chin, then tried even harder to look empathetic. Finally, he couldn't help himself. "That's a real high-class problem," he said. It's the last time we complained about our jobs.

What were we supposed to tell Lynne Rossetto Kasper? That we had simply fallen into this job, by happenstance, because we were lucky? That we'd never imagined doing this for a living and didn't particularly want to because wine has always been an intimate pleasure for us, because we're shy—in John's case, deathly shy—and because we weren't sure that this was an appropriate job for people who had dedicated their lives to hard-nosed journalism? All of that would be true.

It would also be true, though, to say that we'd been preparing ourselves for this job for twenty-five years, almost since the first moment we met. We were born right in the sweet spot of the baby boom, in 1951, and while we didn't know it at the time, the years when we were growing toward legal drinking age mirrored a special time for wine in the United States. A visionary named Robert Mondavi, who thought Americans would be willing to pay more money for good American wine, opened his winery when we were fifteen. Sales of table wine in the United States finally passed those of high-alcohol fortified wines for the first time when we were sixteen. California had its first great vintage, with attendant media buzz, when we were seventeen. Richard Nixon took Schramsberg sparkling wine from California with him to China in 1972, amid an explosion of news coverage, when we were twenty-one. Per capita wine consumption in the United States, which had been almost flat between 1960 and 1968, surged more than 50 percent between 1968 and 1974, about the time that our budding interest in wine became a passion. When, as a very young couple, we bought General Foods Minute Brand Spanish Rice Mix, we discovered a special deal on a book called *Cooking with Wine* ("$1.50 cover price, for only 50 cents!"). We got it, of course. "Wine has played an important role in all ancient Western civilizations as a beverage, as a food additive, and as a medicine," it said.

Over the years, we have seen wineries come and go, wine-making legends die and others take their place, wines like Green Hungarian virtually disappear and Merlot appear from nowhere as the red wine of choice, whole new regions of the country become the latest winemaking hot spots, and entire nations suddenly put themselves on the wine map. We have seen Americans evolve from people who valued only imported wine to people who were comfortable only with California wine. We have watched the passage of a time when the most prized wines in America were the great wines of Bordeaux like Château Lafite-Rothschild to the advent of an era of bountiful wealth that led Americans, almost in a frenzy, to pay astonishing prices for California wines with names like Screaming Eagle.

Our path to professional paradise was a long and winding one. We're not sure we could tell anyone how to replicate it—hell, we're not sure we could do it again if we tried—but it's worth considering how a couple of ordinary people landed in such an extraordinary position. It has to do with commitment, hard work, and luck, but ultimately it comes down to passion, and not just for wine. Passion for life, for each other, for journalism, and for the romance and adventure of wine—not so much the liquid in the bottle as the history and the memories. In that sense, a piece of paradise is available, with a little effort, to lovers everywhere.

Finally, in response to Lynne Rossetto Kasper's question, Dottie said, "Actually, we were very serious journalists before we started doing this. I wrote about race in America for twenty-seven years." "And I was Page One editor of *The Wall Street Journal* for seven years," John said. "But we've been lifelong wine enthusiasts. We've been studying and drinking wine since we first met on June 4, 1973. We never thought about writing about it, but twenty-seven years later, here we are."

Lynne paused for a second and said: "Do you actually know what time it was on June 4, 1973?"

As a matter of fact, we do. If you want to understand how we found ourselves where we are today, that's a good place to start.

DOTTIE'S STORY

My parents liked to joke that they had a mixed marriage. Worrell Granville Gaiter was West Indian, one of ten children born to a contractor and a homemaker. His father had left his family in Nassau to get established in New Jersey. He sent for them seven years later. My dad was born in Seaside Heights, New Jersey, where the Gaiters were one of three black families in town. Dad went to high school, college, and then straight into the army and the Battle of the Bulge. Dorothy Ethel Seruby, one of six children born to a farmer and a housewife who was part Native American, lived in Leonardo, New Jersey, surrounded by relatives' homes, fruit trees, a pig pen, a hut where her father smoked meats, and a small grape arbor that he harvested to make wine.

When they met, Dad was a worldly-wise twenty-six-year-old whose friends called him "Luxury." Mom was twenty and a high school graduate, and, while not very sophisticated, was so pretty and charming that Dad immediately broke off his engagement to another woman. After their wedding, Dad taught cabinetmaking at historically black Tuskegee Institute in Alabama. My sister Juarlyn was born there. Then, all-black Florida A&M University (FAMU) in Tallahassee recruited Dad to teach "vocational education" skills such as carpentry, so the family moved there. But to get a master's degree in education, Dad had to move the family again because no Southern university would accept a black man into its graduate program. So Dad hauled the family back to New Jersey and commuted into Manhattan to earn his master's at New York University. I was born during this hiatus.

Our life revolved around FAMU, so I rarely saw white people. My parents gave parties for other young couples from faculty housing, and they served cocktails. I know this because, according to family lore, when Juarlyn was little she crawled around the floor at one of these soirees sipping discarded drinks.

When I was four, my sister Karen was born, and when she was two, our lives changed forever. We moved to Indonesia. A federal agency coordinated a program that sent black professors from Tuskegee to work with vocational education teachers in Indonesia, setting up technical training centers and developing curricula and machines so that Indonesia's rich natural resources could be better used. Dad was invited to go, even though he was at FAMU. He found a house and servants in Jakarta, and we followed. It was 1957. So rare was it for black Americans to travel abroad that people assumed we were African dignitaries. In Tokyo, curious people touched our kinky hair so often that Mom bought us snug-fitting caps.

I had gone to segregated schools in Florida, but at the International School there were children from about thirty different countries. It was wonderful. It was as though someone had given me a bowl of jelly beans and each one was a different color and flavor. So many friends to make, so many possibilities. Because there were so many nationalities and cultures, none was dominant, although fluency in English was required. I had friends from everywhere. Here, thousands of miles from America, my skin color was of little consequence. To my classmates, I was just their friend Dottie, first and foremost an American.

President Sukarno invited my parents to grand parties where Champagne, the real stuff, was served. Although my parents had a well-stocked bar for entertaining, there was never wine in it.

Sometimes it did contain surprises, like crème de menthe, an emerald-green liquid that was poured over chipped ice in small, pretty glasses. I sneaked a sip of it once, and the strong menthol taste cut off my breathing and made me cry. Adults enjoyed this?

When our two-year stint ended, my parents requested another overseas assignment. While that was being considered, we returned to Tallahassee, to second-class citizenship. School officials suggested we skip a few grades because the International School had pushed us ahead, but my parents thought we should rejoin the classmates we'd had before, so we did. It was a difficult readjustment, and I never did quite regain my footing. Many of my old classmates thought I was a little weird, and I'm sure I was. So I turned to books and became a voracious and precocious reader.

My parents had their own difficult adjustment to everyday hassles. When Mom became ill and needed to see a specialist who was white, she and Dad refused to sit in the colored waiting room. Their presence in the white waiting room made white patients so uncomfortable that the doctor saw her immediately. Brilliant. When we went to New Jersey to visit relatives for Christmas, we'd drive straight there, stopping only at gas stations to use the bathroom. Restaurants wouldn't serve us and hotels wouldn't put us up.

When we got to Grandpa's, we'd have so much fun. The adults drank his sweet red wine, and even we'd get a sip. On the only other occasion when we had wine, at home for Thanksgiving in the formal dining room, it was Mogen David Concord wine poured by Dad from that strangely shaped bottle with a screw cap. It's probably the reason I still love grape juice.

Finally we heard we could move to New Delhi, but Dad fell ill, so we stayed in Tallahassee and adjusted. Some stores wouldn't let blacks try on clothes, and they insisted they had no bathrooms. The bus company refused to serve blacks at its lunch counters, and that became a lightning rod for protests. Martin Luther King Jr.

came in and out of town to raise money and consult with one of his local lieutenants, Rev. C. K. Steele, who led the campaign—eventually successful—to desegregate city buses. Blacks had been arrested for sitting in "white seats" in the front of city buses. Now, in front of the new bus station in downtown Tallahassee, there is a statue of Reverend Steele. My parents didn't demonstrate, but they gave money and food to those who did.

Dad and I followed the news together. We watched terrible footage of demonstrations broken up by dogs and then read about them in the newspapers the next day. It struck me even then that the world could be changed by what reporters did, that whites could be touched to the point of understanding and maybe to action by what a reporter wrote about the aspirations of black Americans.

When I was twelve, doctors discovered Dad had a rare form of cancer. He'd been misdiagnosed and treated for ulcers for years. Now, doctors told us he had four years—tops. I stopped believing in God. But incredibly, we learned to laugh again. And we had Dad for eleven more years.

When integration finally came to Tallahassee schools in 1967 and my high school was closed, I got into Florida High, on the campus of virtually all-white Florida State University. I was the only black girl in the eleventh grade. I worked on the paper, on the yearbook, and in the theater, which helped me battle my shyness.

One Sunday not long after school had started, Mom asked if I'd like to go with her to hear Martin Luther King Jr. speak. I told her no, that I'd catch him next time. There was no next time. A few months later, while we were watching the evening news, there was a bulletin: Dr. King had been killed. Dad grabbed his keys and sped to FAMU's campus, where, as he expected, students, fueled by grief and anger, were milling about, looking for a way to vent. He was gone all night.

A few weeks later, when there was a statewide civil rights march on the Capitol, I joined it. With hundreds of other marchers around me, I was nevertheless terrified just looking at all of the armed highway patrolmen who surrounded us. My respect for people in lonely, isolated places who put their bodies in harm's way to press the cause of freedom grew immeasurably.

I applied that year to the University of Missouri, which has a famous school of journalism. I was on the campus in Columbia for three days before I saw another black person. Two weeks into my freshman year, I met a tall young black man named Nathan, who loved books as much as I did. As we grew closer, he'd often tease me, gently, about my sweaty palms. Other boys had noticed this, too, and said "Yuck!" before letting my hand go. Nathan took me, sweaty hands and all, to my first off-campus party, where I discovered Boone's Farm Apple Wine. It was sweet, light, not obviously alcoholic, and one glass lasted the whole night. If this was how to socialize in college, I was going to be all right.

The wine was made by Gallo—wasn't everything?—and it was 100 percent fermented apple juice. Gallo introduced it in 1961 and it was a major hit. In 1971, Gallo introduced Boone's Farm Strawberry Wine, which was apple wine with natural flavors of strawberries, my favorite fruit. In that wine's first year, Americans bought 7.5 million cases of it, 6.5 million cases more than projected. But in just a few years, both wines fell from favor. A small winery in California called Sutter Home introduced something called White Zinfandel that was a more sophisticated alternative for people who liked their wine simple and a little sweet.

Some journalism majors were starting a black student newspaper, *Blackout,* and needed volunteers. I was in. But Nathan was out. A heart ailment forced him to leave school. My first summer home, I found the *Capitol Canon,* a spunky, muckraking weekly, which was populated by people—"Jews, hippies, and freaks," the editor called them—who'd been rejected, like me, by the city's big paper, the conservative *Tallahassee Democrat*. I don't remember my salary, but I brought in my own typewriter and posed when they needed a model. I interned at the *St. Petersburg Times* the following summer and then at its afternoon sister, the *Evening Independent*. Both summers, I won a coveted Poynter Scholarship, named for Nelson Poynter, a small man of titanic integrity and courage who made those papers great. Missouri also gave me a scholarship and a work-study job.

My social life at Missouri wasn't bad. Near the end of my junior year, I met a cute guy named Jim who had a modest Afro. Unfortunately, he didn't like my huge Afro, or my African-print clothes, or my sense of humor. My hands sweat when he held them. For a while, I tried to be the woman he wanted, even perming my hair. But occasionally, the real Dottie would surface and all hell would break loose. As graduation loomed, the question of what should we do next came up. Neither of us could manage "that was nice, good-bye." We decided to get engaged.

Dad's health was worsening, so I thought it would be a good idea to return to Florida to be near him. Ron Martin, *The Miami Herald*'s managing editor, interviewed on campus and hired me on the spot, for $170 a week. Jim, of course, went ballistic. I hadn't even consulted him. If we were going to get married, obviously where I worked should be a joint decision, he said. I thought that should tell him something, but we nevertheless made plans for him to join me in Miami. I thought that would never happen and I was fairly certain that he didn't want it to happen. But we continued with our plans until months later, when I finally called the marriage off, much to the relief of my parents.

On June 4, 1973, at the age of twenty-one, I was the first of three new hires to arrive at *The Miami Herald*'s newsroom. As I surveyed my new digs, Steve Rogers, the metro editor, walked up with a young man at his side who was wearing gray flannel pants, a navy blazer, and dark-rimmed glasses. His eyes twinkled when they met mine. "This is John Brecher. He was editor of the *Colum-bia Daily Spectator*," Steve said. The *Columbia Daily Spectator* has cult status among college newspapers. Standing before me was its most recent editor. And, God, was he handsome. What's a girl to do? I raised my hands over my head and bowed three times. "Salami, Salami, Baloney!" I said. We laughed and I looked into those eyes again. It was as though I was looking into myself. I felt in my bones like I had known him forever. And there was another thing: When we shook hands, my palms were dry.

JOHN'S STORY

*M*y parents always liked to say that they had a mixed marriage. Ben Brecher was a Russian Jew and Ruth Osterweis was a German Jew. He lived in the South Bronx and she lived on Man-hattan's fashionable West End Avenue. They met and married dur-ing World War II. After the war, my father got a job as an accountant with Schenley, the liquor company, and my mother stayed home. When I was born, my parents decided that they didn't want their kids—my brother Jim was three—raised in New York City. So my father jumped at the chance when Schenley asked if he'd like to help open the new office in Jacksonville, Florida, which at that point seemed like it would become a major Southern hub for big companies.

Schenley was an odd place for my father to work because he didn't drink. He didn't like the taste of alcohol. Not even wine. Like most Americans in the 1950s, we never had wine in the house. When people entertained, they had highballs. Even my

mother occasionally had a slug of Southern Comfort at a party.
Wine wasn't rejected, it was just ignored—except at Passover, of
course, when my father would buy a bottle of Manischewitz Concord wine for the four cups of wine ritually served at the Seder.
Even the kids got four small sips. The first sip always tasted
great—sweet and grapy. Each successive sip tasted less great—
cloying and heavy.

Thanksgiving was different, too. Each year, on the day before
Thanksgiving, my father would come home with a brown paper
bag, and we'd all gather around. He'd open the bag and slowly pull
out the treasure inside. It was a bottle of champagne, Korbel from
California, heavy and strangely shaped, with foil at the top. On
Thanksgiving Day, after Grandma Helen had brought out the
turkey, it was my father's turn. He'd tear the green foil off the
champagne and we'd all cower in fear of what would happen next.
He'd point the bottle into the formal living room, which we never
used, unwrap the metal, and—*pop!*—the cork would fly into the
other room. The champagne was open. Thanksgiving had officially
begun.

When Schenley wanted my father to move back to New York,
he quit. He later became a car salesman at Gordon Thompson
Chevrolet ("Get Your No. 1 Buy on the No. 1 Car from Jacksonville's No. 1 Chevrolet Dealer!"). He may have been the only
Jewish car salesman in Jacksonville, a place where Jews were so
foreign that a neighbor once invited us over for dinner and told us
when we arrived: "I know you don't eat ham, so I made lobster."
My father worked six days a week and earned only commission,
which was usually about $25 per car. Money was very tight for a
very long time, but my mother worked hard to make sure we
never knew how bad things were.

In the long run, though, Chevys put me through Columbia. I
had wanted to return to New York since I was a little boy sitting in
Grandma Helen's window on West End Avenue watching all the

excitement pass by. I always knew I wanted to write, and I'd been increasingly drawn to journalism. It was the sixties and journalism was cool, thanks to the heroic efforts of some journalists covering civil rights. Not only that, but the Jacksonville paper, the *Florida Times-Union,* which was owned by the local railroad, was so awful that I was convinced it helped keep the city down. Indeed, Jacksonville developed a national reputation as one of the nation's more backward cities during the civil rights struggle. It closed its public pools rather than integrate them. I went to elementary school just on the edge of a black area—"Colored Town," white people called it—but the black kids were bused to a school far away. I never went to school with a black person until my senior year in high school, when a single black boy entered the school of two thousand. He seemed pleasant enough, but I never spoke to him. I remember that his last name was White.

I was accepted by Columbia, to my surprise, and arrived in New York alone, in a coat and tie, while students watched the Miracle Mets in the lounge. Only days later, a big redheaded guy from across the hall named Lou Dolinar knocked on my door. "There's a sit-in at P and S," he said. "I'm covering it for *Spectator.* Let's go." A sit-in! Wow! *Spectator* was the school newspaper, but I had no idea what P&S was. It turned out to be the Columbia University College of Physicians and Surgeons, the medical school. Lou and I walked into the office of an administrator, where a handful of longhaired students were sitting on the floor, languidly, in solidarity with a union. Right on! I was pretty well hooked on journalism right there. My first byline appeared the next morning, on the front page of the *Columbia Daily Spectator.*

I spent the next four years of college working at the paper and exploring New York as best I could on my budget, which was $37.50 a week. This was the high point of the sexual revolution, but I didn't know it at the time. I was shy and didn't know anything at all about women except what my mother had told me, which was basically this: Stay away from the wild ones. And stay away from the quiet ones, because they're the wildest of all. I spent all of my time at the newspaper, and rarely had a date. But when I did, I knew this: Take Mateus. If you really want to get lucky, take two bottles of Mateus. If the relationship ever gets serious, take Lancers.

Mateus is one of those names that bring a combination of warmth and horror to many people around our age. For so many of us, it was our first wine. The famous rosé from Portugal in the squat little bottle burst upon the world in 1942, the brainchild of Fernando van Zeller Guedes, whose family was a well-known producer of Port and vinho verde, a delightful white wine. He had been casting about during the war years for something new to offer wine drinkers who were hungry for new tastes and open to trying something from abroad. He came up with the idea of a medium-dry rosé. The wine grew extremely popular in the late sixties and early seventies and, at its peak, accounted for 40 percent of Portugal's export income.

Lancers was even more special. It was "imported," as the ads said, "the wine that puts a little class in your glass." At its height, in 1974, almost 700,000 cases of Lancers were sold in the United States. It's impossible to know how many children were conceived with Lancers in their bloodstream. We heard not too long ago about a Lancers representative who was pouring the wine at a promotional event when a middle-aged woman kept coming up, time and again, to request just a little bit more wine. Finally, the Lancers man said to her, "You really like this, don't you?" She looked at him wistfully and said, "This is the wine that I lost my virginity over."

I became editor in chief of the *Columbia Daily Spectator* just before the Watergate break-in. I was working as a summer intern for *The Wall Street Journal,* as a reporter in the Cleveland bureau, when it happened. I'd loved the *Journal* since I was seven years old, when a neighbor gave me a copy once as a joke and then was so charmed by my interest that he gave me a stack of his old copies every week. The *Journal* had a well-known intern program, so I applied and was assigned a reporting job in Cleveland, which I knew to be somewhere in the middle of the country.

This was a great time for journalism. No one was cooler than Woodward and Bernstein. I knew what I wanted to do with my life, and now I was pretty sure I knew I wanted to do it at the *Journal*. Not only was the journalism serious and seemingly incorruptible, but the people who worked there were nice, too. Some of my liberal friends at Columbia wondered why in the world I'd want to work for a tool of the capitalist establishment, but I always thought that truth wasn't political, and the *Journal* newsroom seemed committed to the truth.

When I graduated, I tried to stay in New York. I applied to the *Journal,* but they said I'd have to start someplace like Cleveland or Pittsburgh. *The New York Times* wanted me to start as a copyboy, which seemed insulting to the editor in chief of the *Columbia Daily Spectator.* So, because I knew Florida, I applied to papers there. Then the phone rang in my dorm room. It was Steve Rogers, metro editor of *The Miami Herald.* He wanted me to start immediately after graduation as South Dade bureau chief at a starting salary of $175 a week. Bureau chief! And I hadn't even turned twenty-two yet. I accepted the job on the spot.

The mailboxes at Columbia's dorms were all lined up along a wall. One day, just before graduation, I looked into my mailbox and found a small envelope. I tore it open and found a thin paperback book. It was *The Signet Book of Wine* by Alexis Bespaloff. "America is not a wine-drinking nation," it began. "In France, Italy, Spain, and Portugal, for example, wine is taken for granted as the daily beverage of its citizens. In America, the most popular beverage is milk, followed by soda and beer. The annual consumption of wine in France and Italy is more than 200 bottles per person;

the average American drinks two bottles a year of table wine." The book arrived with no note of explanation. I packed it in one of the two pieces of hard-sided brown Samsonite luggage I took to Miami that included all of my worldly possessions.

For graduation, my parents gave me $1,000, so I was able to find an apartment ($150 a month) and rent furniture ($25 a month) before I started work. Promptly at nine A.M. on Monday, June 4, I showed up.

The *Miami Herald* newsroom looked just like a newsroom was supposed to look, with plain desks lined up in a big room. Back then, it was filled with smoke, the sound of IBM Selectric type-writers, and tough reporters asking tough questions on tough deadlines. People still yelled "Copy!" to copy kids, who rushed their stories to the editing desk and then got coffee for the re-porters. When I walked in, Steve Rogers met me, shook my hand, and told me he wanted me to meet two other reporters who had started the same day.

There was one big aisle between the desks in the city room. We walked down it while reporters all around seemed to be breaking the latest Watergate news. On the left side, two rows from the back, Steve stopped. "This is Dorothy Gaiter," he said. "She's from the University of Missouri."

I was frozen. In front of me was a young woman with a medium-length Afro, huge eyes, and a massive smile. She was, simply, the cutest person I had ever seen. Her body seemed covered in sparkles that exploded all around her, and everything else in the room suddenly looked flat and dull. But there was some-thing more than that. I felt the instant I saw her that we had always been together, and knew we always would be.

LOVE BY THE GLASS

André Cold Duck

· · ·

THE FIRST WINE WE SHARED WAS ANDRÉ COLD DUCK. HEY, don't laugh. Okay, go ahead and laugh. It was a big deal then, a bizarre concoction with a bizarre label. The name *cold duck* was derived somehow from the German practice of blending already opened bottles of red, white, and sparkling wines so they wouldn't go to waste. The resulting cuvée was called *kalte Ende* or "cold end," which sounds like *kalte Ente,* which means "cold duck." In the early 1960s, David Gallo, who was co-president of the E. & J. Gallo Winery and the oldest son of Ernest Gallo, figured there was room in the market for a nationally marketed, inexpensive "domestic Champagne." So in 1965, when he was working in marketing, he oversaw the development and introduction of André Champagne. Two years later, he developed André Cold Duck, which was a red, sweet sparkling wine made from Concord grapes. By 1971, the winery was selling two million cases of it a year.

John's parents gave him a bottle as a housewarming present, and it sat in his refrigerator for months. John was posted to South Dade County, then the more rural part of the county. It turns out that being "South Dade bureau chief" meant he got a tiny little office in a town called Homestead and a massive area to cover by himself. Dottie was a general assignment reporter in the main office, a lumpen structure on Biscayne Bay, where we worked together every Sunday. As the weeks went on, we found it was fun to have lunch together along with a couple of other new reporters. Then we started to wait until the other reporters were out of the office and we would rush off to lunch alone. We could talk for hours, as though we were the only people in the world. We were so much alike in our outlooks and values that it was as though we'd been raised by the same parents. We even had a joint byline together, on a story about the annual New Year's Eve riot on Miami Beach. While we were dodging tear gas, a sweet thing happened. A drunken reveler stumbled up to us and drawled, "You two are beautiful together, man." Was it that obvious that there was something between us?

After months of rushing off together whenever we could, John mentioned to Dottie a story he was doing about U-Pick fields. Those were South Dade farms where you could pick your own food. It was fun, it was cheap, and it was a great story for the *Herald*'s weekend section. Maybe I could show you the U-Pick fields sometime, John suggested.

Without knowing it, John had touched Dottie's most vulnerable area: fruits and vegetables. Dottie is passionate about them. She had inherited that from her mother, whose father had grown cherries, peaches, mint, and corn. The date was set. On a beautiful winter day, we picked squash and lima beans and snap peas and eggplant and the most beautiful strawberries Dottie had ever seen. She sat on the ground and ate them, still warm from the sun, right off the plant. John thought he'd never seen anyone so pure, happy, and beautiful. We took all of the bounty to John's little one-bedroom apartment. Dottie simply sautéed the vegetables in butter and served them over rice that John had cooked.

Sweet, sparkling red wine is not a classic match with sautéed vegetables over rice, but that night, on our first date, no wine could have been better. We woke up the next morning as a couple.

It wasn't long before we told our parents.

John: *I had mentioned to my parents on the day I arrived at the* Herald *that I'd started work with two black women, and one was really cute. One night, when my father answered the phone, I said, "I'm actually dating someone." This surely pleased my father, who was concerned that I had been lonely for all of those months down in Homestead. My parents had visited a couple of times, and they were pretty much appalled by my rental furniture and solitary life. "That's great!" said my father. "Who is she?"*

"She's one of the reporters I started with," I said. "The cute one."

There was a momentary pause. "She's black, isn't she?" asked my father. "Yes," I said. My parents didn't raise the issue again.

Dottie: *When I called home, I told my father I was dating a colleague named John. "We started on the same day, he went to Columbia, and he's white and really nice," I said, rushing through the salient part. There was a momentary pause. "Well," my dad said, selecting his words carefully, "we always taught you to choose your friends by the content of their character." He had paraphrased Martin Luther King Jr. And that was it.*

In our first years together, we moved around a lot within South Florida. John became an editor and moved up the *Herald's* career ladder, from South Dade to North Dade to Palm Beach

County and back to Miami. Dottie moved up to bigger reporting jobs, from general assignment in Miami to school reporter in Fort Lauderdale to beat reporter back in Miami. We worked all the time—we were journalists, committed to changing the world, after all, and it was an exciting time for journalism. John's first front-page byline was about a gas station owner during the Arab oil embargo who forced motorists to buy his daughter's Girl Scout cookies if they wanted a fill-up. Our nascent interest in wine was our respite.

We started with Blue Nun. In Florida, supermarkets can sell wine, so when we shopped, we'd walk down a long aisle of so-so wines. In 1974, we certainly didn't know much about wine, though *The Signet Book of Wine* had piqued John's interest, and then Dottie's. When we were in the grocery store one day, we picked up a wine we'd seen advertised and that we knew to be popular: Blue Nun.

Blue Nun was a German wine that few Germans drank. It was a Liebfraumilch, which means "Milk of Our Blessed Mother." It is, in many ways, simply a low-end, generic German wine. As far back as 1910, an official body in Germany declared that Liebfraumilch was nothing but "a fancy name." The Sichel family of Mainz, Germany, made Blue Nun, and some of it was sold in the United States, even during Prohibition. The label back then showed a nun in a brown habit on a blue background. Peter Sichel, who represents the fourth generation of the family, which later became importers, says that as the wine became popular, customers and distributors started referring to it as "that wine with the blue nun label." After Prohibition was repealed, sales took off in the United States and the label was changed to read "Blue Nun Label." But there was a hitch. Because of religious concerns, the federal government which has to approve all wine labels, decided it couldn't really allow a nun on the label, so post-Prohibition labels sported a picture of farm girls, Mr. Sichel says. After arguing that other countries with large populations of Catholics allowed the labels to have a nun on them, Mr. Sichel got his way. It wasn't until 1963, though, that the word *label* was dropped from the label.

Blue Nun was low in alcohol, inexpensive, and slightly sweet. For a country that, on the whole, still didn't know or much like the taste of real wine, it was perfect. Sales went crazy. In 1959, ten thousand cases of it were sold in the United States. By the late 1980s, two million cases of Blue Nun were bought worldwide, 1.2 million of those cases in the United States. In fact, Blue Nun was so popular that one day we even bought a knockoff called Blue Monk. Then White Zinfandel entered the market and started sinking Blue Nun, says Mr. Sichel, who sold the company in 1995. Sales in the United States are now around 250,000 cases, he estimates, adding that the wine still does well in England and Ireland.

We felt very grown-up with Blue Nun. With cookbooks in our laps, we looked for the right dish to complement the wine. Thick-cut pork chops with sauerkraut and sautéed apples was perfect. With our dinner and a bottle of Blue Nun, we felt very romantic.

Alone in his office in South Dade, John had the culinary choice each day of either Burger King or McDonald's, which were across from each other on U.S. 1. One day, a new strip mall opened near the McDonald's. In a town where very little ever happened, this was news, so John dropped by to check it out as a possible story. He went into one of the stores, which was called Crown Liquors. The store was overwhelming but exciting. All those different wines. All those different labels. He had no idea what he was doing, but he knew there was no reason to buy Blue Nun, since we could buy it at the supermarket. So he picked up a bottle of wine that was featured next to the cash register. It was white, French, and cheap. That's pretty much all we remember. It was some sort of generic French wine, three for $9.99. John took three. "If you take a case," said the man behind the register, "I'll give you fifteen percent off." It seemed like a very good deal—that meant it was

$2.83 per bottle—and John said sure. The man asked whether he wanted all generic white, or a mixed case with generic red. John took half and half. It was the first case of wine we ever bought.

When John brought it home, he took all the bottles out of the box and stood them up on his green shag carpet. He waited with even greater anticipation than usual for Dottie to drive up in her little white Toyota, which was less a car than a metal box on wheels. Seeing that clunky car putt-putt up the street always made John smile, and not only because Dottie was in it. Whenever John's father tried to talk his customers out of buying a Toyota, he'd laugh and say, "Do you know why it's called 'Toyota'? That's what the Japanese called it because it's a 'Toy Auto.' " When Dottie's Toy Auto finally arrived that day, John brought her in and showed her the wine. "A whole case!" she exclaimed.

We had a bottle of white the first night and a bottle of red the second. We had never tasted dry wine before. It was like nothing we could have imagined—crisp and fruity and interesting, yet as real and plainspoken as water. Every night for twelve nights, we opened a bottle of wine to have with dinner. We felt so very grown-up. We began to imagine ourselves as everyday wine drinkers. We imagined a new way of life.

That life really took hold a few months later, when we met a woman who became very important to us, but whose name we never knew.

We weren't living together yet—that would be a huge step, and we weren't ready—but Dottie spent more time at John's place than at her own. Sometimes, on assignment, John drove by Dottie's apartment to see if she was there. If not, he left a note on her door with a drawing of her face on the front, or at least her face as he saw it. There was a small forehead topped by a tiny, somewhat angular Afro. Then there was a big round face, with massive cheeks, huge eyes, and a little nose and a smile. Later, Dottie thought the sculpted hair made her look a little like the

Olympic medalist Carl Lewis. John knew it wasn't perfect yet—
those adorable cheeks weren't quite right—but it was a start.

A friend at the paper and his wife were renting part of a
triplex house in the very hip Coconut Grove area of Miami and
asked John if he'd like to rent another part. The house was owned
by a man who bought and sold buildings that sometimes burned
down under mysterious circumstances. The third part of the house
was occupied by his son. "Hi," the son said when we first met him.
"Call me Match." We rented the third part anyway, though Dottie
still kept her own apartment.

Coconut Grove has always been a patchwork of nice homes
and businesses, pretty much side by side in some areas. Right off
Bird Avenue, near the Bird Bath, where we did our laundry, there
was a small clutch of tiny shops nestled among little houses with
beautiful bougainvillea all around them. One of them was a wine
shop and one day John nervously walked in. We bought wine from
time to time, but usually at the supermarket. Even Crown Liquors
seemed a bit intimidating. John was just curious. The store was
really small, maybe twelve or fifteen feet wide and not very deep.
There were no racks. Instead, wines simply sat, or were tilted up,
in wooden wine boxes, all over the floor. Something about whole
cases of wine, just sitting there, seemed particularly pretty and
inviting. There was no cash register, just a woman sitting at a table
in the back of the store. When John walked in that day, he was her
only customer. There was no escape. He would have to say something, and probably would have to buy something, too. So he asked
for a bottle of red wine.

It was a remarkable store. This was long before a wine's status
became more important than its taste and before stores stocked
up on famous wines at astonishing prices. This shop might have had
a hundred different wines, but they were mostly from countries
like Chile and Greece. The French wines were mostly simple and
inexpensive. There were few California wines because it seemed

there were few worth buying that weren't expensive. The explosion was happening just underneath the surface. This was 1974, the year that Gallo, which always seemed to sense trends first, made its first "varietal" wines, wines named for their grape types instead of ripped-off foreign names like Burgundy and Chianti. There was a whole line of varietals featuring a white Ernest & Julio Gallo label—French Colombard, Ruby Cabernet, Barbera, Sauvignon Blanc, Zinfandel, Riesling. It hadn't caught on yet, but the Gallo line was a potent signpost of things to come.

The wine lady picked out a bottle from someplace abroad, said, "I think you'll like this," and handed it to John.

We're not absolutely sure what the very first wine was that we bought from the Wine Lady of Coconut Grove. We think it was a Goyenechea Cabernet Sauvignon. It had a very rustic label—so many of her wines did—and said it was *vino fino tinto,* which at least looked like "fine red wine." It was from the Mendoza region of Argentina. Argentina now is well known as a wine-producing country, and its Malbec wines, which are perfect with grilled meats, are on the verge of breaking into the American consciousness. But then, wine from Argentina simply seemed weird. John bought it anyway—how could he not?

It was a miracle. We tasted things in that wine we had never tasted before. It somehow seemed crisp, but when we swallowed it, we could almost taste something dark in our mouths, like the soil in the U-Pick fields of South Dade. We couldn't believe a wine could have so many tastes. We had never been to Argentina and knew little about it, but we felt we had been transported there. Years later, we learned this is what wine experts refer to as *terroir,* the unique quality that a certain geography, with its particular soil and minerals, can bring to a wine's taste. Back then, though, we merely knew that we had sipped a wine whose taste seemed so demonstrative of its origin—its actual soil—that we felt we had traveled to the very place where it was made.

The next time John went, he bought an entire case of wine, from all over the world. We had a budget: $72 for the case. It was a lot of money—we were still both making under $200 a week—but $72 allowed us to splurge on a couple of $10 wines and still stay under budget with $3 and $4 bottles. We bought our first Greek wines there (Demestica, red and white, which we had with large Greek salads), our first Chilean wines, usually with lasagna or meat loaf, our first rosés from Provence, which we sipped alone, and our first Egri Bikavér—"Bull's Blood"—from Hungary, which we drank with rough stuff like steak. And there were our first wines from châteaux in France.

God. Actual châteaux in France. Dottie had lived in Indonesia. She had traveled to exotic places. John had never left the United States. To him, this was as close to traveling the world as he could imagine. We went out and bought a wine book for the very first time, *The World Atlas of Wine*, by Hugh Johnson. It didn't seem very scary because it was filled with maps and pictures of labels. Johnson wrote in his introduction: "Bit by bit it dawned on me that maps on a large enough scale are more than aids to navigation: they are pictures of the ground and what goes on on it. That it was possible, as it were, to take a reader up into a high mountain and show him all the vineyards of the earth."

John usually did the wine shopping. It wasn't something we planned, and we never discussed it. But John had no problem lifting boxes of wine, and it took Dottie a while to be comfortable walking into a liquor store. It didn't seem like something a nice young lady would do alone. What would her mother think? John would come home with the case in the trunk of his gold Camaro and rush inside with it. Then he would run to get the *World Atlas*. Together we'd sit on the shag carpet and look at each treasure, then see if we could find it in the book. "Look! It's right across the river from Château Latour!" Each bottle was gloriously different and usually from a whole different place. We never bought the same bottle twice. Maybe two times a month, John went to see the Wine Lady, and she picked out twelve more bottles for $72. Some were good and some weren't so good, but every one of them was, in its own way, a revelation. That's how we began to collect wine. We never intended to. We never figured out what bottles we wanted to save and how much of what kind of wine should go into a collection. We simply began collecting wine because we bought it faster than we drank it.

We were lucky. This was long before there were so many wine writers and experts telling us what we should like and what was plonk. There was no national obsession on the quality of the vintage in Bordeaux. Perhaps most important, because California wines hadn't yet burst upon the scene in full force, the first wines we discovered were from all over the world. We didn't develop a specific taste for any one wine from any one place and stop there. We knew from our first purchases that the world of wine was a very big place, and we were intent on sampling everything we could, from one corner of the globe to another. We bought one of those little accordion wine racks and set it in the living room on the white shag carpet of our part of the Coconut Grove triplex. In our tiny little kitchen, we made multicourse meals to go with our wine, like beef Stroganoff and veal Marsala.

In late 1974, John's parents met Dottie. They were coming down to visit anyway, and it seemed like it was time. For John's parents, and especially his father, Miami Beach provided a little bit of New York. There was cheesecake and deli food and there were people with New York accents. One of the temples of this was a place on South Beach called The Famous. The waitresses were loud, the food was heavy, and the seltzer on the table was a throwback, but everyone had a good time there, and we knew John's parents would. We figured it would be a good introduction. When John and his parents picked Dottie up at her apartment, she greeted John's mother with a red rose. The ice was broken.

John's father drove to Miami Beach and parked at The Famous. Dottie seemed to be getting along well with John's parents, which primarily meant getting along well with his mother, who was interviewing her in an impressively thorough manner. We sat down at a table with a seltzer bottle and a loud waitress. For the next hour, John's father ordered every Jewish food he had missed for so many years—pickled tomatoes, gefilte fish, and all sorts of things John had rarely seen before, couldn't pronounce, and didn't want to touch. But Dottie kept up with John's father, bite for bite, through the chicken fat and herring and the chopped liver. There was nothing she didn't try.

Dottie: *I had learned an important lesson as a child overseas: Sharing another culture's food—sugar on rice in Pakistan, a cracker with baby octopus in Japan, or in this case, pickled herring—demonstrates trust and respect. It is a good way into that culture's heart. This was easy for me anyway: I found that I loved new tastes.*

John's mother was amazed. His father just beamed. John's father had always wanted a girl. When John's younger brother, Kris, was born, making it three sons, it was time to stop trying. If John's mother had been younger, they would have kept having babies until they had a girl. By the end of the night, John's father felt he finally had a daughter. It was John who was chopped liver.

John never got to meet Dottie's dad. When Dottie went home for Thanksgiving in 1974, he was deathly ill.

Dottie: *No one told me that he had had such a rapid decline. As a family, we never talked about Dad's health very much or, in general, about our feelings. Years later when I asked about that, asked whether it would have been better for Dad and for us all if we had talked about his illness, Mom said no, that he wouldn't have wanted it that way. So I was shocked and frightened when I found him near* *death. I had come up a few weeks earlier when he was in the hospital. He had been losing weight for some time, but when he saw me he smiled and promised me that he would put some pounds back on. There were times when I would come home and he would be mostly bedridden, but he always bounced back. He always found the strength to come out into the living room in his blue and white robe, smile for us, and sit in his favorite leather chair.*

Now he lay in a hospital bed that my mother had had erected in their bedroom. A slight and gentle presence, he slipped in and out of consciousness. I came from the airport and went straight to his side. He woke up, looked up at me, and smiled. "You're here," he said, then went back to sleep. As he slept, I hoped that somehow he could hear me. I told him I was so lucky to be his daughter, and I promised him that I would look after my mom and my sisters. He had told me the day I went to college, in an uncharacteristically emotional moment, that I didn't owe him and my mother anything. I guess I must have told him that I would try to make them proud. He said that they were already proud of me. He told me that I was sweet and trusting and that the rest of the world wasn't like that and that he hoped I'd never change. When I came home that first Christmas from college, he marveled that I seemed the same.

One summer during high school, I had gotten a job over the phone to wait tables at Howard Johnson's. A Jewish classmate had recommended me. That first morning, Dad had driven me to work and told me he'd wait for a few minutes in the parking lot. He must have suspected something. And sure enough, the manager took one look at me and the job vanished. I walked outside in a daze and climbed in the car beside him. He turned me around to face him and told me to always remember that not all white people were like that. A couple of days later, the same manager called and offered me the job. Had Dad called someone?

All of those thoughts and memories now came rushing back as I watched his thin chest rise and fall. I think he was waiting for all of us to be together. He died on December 3, 1974, and was buried in a beautiful wooden casket carved with a craftsmanship he would have admired. He had seen only pictures of John and thought he had a kind face.

After Dottie's dad's death, his fraternity planned a program to honor him on a cruise that it was taking from the Port of Miami to the Bahamas. Dottie and her mom signed up for it. When her mom flew down for the cruise, we thought that was a good time for her to meet John. When John picked them up at Dottie's apartment to take them to dinner, he knew he could relax. Out of the bedroom came an older, mellower version of Dottie. She even had plump cheeks and eyes that sparkled. At the end of the evening, after John had dropped them off, Dottie's mom turned to her and said, "Dorothy Jean, he's very nice. Have you met his parents?"

For Christmas 1973, John's parents had given his brother, Jim, a home winemaking kit. Welch's, the grape juice people, made it. They called it "Welch's Wine Country," and it included everything except the wine bottles. This was ironic, considering that Thomas Bramwell Welch invented Dr. Welch's Unfermented Wine in 1869 because he was such a fervent believer in temperance. Jim had no interest in the winemaking kit and gave it to us. It seemed like an interesting project to help distract Dottie a little after she returned from her father's funeral. We followed all the directions. Fermentation began on December 7, 1974. We racked the wine— took it off the sediment, as directed—on January 11, 1975. We bottled it in several used wine bottles on January 26, 1975, and aged it for a few weeks before trying it. It wasn't very good, but it was drinkable, and it did give us a certain point of reference. To this day, we sometimes taste a so-so wine and say, "That tastes like the wine we made."

That Christmas was memorable for another reason. Over time, John's fascination with Dottie's face had grown. He studied it endlessly. He could tell when she was tired, when she was happy, when she was hungry. He always knew she was cold before she did. Our colleagues at the *Herald* had grown accustomed to the elevator door opening and seeing John's hands all over Dottie's face. His drawing of Dottie's face had become more refined, too. The forehead grew bigger, the cheeks rounder. It was "the Dottie face." That Christmas, John found a Cuban glassblower who made a blown-glass Dottie face, sitting on a delicate glass pedestal. It was the first Dottie present.

We moved in together in 1976. It was a very big step, especially for Dottie, who was more comfortable living alone than John. Dottie did wonder sometimes if John loved her or her face. John liked to say that her face was just an outward manifestation of her inner beauty. But it is true that for Christmas, he gave Dottie a copyright of her own face. At the Copyright Office of the United States, registration number GU58427 is "Caricature of the Head of Dorothy Gaiter."

We moved into a two-bedroom apartment in North Miami Beach, an old area filled with traffic, delis, and a little wine-and-cheese store called Le Château in a strip shopping center. We lived too far away from the Wine Lady of Coconut Grove to visit very often, but we were still buying inexpensive wines wherever we could find them. Le Château had interesting stuff—we bought a "Champagne" from Russia, and some interesting California wines were beginning to show up. It was a period of remarkable experimentation in California, with the wine industry still caught between the past and the future.

Despite Gallo's leap into "varietal" wines, many California wineries were still giving their wines foreign names because they were more familiar to Americans who drank wine—"Chablis" for whites, for instance, and "Chianti" for reds. Even some good wines were called "Burgundy." Inglenook produced something called "Vintage Burgundy," which is an interesting contradiction: The label said the wine was from the 1976 vintage, but gave no idea what kind of grape or grapes the wine was made from. Real red Burgundy, from France, is made from Pinot Noir. California "Burgundy" back then was often made from a grape called Petite Sirah.

By calling the wine Burgundy or Chianti, the wineries gave the wine some context that they thought American consumers needed. This drove other countries crazy, of course, and as a practice it began to decrease in the late 1970s as varietal designations, using the name of the predominant grape, became more popular. But this was an interesting period when American wines were in transition. Hence a winery named J. Lohr could call a wine "Chablis" on the front but on the back say: "You will find this Chablis to be dry, soft and very palatable. It is a blend of four premium varietal wines: 54% Semillon, 9% Chardonnay, and 5% Pinot Blanc lending character and body, and 32% Johannisberg Riesling contributing a flowery nose and delicate softness. Since each wine was aged in small Limousin and American oak barrels, there are sophisticated notes of oak in the bouquet and tastes." Real Chablis, from France, is made from Chardonnay.

Winemakers felt they had to tread carefully with a still-suspicious American marketplace that was more comfortable with French stuff. Consider this label, on a 1976 "White Table Wine":

Fifteen years ago, we at Château Winery dedicated ourselves to making a wine worthy of our name. In order to achieve our goal, we decided to emulate the productive methods of the great Bordeaux Châteaux. The result is a vintaged wine which has a lot number, a lead capsule, a two-inch branded cork, an appellation, and wine which is aged in wood.

We honestly believe these wines to be superb, and, therefore, cordially invite you to enjoy our creation.

Vôtre santé.

...

California vintners were desperately trying to figure out what kind of wine Americans would ultimately like best. Sonoma Vineyards made a wine called Ruby Cabernet—a cross between Cabernet Sauvignon and a grape called Carignane that had been big in the United States before Prohibition—and on the back label called it "an emerging wine that is creating more interest each year."

We tried as many different wines as we could afford. One day we walked into Le Château and there on the floor, in wooden wine boxes, was something we'd read about but never seen: a case of Château Lafite-Rothschild, one of the storied "first growths" from Bordeaux, the most famous wines in the world. We knew that Bordeaux wines had been classified in 1855 and that there had been four "first growths"—Châteaux Lafite-Rothschild, Latour, Margaux, and Haut-Brion—and that one more, Mouton-Rothschild, had recently been added. But we'd never held one in our hands. The Lafite label was so very elegant and simple. It said very little, because it didn't need to say more. When we looked at the handwritten sign stating the price, we couldn't believe our eyes: *Eight dollars!* Eight dollars for a Château Lafite-Rothschild. We could afford to own one. There was, of course, a catch: The Lafite was from the 1968 vintage.

Every year is different for grape growing, just like growing anything else. Some years are sunny and dry, some are wet and cold. That means sometimes grapes get very ripe and other years they don't. So the vintage of a wine does matter, but not nearly as much as the obsession with the subject would indicate. Some properties make bad wines in good years and vice versa. What's more, every region in the world seems to declare every year "the vintage of the century." Even in years with awful weather, press releases explain defensively why that actually made the grapes better and how the winemaker's skill triumphed over the elements.

Nineteen sixty-eight, however, was an exception. Just as it was a spectacular year in California, it was universally agreed to be an unmitigated disaster in Bordeaux. It rained like crazy in August, and the grapes never did really ripen. "This sort of vintage exposes as sheer nonsense the glib saying that some good wines are made even in a poor vintage," wrote Michael Broadbent in *The Great Vintage Wine Book.* He wrote of the Lafite: "It is of course arguable (and none of our business) whether a premier grand cru does its reputation—or that of Bordeaux—any good by selling a wine under its own name in a vintage like this. But in the 1971 to 1973 wine boom period, when this and other '68s were put on the market, the ignorant and the gullible would buy anything."

Being ignorant and gullible, we bought three. It was the most exciting purchase we had ever made. We'd drink one and save two. That meant our little wine collection, the accordion wine rack on the floor, would include Château Lafite-Rothschild.

There was a large Italian-American population in North Miami Beach, and a great Italian supermarket called Laurenzo's. It had a fine collection of Italian wines just sitting on the shelves like bread, and it's where we first began to dabble in Italian wine. It also had a great meat department with kind butchers who helped teach Dottie how to cook. They told her everything she'd need to do, and even wrote it down on white butcher's paper. A week after we bought our Lafite, Dottie went to Laurenzo's and bought two massive veal chops. At the butcher's direction, we prepared them with parsley, butter, and a little lemon zest. We spent hours making the meal, preparing new potatoes, asparagus, and a salad. We even splurged on a can of Pepperidge Farm strawberry soup for an appetizer. We served the food, then set the Lafite on the table. We were so excited we could hardly sit still.

John opened the bottle in silence as we both drew close. Not only was this wine from a terrible year, but it was now eight years old. Eight years is nothing for a fine red, and especially a Bordeaux from a great château. But these wines, everyone said, were dead on arrival, and simply got thinner, with less fruit and even less charm, with each passing year.

We'd never pulled a longer cork. It seemed to take forever to come out. But the second the cork came out, we knew we were experiencing something unforgettable. There was no turning back. This wine was about to touch our souls, take us to another level. A bouquet of cedar, leather, and the richest fruit we'd ever known rose from the bottle. We poured a small amount into our glasses and smelled it. It was pure heaven, with a complexity of aromas we never could have imagined. Demestica and Bull's Blood were delightfully simple and rough. One whiff and you'd smelled it all. But this was different. With each swirl and each sniff, we could sense something new, a different nuance. Finally, we clinked glasses. "To your face," said Dottie. "To your bottom," said John. Cedar, vanilla, cherries, blackberries, and all of the wines we'd ever tasted seemed to be captured in that glass. Each sip seemed like a whole world.

We'd been living together for a year when John was named Palm Beach bureau chief. It was not just a big job—running a bureau of eight people in a growing area of South Florida—but another important step on the *Miami Herald* career ladder. It meant, though, that we would have to live apart for a while. Dottie stayed in North Miami Beach, in a new one-bedroom apartment, and the drive was not that long. It was sixty-one minutes. We timed it.

Not far from his office John found a little shack called the Blue Front, in a pretty rough black area of town, that had the greatest take-out ribs, one of John's greatest loves. Growing up in Jacksonville, he'd developed a taste for Southern food, and these were the best, meaty and lean and perfectly cooked over a fire. When he expected Dottie, he'd drop by the Blue Front on the way home

and pick up more ribs than could ever be consumed by two people, and a cold six-pack of Budweiser at the 7-Eleven. The only
thing that kept the ribs from being perfect was the sauce. It
was flavorful—vinegar- and mustard-based—but not nearly hot
enough. Every time John went in, he asked for hot sauce, and
every time, the sauce was tasty but mild. One night, when John
was especially late, Dottie suggested that she pick up the ribs. John
reminded her, "Be sure to ask for hot sauce." When John got
home, we placed the huge platter of ribs in front of us and bit in.
The sauce almost blew off the tops of our heads. It was like fire. We
realized then that there were two "hot" sauces—one for white
people who thought they knew what hot was, and one for black
people. From then on, when John went in, he looked at the man
behind the counter and said, "I want hot sauce. The *real* hot sauce."

Aside from bizarre issues like that, it never made any material
difference, as far as we knew, that we were a racially mixed couple.
Miami was a diverse place anyway, we were in prestigious jobs
with the powerful *Miami Herald,* and we made enough money
every week to live pretty well. It's true that when we walked into
some restaurants, little old ladies stared from time to time, but
that didn't bother us because we knew our own mothers would
probably stare. People were curious, not necessarily disapproving,
and what if they were? So what? Sometimes a maître d' would look
at us and ask, "Two?" When he did, John would glance around for
that imaginary third person who must be confusing the poor fel-
low and then say, "Yes, two." Once, a Black Muslim, as they were
called then, yelled at Dottie, "Sister, you're going to hell!" because
she was with John. Dottie yelled back, "Then I'll see you there." If
anyone is really interested in the true number of interracial couples in America, they should ask the Black Muslims. We're sure
they've greeted every single one of them.

For Christmas that year, John found a clock maker in West
Palm Beach who made a clock shaped like Dottie's face. Dottie

bought John a case of wine that included a bottle of 1974 Louis Roederer Cristal Champagne, all wrapped up in gold cellophane.

North Palm Beach, on the other end of Palm Beach County from Boca Raton, was just beginning to be developed back then. John drove up one day to scope out the scene and happened upon a little wine shop called the Wine Cask. He walked in. It was the most serious wine store we'd ever been in. The Wine Lady of Coconut Grove sold mostly inexpensive wines in a tiny space. Le Château specialized in gourmet food more than wine. The Wine Cask was different. It had racks and racks of fine wine, really expensive stuff, the kind of wines we'd read about but never seen, and the kind of wines we'd never read about and never imagined. John dropped by a couple of times and bought single bottles. On his third trip, the owner asked, "Do you like German wines?"

German wines. Yech. We'd long since outgrown Blue Nun. It was sweet and simple and one-dimensional. German wines were cloying, like Manischewitz Concord. "Not really," said John.

"Try this," said the owner. It was a lovely bottle with a simple, elegant label. "Steinberger," it said. "Kabinett." It didn't say much more. But John—still, frankly, a little nervous and a bit intimidated in such a fine store—took it home.

Dottie was skeptical, too, when she arrived that night. But it was well chilled and she was ready for some wine after the hour-long drive, dodging highway patrolmen and singing along to the radio as she sped. She would arrive on Friday night and it sometimes would take an hour or so for us to get into our old rhythm. We had pretty separate lives, Monday through Thursday, and it was sometimes awkward seeing each other after time apart. Having the wine to drink and discuss helped usher us into our intimate little zone.

The best German wines are made from the Riesling grape, which is flowery, fruity, and clean. Because Germany's wine-growing regions are northerly, the grapes generally don't get very

ripe, which leaves the wine with somewhat low alcohol and somewhat high acidity. That makes them good with food and generally
appropriate for long aging. Mosel-Saar-Ruwer is the best-known
area for German wines. The wines from there tend to be especially
flowery and delightful. Another area is Rheingau, where the Riesling grape creates a wine of a bit more power and a little bit of
pepper and spice. We knew nothing about this at the time. We
didn't even know that the Steinberger was a Rheingau wine. But
with our first sip, we knew that, as Patty Hearst had said not long
before, we could never go back to the life we once lived. It was the
most delicate wine we had ever tasted, with melons and other
fruits on the "nose," yet a spiciness in our throats that almost
seemed to tickle. After we swallowed the wine, we didn't need another sip for several minutes because the taste lingered for so very
long. Yet the wine was so light that it seemed ephemeral.

This was one of the most important moments of our wine
life together—not just because we fell in love with German wines
and the Riesling grape, but because we learned a lesson that was
crucial to us in the future: Never bring preconceptions to any
wine. That was important a few weeks later, when Art, the owner
of the Wine Cask, insisted that we try a Chablis. We knew Chablis:
It was a flabby, slightly sweet, pineappley wine that often came in
big jugs. But Art insisted. Real Chablis, he said, is from France,
made from the Chardonnay grape, and a classic combination with
seafood. We had it that night with creamy, succulent lobster New-
burg, rice, and broccoli, and we couldn't believe it. The wine was
green-gold and the taste was exceptionally clean and acidic, but
assertive and almost steely. It was so crisp in our mouths that it
tasted like ice. Our whole bodies seemed to come alive as we
swallowed it.

If this is what Chablis really tastes like, we thought, what else
are we wrong about?

Robert Mondavi Cabernet Sauvignon 1974

· · ·

WE SPENT SOME NIGHTS APART, SO WE HAD TIME TO BUY and read several wine books. Our favorite was *The Signet Encyclopedia of Wine* because we could tell that the author, E. Frank Henriques, had a good time writing it. It was simple, alphabetical, and delightful to read. "Folks have argued for centuries over which is the greatest red wine on earth, Bordeaux or Burgundy, but true wine lovers don't expend precious energy—we're running short on that commodity, you know—in bootless speculation; they simply love and enjoy both of these splendid gifts of God, as one loves and enjoys one's two-year-old son and five-year-old daughter."

There was also Terry Robards's book *The New York Times Book of Wine,* which was snootier but comprehensive. *The Wines of America* by Leon D. Adams made all the wineries, and winemakers, seem so real, so very rooted in American history. He explained that winemaking in the United States has a very long history, though not necessarily a glorious one. He wrote that the first wine in America was made in Jacksonville, of all places, in the early sixteenth century. Immigrants, especially Italians, created a thriving wine industry in California in the early twentieth century. Some very good wines were made. But Prohibition killed the industry. Some wineries survived by selling grapes for home winemaking or by making legal "sacramental" wine, but the fine-wine industry was devastated. It picked up the pieces and made some good wine after Prohibition, of course, but people generally drank cheap California wine. If you wanted the good stuff, you had to buy imported. Get Lancers.

The books were helping us begin to put wines, and wine, in context. It seemed to us, though, that if we were ever going to really understand wine, we'd have to go to the source. We decided to visit San Francisco and Napa Valley. It was a perfect time to do it. The number of Americans who said they drank any alcohol at all had risen to an all-time high of 71 percent, according to the Gallup Poll. Money was pouring into Napa. And lightning had struck. In 1976, French experts conducted a blind tasting of some American wines versus great French wines. The winners were American: a Chardonnay from Château Montelena and a Cabernet Sauvignon from Stag's Leap Wine Cellars. The wine world was agog. American wine had arrived.

The 1968 vintage had been great, but the 1974 vintage put California over the top. It was not only another great year, but the vineyards that year had yielded a big crop, which meant that a country that was just beginning to get a taste for good California wine could generally find a good wine from an outstanding vintage made by an up-and-coming winery. The 1968 and 1974 wines from Beaulieu Vineyard and Heitz Cellars were hailed as spectacular. A Russian émigré named André Tchelistcheff became famous in the wine world with Beaulieu's Cabernet Sauvignons, and Joe Heitz's "Martha's Vineyard" Cabernet acquired near cult status.

Great Cabernet was critical to California's rise. The wines by which all others had been judged for centuries were red Bordeaux wines, which are primarily Cabernet-based. If California was ever going to be taken seriously in the wine world, it would have to make great Cabernet. Now it did.

The most famous 1974—the one with huge buzz that even wine amateurs couldn't miss—was the 1974 Cabernet Sauvignon from Robert Mondavi. From our own perspective, if any single California wine can be said to have planted fine California wines firmly in the consciousness of America, it was Mondavi's 1974 "Reserve" Cabernet Sauvignon. This doesn't mean it was the best wine California had made, or even the best wine of that year. But this was a much simpler time in wine, a time when an importer like Frederick Wildman and Sons could import a modest Saint-Julien wine from Bordeaux and describe it this way on the back label: "Wildman Selected Generic Wines . . . We have made a careful selection from this area to give you this truly traditional generic wine." More than with other products, the way wines were presented to the buying public truly mattered. Mondavi made a fine wine, made plenty of it, and marketed it well enough to create real excitement.

We flew to San Francisco and checked into a little old hotel in the middle of town called the Cartwright. San Francisco was everything we'd imagined—the cable cars, the hills, the charm, the hippies, Chinatown. On every corner, it seemed, were vendors selling fresh-cut flowers. Dottie kept commenting on how special the sunlight there was. Remember how in *Star Trek* pretty women would be shown in soft focus, filtered light? Well, that's how Dottie saw San Francisco. It was a magical place. Our first morning, we had a Champagne brunch at the Carnelian Room, a restaurant on top of the Bank of America building. As we looked out the window, the fog lifted off the Bay Bridge, showing just a tiny bit more of the bridge every minute. It was a spectacular sight.

Everyone had told us that the very first place we had to eat was Ernie's, so we went ahead and made reservations while we were still in Florida. Just like they all said, it looked like a whorehouse. Red velvet everywhere, even on the walls. Just like they all said, it had a great list of California wines. And there it was, smack in the middle of the list—the 1974 Robert Mondavi "Reserve" Cabernet Sauvignon. We'd never actually seen one before.

We had yet to experience a great wine from California. Partly it was because great wines from California were still precious then. We rarely saw the best ones and couldn't really afford them when we did. Partly it was because we'd gotten to know wines from other winemaking regions first. When we went out to dinner, we almost always ordered French or Italian wines, because they were cheaper and more familiar to us, and there were plenty on local restaurant wine lists. We found a restaurant in Miami called Victoria Station that had a railroad motif and good prime rib. We always started with stuffed mushrooms and a bottle of a cheap red wine from France called Marquisat, in a strangely shaped bottle with a drawing of a man—the Marquis, we guess—on the label.

The Mondavi was huge, with massive fruit and real weight, very different from the elegant Bordeaux wines we'd tasted. It seemed to us to be very American in its big, bold tastes. It had the layers we found in a Bordeaux, but everything seemed magnified, pumped up. With John's veal and Dottie's steak, it seemed to leap right out of the glass. The meats and the wine seemed to make each other taste better. The wine was so remarkable that we lingered over it for what seemed like forever. Our dessert, an orange soufflé, had to wait. We immediately became convinced that Robert Mondavi made the greatest wines in America. The next night, when we went to a Chinese restaurant called the Imperial Palace, we had a Mondavi Fumé Blanc, which is a name that Robert Mondavi invented for his wine made from the Sauvignon Blanc grape. It was perfect with our shrimp in rice paper.

Later, we became big fans of the Sauvignon Blanc grape, which is amazingly versatile. It makes terrific dessert wines in France— it's one of the grapes in great Sauternes—and crisp, grassy wines in Sancerre. It makes some woody, nutty, rich wines in California, some refreshing, minerally, quaffable wines in Washington State, and some bold, true-to-the-varietal, green-pepperish wines in New Zealand. But we had never had one, and this one—young and fresh—was a real eye-opener. It seemed to jump around in our mouths, and had such fresh green tastes that we felt we were in the middle of a field. The juicy acidity of the wine made the shrimp seem fresh enough to swim.

The next day, our very first stop on the very first day of our very first visit to Napa Valley was the beautiful Robert Mondavi Winery in Oakville, on Route 29, the wine road. People must have thought Mondavi was crazy when he built a huge, tourist-friendly winery right at the beginning of the wine road, but it quickly became a destination for thousands of people, including us. The first thing we did was pick a grape from a vine right in front of the winery. For years afterward, we'd point to Robert Mondavi's pretty label that featured a drawing of its winery and put our finger on that very vine.

We drove up Route 29 to the Louis M. Martini Winery in St. Helena, where then—and now—they sold a wine only at the winery called Moscato Amabile, a sweet, light wine that's so fresh and unstable that it must be drunk virtually on the spot. Now, California wineries have come to focus primarily on the very best, and best-selling, grapes, like Chardonnay and Cabernet Sauvignon and Zinfandel (with a few pioneers making wines from unusual grapes such as Mourvèdre). Back then, everyone was experimenting with new things, even while embracing the old. So we tried Louis Martini's Barbera (a grape from the Old Country, Italy), Claret (which could be anything, since claret is actually what the British call red Bordeaux wines), and Cabernet Sauvignon. We dropped in on a sleepy little winery called Sutter Home and tried its 1973 Zinfandel.

We took the tram up to Sterling Vineyards and bought a bottle of 1971 Cabernet Sauvignon sold only at the winery. We went over to Sonoma County and visited Korbel—a toast to John's father—which was then making not only sparkling wines but still wines like Grey Riesling ("a welcome treat with seafood," said the label), and a very old-line winery called Sebastiani.

August Sebastiani was another of those crusty old winemakers who brought personality to wine country, and to his wines. In a book called *Great Winemakers of California,* he was asked how he made his wines. He replied: "Look, my dad taught me this stuff and some of it I don't tell anybody but my kids. This is the difference between me and some other guy. What else do you have? Anybody can send to the university and get an oenologist trained by . . . the professors up there. They all go through the same school, same books, same methods. What have you got? You've got a bunch of canned peas."

Sebastiani had a tasting room with a long wooden bar and, it seemed, about a million wines to taste. There was Mountain Chablis and Petite Chablis and Arenas Dry Sherry and "Burgundy" ("the skillful blending of properly selected grapes is the most important factor in making a great California Burgundy"). As we worked our way through the wines, we came across one that stumped us: Gewürz Traminer. First, we asked how to pronounce it. Then we asked what grape the wine was made from. The woman behind the counter looked at us blankly and said, "Well, Gewürz Traminer." Gewürztraminer is the great white wine of the Alsace region of France. It has a very special peppery taste that makes it the perfect wine to have with pork. We had never heard of it.

As we went from winery to winery, what amazed us was the informality and friendliness of every one of them. We just showed up at these places and someone took out a couple of glasses and started pouring wine. We usually didn't buy anything—how could we carry it?—and no one really seemed to care. We were then in our mid-twenties, terribly shy, certainly didn't look prosperous, didn't know too much about wine, and had no appointment or introduction. What was our secret? We were curious and sincerely interested. We saw visitors to the tasting room who tried to impress the wineries with their knowledge—one actually asked about glycerin content—and they were brushed off like flies. We saw other people—most people, in fact—who were interested only in getting a free glass of wine. They came in, declared that they liked only white or red wine, drank a glass, said nothing, and left.

We quickly realized that it took only our interest to coax winemakers into talking to us all day, and they were so interesting, all of them. We didn't need wine-speak. We described things the way they tasted to us. If the person pouring the wine gave us a fresh white, we'd just say something like "This is so fresh. It tastes like flowers in spring. How do you do that?" Their eyes would get big and they'd start talking—and pouring—and never stop. We realized that visiting a winery was very much like visiting an art gallery. Would you walk in and say to the artist, "I only like paintings with green colors"? Of course not. And wouldn't you say something nice to the artist about the work? "Gee, I love your use of color there. How did you do those brushstrokes?" Winemakers are artists. They love to talk about their art. We realized that all we had to do was give them the opportunity to do so.

Nowhere was more remarkable to us than Hanns Kornell Champagne Cellars, where the stocky, energetic man behind the counter turned out to be Hanns Kornell.

Hanns Kornell's life and sad death are, in many ways, the story of winemaking in America. He was born in Germany, where his family had been known for a hundred years for their wines. He worked in wineries in Italy, France, and England, but the Nazis sent him to Dachau just as he was about to take over the family winery. He survived, fled to the United States virtually penniless, and worked in various American wineries in places like Kentucky, back when states like Ohio and Michigan made a great deal of America's wine. He worked for Cook's Champagne in St. Louis, which is a venerable name in American winemaking, but left there just about the time John was born when the company was bought by Schenley, the company John's father worked for.

Kornell moved to California, worked in the wineries there for a while, and, in 1958, bought the old Larkmead Winery, part of whose vineyards were once owned by Lillie Hitchcock Coit, the donor of Coit Tower in San Francisco. His was the only winery besides Korbel that specialized in sparkling wine, and his were special. He made a whole variety, each with a different-color label: Rosé was pink, Extra Dry was black, Brut was green, Demi-Sec was purple, Muscat Alexandria was white, and the very special Sehr Trocken was golden. The Sehr Trocken even had, on the back, the hand-printed date that the wine was "disgorged." On the front of each bottle was this: "Naturally fermented in this bottle."

That was a really big deal for Hanns Kornell Champagne Cellars. The way real Champagne is made, in the Champagne region of France, is this: Pinot Noir, Pinot Meunier, and/or Chardonnay grapes are picked and made into a regular, still wine. Then some sugar and yeast are added, and the heavy bottle is tightly capped. This sugary mixture breaks down into carbon dioxide, which makes the bubbles. But all of the sediment that the process creates is trapped in the bottle, too. So for months or even years, each bottle is carefully turned and twisted with the head down so that all of the sediment will sink to the neck of the bottle. Finally, the neck of the bottle is frozen to fix the sediment in one place, the temporary cap is popped, and the sediment is "disgorged," removed. This process is very expensive. Many California sparkling wines, even today, are made in a bulk process in huge vats. Hanns Kornell's sparkling wines were made the way Champagne is made. As the label said: "Hanns Kornell eschews modern mass-production methods in favor of time-honored traditional practices . . . A wine-yeast-sugar blend was placed in 'THIS' same bottle and has been hand-tended by skilled workers through the years of fermentation, clearing and aging, under the personal supervision of Hanns Kornell."

But just about the time we met Hanns Kornell, the world was shifting underneath him. Schramsberg Vineyards had started up in 1965, producing better sparkling wines than Kornell's. Their wines had a finesse that his didn't. That's the wine Richard Nixon took to China. In 1973, Moët & Chandon opened a beautiful winery in Napa Valley that produced large quantities of outstanding sparkling wine at reasonable prices, and with the distribution heft of a large company behind it. One big Champagne house after another followed into California. Hanns Kornell's winery became quaint and old-fashioned, and his wines suddenly seemed clumsy.

It was clear that Hanns Kornell Champagne Cellars had to grow to survive. In the early 1980s, he borrowed $4.5 million for expansion. But, like so many of the pioneers in California, Hanns Kornell was a winemaker, not a businessman. In 1991, he filed for bankruptcy. The banks foreclosed on his winery the next year. By 1994, he was virtually destitute. When Kornell and his wife were faced with eviction, Robert Mondavi and his sons bought their house and told them they could stay there as long as they wanted. Hanns Kornell died later that year.

The winery was sold. In June 2000, a terrible fire swept through a newer part of the Hanns Kornell Champagne Cellars, almost destroying it. The original structure was spared.

On September 8, 1977, we stood across the tasting room

counter from Hanns Kornell, a ruddy white-haired leprechaun of a man with a quiet, gracious manner, and asked him to sign a bottle of his Muscat Alexandria, with the white label. "Thanks for your kind visit," he wrote. "Hanns Kornell." It is one bottle we will never open.

THREE

Taittinger Brut "La Française"

. . .

WE STILL WENT HOME FOR CHRISTMAS EVERY YEAR, JOHN to Jacksonville, Dottie to Tallahassee. Sometimes we visited each other's house for a day or two. The first time we drove up to the house in Jacksonville together, John's mother ran outside, grabbed both of Dottie's cheeks, and then hugged her for a long time before she even said hello to John. That night at dinner, John's brother Kris, meeting Dottie for the first time, stared at her for a while and finally said: "When you talk, do your cheeks go down?"

The most amazing thing about the visit was that when Dottie walked into the house, she knew where everything was. John's parents had designed their house in Jacksonville, and Dottie's had designed their house in Tallahassee—and they were essentially the same house, even down to the carpet in the formal living room where the kids and pets were banned. Only grown-ups could spend serious time in that white-carpeted room, which usually meant our dads on Sundays. That was the day John's father went in there to listen to Sinatra and Dottie's went in there to listen to Nat King Cole.

Our drill was that at John's home, his Jewish mother would quickly drag Dottie off into the kitchen, close the door, sit her down at the table, and ask, "So, how's my son getting on in the world?" As Dottie rattled off John's accomplishments—he really was incredibly young to be doing just about everything he was doing, she enthused—John's mom listened and smoked one cigarette after another. We were in love. Our friends all said we twinkled when we talked about each other. So Dottie would sit there and twinkle at John's mom and she would twinkle back at Dottie.

It soon became clear to John's mom that Dottie was open to talk about anything and everything. They'd talk about values, morality, religion, and politics. They'd talk about race. John's mom thought that class was more important than race, which in our case was certainly true. Nothing was off-limits. And it was immediately clear to Dottie that John's mom was an expert wife, mother, and friend—that was her job, after all—and she loved talking about all of those roles. Most important, she was an expert on John. Dottie and John's mom would talk and talk and talk until John's dad would finally open the door and say, "Ruthie, give the poor girl a break!"

That first evening, John's mom surprised everyone by insisting on eating in the dining room on the good dishes her mother had given her on her wedding day. Dottie's ritual with John's dad consisted of his reading to her from some of his first editions, which he had collected years before, mostly in New York. She would sit perched by his side and he would just as much act as read to her. He was a gifted comedian and a great storyteller. At the end of Dottie's first visit, John's little brother Kris pronounced her a keeper. The only other girl John had brought home, during college, had yelled at Kris because he had left the toilet seat up.

We still weren't allowed to sleep in the same bed, though. We were almost married before John's mother surprised us during one visit by picking up Dottie's suitcases in the guest room and, without a word, carrying them into John's. We didn't sleep together in Tallahassee until we were married.

Dottie's parents were more social than John's. They had lots of friends. So part of the drill of a visit to Dottie's mom's house meant sitting on the sofa in the family room while Mrs. Gaiter's friends, people Dottie hadn't seen in years, looked John over. In truth, some of these people had been trying to catch Dottie during a visit home for years. Unlike most kids who came home after college during the summer, she was always off somewhere working for a newspaper. As a young kid, she had always made herself scarce when company visited. Now with her name in the newspaper, the largest paper in the state, she had assumed a higher profile. The family's circle of friends had produced doctors and lawyers, even second- and third-generation ones, but she was the first journalist. Besides, visiting people was, well, what was expected when you lived in Tallahassee. It was the neighborly thing to do. And Dottie with a white boyfriend just had to be seen. In very sweet visits, some of Mrs. Gaiter's oldest friends came by for quick chats. As her mom's friends left, Dottie could see them squeezing her mom and pronouncing John a fine young man, good-looking, too. Ah, the rituals of mating.

Soon after we met, we'd visited New York for the first time. John showed Dottie around the Columbia campus. He bought her a meatball hero with sweet sauce from Ta-Kome, the greasy spoon that kept him fed for four years. Dottie could eat pickled herring and octopus, but *that* grossed her out. We didn't have enough money to do anything that required it, but so little really cost money. We walked around Times Square, Greenwich Village, the Upper West Side. We thought the city was incredible—so full of energy, with so much to do. We decided then that someday, somehow, we would live in New York. For our second trip, we decided to take the train. John's sainted Grandma Helen used to take the *Silver Meteor* to Jacksonville for her annual trip. This was always a special time for John, who would sit in the kitchen for hours with Grandma Helen while she made her famous brisket in a very heavy, jet-black pot. John told Dottie close to a million times how exciting it was to stand on the platform and wait for the *Silver Meteor* to arrive, so big and shiny and powerful. A train trip seemed like it might be fun, and romantic. We reserved a sleeper on the *Silver Meteor* from Miami to New York.

We had never been in a sleeper car, so we didn't quite know what to expect. But it seemed appropriate to take along a bottle of Champagne. We didn't know a lot about real Champagne—it was expensive, and Hanns Kornell had been fine enough—but we went out and picked up something called Taittinger Brut "La Française." Taittinger is one of those great Champagne houses of the Champagne region of France. Like most Champagne, Taittinger "La Française" is nonvintage—it's blended from several vintages for a consistent taste—but Taittinger also makes a "prestige cuvée" called Taittinger Comtes de Champagne, which is expensive. Vintage Champagne is only made in the best years, and from the best grapes. We didn't know any of this at the time. We picked up the Taittinger only because it was on sale.

We arrived at the train station with tickets, one piece of luggage, and a bottle of bubbly in hand. Finally, we boarded and found our bedroom. It was tiny, and all metal. Everything had a function, each little knob and hanger. There was an adorable, thin little closet—with a space up top that opened into the hallway, so we could leave our shoes there for the attendant to polish—and a very small bathroom with a sink that folded up in order to use the toilet. The bottom bed—it had bunks—folded right out of the wall and lay parallel to the large window. It didn't take us long to realize that there was no reason to be sitting in the seats when we could be lying in bed. We had the porter put the bed down and we never let him put it back up. The bed was just thirty-one inches wide, but that was more than enough for us. We could lie together in that tiny bed all day and watch the world go by.

We asked the porter for ice and then chilled the bottle of Champagne in the fold-up sink. When we popped it open, to celebrate the start of our trip, a remarkable smell filled that little cabin. Yeast and chalk and soil and citrus all wafted out of that single bottle of Champagne. We poured the Champagne into the glasses we'd brought, and the smallest little bubbles we'd ever seen appeared, rising like little DNA strands. "To your face," said Dottie. "To your bottom," said John. Then we sipped it. It was like nothing we had ever tasted, far more elegant than Hanns Kornell. It didn't taste like wine with bubbles. The bubbles themselves were the taste, or, perhaps, all of the taste was within the bubbles. We were lying in bed naked, headed to New York, with the world passing our window, rhythmic clicking underneath, and real French Champagne in our glasses. We couldn't imagine anything—or any wine—more wonderful.

We had a whole week in New York all to ourselves. We ate at Mama Leone's, where we had a 1973 Grignolino from Italy. We ate at Luchow's, in honor of John's parents, who said they never ate there because they didn't like Chinese food (it was German). We had lunch at Gage & Tollner, the venerable seafood restaurant, where the waiters wore stars indicating how many years they had worked there. John watched with awe as Dottie ate raw oysters and then moved on to shad and shad roe. He had the trout amandine, which was done just right. We ordered a Muscadet, the inexpensive white wine from the Loire Valley of France. We'd had it before and thought it was okay. When we had it with perfectly cooked seafood, we understood the true magic of Muscadet.

While in college John had seen a few Broadway plays from the cheap seats—*Raisin* with Virginia Capers, *Play It Again, Sam* with

Woody Allen, and *1776* with William Daniels—and he must have told Dottie about each of them a thousand times. He'd even played cast albums for her. Now we'd go together. We got tickets to *The Wiz,* an all-black remake of *The Wizard of Oz.* It was simply fabulous, brilliant. Not only that, but at the end, after a thunderous ovation, the new Dorothy, a young singer named Stephanie Mills, parted the curtain and came out with Margaret Hamilton, the original Wicked Witch of the West. The audience went nuts. When the applause died down, Margaret Hamilton simply said to the crowd: "Oz was never like this!"

We loved that experience, and the audience. The people in the theater were so elegant, so respectful, so sophisticated, so smart, so stylish. We wanted to be like them, but didn't think we ever could be.

When we next visited New York on the train, we made reservations at a new restaurant called Cellar in the Sky in the World Trade Center. Every Wednesday in *The New York Times,* which Dottie had delivered daily as a present for John, Cellar in the Sky had a little ad in which it simply printed the names of the five wines it would be serving with its $45 prix fixe dinner for the next two weeks. Week after week we'd see that ad and fantasize about eating there someday. This would be it.

Cellar in the Sky was an orphan space in Windows on the World. Windows was famous, of course, for its view from the 107th floor of the World Trade Center. But there was a little space that had no view, and someone must have come up with the idea that the only way to get people there was with something special. So they lined the glass walls with wine in thin, metal wine racks, put in enough tables for just thirty-five people, and called it Cellar in the Sky. The concept was then so new that they printed an explanation—typed on a manual typewriter and photocopied—that they sent us after we made reservations:

THE CELLAR IN THE SKY

The Cellar in the Sky is a small, romantic dining room within the larger restaurant that is Windows on the World. It is the working wine cellar for the entire restaurant and the setting for a spectacular dinner designed around wines. The single, seven-course menu provides a harmony between the five wines selected by Kevin Zraly and the food, chosen from among the best of the world's cuisines by Chef Andre Rene and Director Alan Lewis. Careful attention to the balance and succession of the foods and wines is usually done only for wine and food societies' dinners. Here, the adventure of a wine-lavished dining experience is available to thirty-five diners each night (except Sunday). Captain Pepe Enriquez presides over the room, lovingly presenting and describing each of the wines poured, each of the courses offered.

Jackets and ties are required! Denims? Never!

When we walked into Cellar in the Sky, the handwritten menu was resting on a frame.

CELLAR IN THE SKY

EGGPLANT, ORIENTAL
Wisdom & Warter Fino Sherry Solera 1908
MUSHROOM CONSOMMÉ
SEAFOOD FLAN, LOBSTER SAUCE
Domaine de Goulaine, Muscadet 1976
ROSEMARY ROASTED RACK AND SADDLE OF LAMB
JERUSALEM ARTICHOKES PROVENÇALE
Simi, Cabernet Sauvignon 1973
ARUGULA AND RED LETTUCE SALAD

ROQUEFORT, COROLLE, AND FONTINA CHEESES
Château Beychevelle, 1966
CHOCOLATE STRAWBERRY TART
Niersteiner Auflangen Auslese, 1976
COFFEE

Kevin Zraly was there—then just a young wine geek, now the famous wine expert and author of *The Windows on the World Complete Wine Course*. He explained each of the wines to us as the waiters poured them endlessly: the sherry that was lighter than air, the crisp Muscadet, the rich Simi Cabernet Sauvignon from one of America's most venerable producers, the German from a great year that would probably last forever, and the Beychevelle.

The Beychevelle. Château Beychevelle is a Bordeaux wine from Saint-Julien. It's a "fourth growth," which means that when Bordeaux wines were officially classified in 1855, at the direction of Napoléon III, it was considered in the fourth rank. But it's really better than that, and in an excellent year like 1966, it was terrific. Not only that, but by the time we tasted it that night, more than a decade old, it was nicely mature—supple, deep with fruit, with layers of complexity and a long finish that tasted almost majestic to us. It was the first well-aged fine Bordeaux we'd ever tasted from a good year, and it was magnificent. There was a comfort to it, almost a kind of wisdom of age, that we'd never tasted before. It wasn't trying to be anything. It simply was what it was. The good wines we'd tasted until then seemed to be going somewhere. This wine had already arrived.

We have always been demonstrative at restaurants. We get excited about the food and the wine and aren't embarrassed to show it. That, in turn, sometimes excites the people who work there,

who then drop by to talk. Cellar in the Sky had a particularly intimate atmosphere—there was even a classical guitarist playing
softly in the back, and a little bathroom just for us—and it was
carefully watched over by the great New York restaurateur Alan
Lewis. It was said that Alan Lewis, who ran Windows on the
World, had a soft spot for black women. Maybe that was it. Maybe
it was just that we were so clearly having the greatest meal of our
lives. For whatever reason, Alan Lewis came by, pulled up a chair,
and started talking to us while smoking a cigarette. He told us
about Windows and about Cellar and seemed genuinely interested
in our stories about Miami. It was, in all, a most remarkable experience. When we returned to Miami, we made a pact: Whoever
got a job in New York first, the other would follow.

For Christmas 1978, Dottie gave John a copper Dottie cookie
cutter and John gave Dottie a Dottie-shaped mirror. John's
mother joined in, too. She had taken up pottery. She made a nap-
kin holder with Dottie faces on both sides.

FOUR

Louis Roederer Cristal 1974

. . .

IN 1978, JOHN WAS TRANSFERRED BACK TO MIAMI AS AN assistant city editor. Dottie, meanwhile, had left reporting and joined the state desk as an editor. John's return meant that we would be living together and working together in the same office for the first time. We decided that we wanted to live in Coconut Grove again and went looking for an apartment, or maybe even a house to rent. Our first stop, of course, was the Wine Lady of Coconut Grove. With John in West Palm Beach and Dottie living in North Miami Beach, we hadn't gone to see her in two years. She was gone. The shop was gone. There was no indication she'd ever been there. We always wondered what became of her, but we never even got a lead.

We found a little house to rent for $450 a month. It had a Persian lime tree for Dottie, orange shag carpeting in the bedrooms, a big sunken bathroom, and plenty of space. This was the clincher:

The man who owned the house was an amateur photographer. He had built a little photo lab, with no windows and its own air-conditioning unit, in the back of the house. With the doors closed, it was chilly and pitch-black. With the lights on, it was cute, with white carpeting and cheap wood paneling. It was perfect for a wine room. Our very first purchase was a pair of metal wine racks that Dottie had found in Tallahassee and had shipped down. Each held sixty bottles. We couldn't fill even one of them.

Each morning, we made the short drive to the office. We worked pretty much all day and deep into the night. We were going to change the world, or at least Miami. The city was already becoming a pretty mean place by then, not only because cocaine money was creating rampant corruption and crime, but because ethnic tensions were beginning to escalate. The community leaders, both elected and behind the scenes, were bozos. Someone came up with a plan to make dying South Beach into a kind of American Venice, with canals. But how to chase out the many old, poor people who were spending their last years there? The city decided to ban any improvements in the area, guaranteeing that it would become a slum. Then, by God, people would leave.

We always suspected that community leaders were slow to move aggressively against the "cocaine cowboys" because, frankly, cocaine money was making Miami rich. High-end restaurants were packed with shady characters who ordered the most expensive wines on the menu and often gulped them down while smoking cigars. (Sometimes they'd drink only one glass and leave the rest of a great bottle. Philistines!) Land prices were soaring. But when warring cocaine lords burst into a shootout at Dadeland Mall, right in the middle of sleepy, suburban Dade County, they made a serious mistake. A top editor's wife was shopping there at the time. There's an old saying in journalism that news is what happens to the publisher, and big news is what happens to the publisher's wife. This was big news. The community decided that it was time to crack down on cocaine in its midst.

After covering this every night, we ate out late or came home with take-out food to a refrigerator that was almost empty except for a bottle of Chandon. We were both too busy to shop for groceries. Chandon was the sparkling wine made by Moët & Chandon in California that was hitting the market in force by then. It was really good, but the best thing was that it was just $8.99 a bottle. There was no reason not to drink it all the time, so we did.

American interest in wine was at an all-time high. Per capita consumption was about to pass two gallons a year for the first time. Frank J. Prial, the great wine columnist of *The New York Times,* put his columns together into a book called *Wine Talk* that seemed written just for us. The very first chapter was called "The Best Bottle."

"When the talk turns to wine," he wrote, "I can usually hold my own. But there is one game of wine one-upmanship that is always difficult to play: that business about the best bottle." He wrote about some of the magnificent bottles he'd had, but concluded that maybe the best bottle was an Almaden Mountain Chablis he'd had in 1954, because he'd just come in from "a wearing, pounding patrol" with the Coast Guard and he had it with his "first decent meal in days." It wasn't just us. Even a real expert understood that there's a lot more to wine than what's in the bottle.

With interest in wine so high, it was the perfect time for a new organization called Les Amis du Vin to be founded. It was an international group with its own magazine and dues of $20 a year. Ron Fonte, a much-decorated authority on wine and food, headed it for seventeen years, and its headquarters were in Silver Spring, Maryland. Dottie gave John a membership for Christmas, so we joined the Miami chapter. What a revelation. We really weren't alone. There were regular tastings that usually didn't cost much unless there was a feast served with the wines, and fifty people just like us would show up, people who were passionate about wine but were not wine snobs. Winemakers poured their wines and we all listened attentively through the first two or three wines. Then the room got boisterous and no one paid much attention to the winemakers. Some of the guests accepted this with humor and inevitability; some did not. We tasted everything—Champagne with Robert Gourdin, who was North American sales director for Moët & Chandon, and Château Latour with Harry Waugh, the celebrated English wine merchant who was director of Latour. We even tasted various beers with Indian food. They told us that the beer would smell like bananas when it warmed up, and darned if it didn't. At its peak, Les Amis had 350 chapters worldwide, but it folded in 1988.

Through Les Amis, we discovered another great wine merchant, Chip Cassidy. We'd go to Chip's store in Miami, Crown Liquors, and he'd run around like he was on fire. "You've got to try this!" he'd say. "It'll blow your head off!" He talked about the vineyards and the people behind the wines. He wanted us to try everything. We tasted sparkling Vouvray from the Loire Valley of France, sparkling Sekt from Germany, Petite Sirah from California, Aurora Blanc from New York State, Est! Est!! Est!!! from Italy, and Medea Rouge from Algeria. We found restaurants with good wine lists and others that let us bring our own. We practically lived at a little antique-filled restaurant called The Affair whose entire staff appeared to be the male couple who owned it. It had two entrées, one meat, one fish, and included in the price of the dinner were two wines, one white and one red. Walking into their restaurant was like entering a grand salon. There was a sitting area with high-backed velvet sofas with lace and silk throws accenting them, and all sorts of curios, including a collection of garnet glasses and antique dolls. The chef, wearing burgundy velvet slippers, presided over everything and helped serve. It was eclectic and cozy, and Dottie just loved the way it looked.

At around the same time, the *Herald* decided to start printing a regional section that would include in its area of coverage a large and vibrant black section of Miami. The newspaper had no black editors at the time other than Dottie, and she felt this was a good opportunity to address the community's worsening racial problems, so she raised her hand for the new job. When the paper turned her down, she quit and went to the *Herald*'s afternoon competitor, the *Miami News,* in the same building. When the executive editor of the *Herald* heard that Dottie had quit, he called John in to ask if she was serious. John told him, "Ask Dottie." The white man the *Herald* gave the job to washed out in about six months.

Dottie's working hours at an afternoon paper were tough on us. She worked either from three A.M. until noon or from six P.M. to three A.M. as the *News*'s night city editor, and we rarely saw each other awake. But Dottie enjoyed kicking the *Herald*'s butt with her scrappy little staff. She'd wait until the *Herald* was well past its final deadline to tell John about some story she had that he didn't.

We began having wine dinners with friends on weekends. Miami has always been a place where people had little in common. It's a transient town in many ways. There's not much of a downtown, either in fact or in principle. The town we covered had Jews and crackers, a vibrant gay culture and Anita Bryant, powerful old-timers who couldn't adjust to the times and newcomers who wanted to make a quick buck and run—not to mention the more recent problems of blacks versus whites versus Hispanics, which isn't even that simple, since there's also American blacks versus Haitians and Cubans versus other Latin Americans. There are also divides between black Cubans and white Cubans. (White Cubans, for example, insist that people who would be considered white Americans in any other city in America be called "Anglos" instead of white.) There was only one thing many people in Miami had in common: They hated the *Herald*. Their reasons were diverse, and often unfair, but it was a fact.

The *Miami Herald* building not only looked like a fortress, but very much was a fortress to those of us who worked there. Inevitably, that meant that the people of the *Herald* turned often to one another for comfort and companionship. That's pretty much how our wine-tasting group got started. Its members included "the two Freds," both of whom were assistant city editors at one time or another and who, after they married, participated with their wives, the two Catherines; Bob, an editor who worked for John, and his wife; three reporters who worked for John, and us. Everyone took turns hosting the dinners, and everyone brought a course and a wine to go with it.

When we were alone at home, we tried everything, but we had our house wines, too. Neither of us ever wanted to open a good bottle of wine without the other, but one of us was often home before the other, and we obviously had to have a glass of something. So we found "house wines"—good, inexpensive, everyday wines that weren't so precious that we couldn't just pop one open. There was a Spanish red, from Rioja, called Federico Paternina "Banda Azul," for instance, and Premiat, a red from Romania. We even had a house dessert wine. Like most Americans, we had avoided dessert wines for a long time, since we figured they were heavy and would remind us of John's father's Manischewitz, thick and sickly sweet and hard to drink. One day we saw a golden wine in an oddly shaped bottle called Muscat des Papes Muscat de Beaumes-de-Venise, and we gave it a try. It was about $8 and it changed forever our view of dessert wines.

Muscat is a very special, honeylike grape that makes good wines all over the world. This one, from France, was a bit heavy, but so very flavorful and lovely that we always kept a bottle in the refrigerator. It even had a screwtop, so we could have a small glass of it for several days. Whenever we offered friends a wine at our home, they would gladly accept it. We were known for serving good stuff. But dessert wines were different. After dinner, we moved our guests to the living room, put out pretty little glasses that Dottie collected, and brought in the bottle of Muscat. It had a beautiful golden glow and in that strange little bottle, it could have been shampoo, for all people knew. Invariably, when we poured it and handed it to them, explaining that it was a dessert wine, they shook their heads, waved their hands, and said, "No, I don't like dessert wines." We figure few of our friends had ever had a dessert wine back then, but we knew what they were thinking. "Just take a sip of this," we said. "It really is good." And a funny thing would happen. Before we knew it, their glass would be empty and they would be pouring themselves more.

We went to both hometowns for Christmas that year. Before we did, John gave Dottie her Christmas present: a gold necklace with a very delicate little gold Dottie face hanging from it. First we drove to Tallahassee, where we celebrated Christmas with Dottie's family. Then we drove over to Jacksonville, 150 miles to the east, and celebrated with John's family. Each of us was very much a member of the other's family. In Jacksonville one day, when Dottie was in another room, John's father was sitting in his favorite chair and John's mother was in the kitchen, as usual. John stood in the doorway between them and said, "I think I'm going to marry Dottie." There was a long pause. "Well?" he said. "It's about time," said his mother.

Later that day, she handed him a box. "You'll need these," she said. Inside were John's favorite Champagne glasses. They were magnificent. They were the old-fashioned bowl glasses, and the glass was so thin and light that it seemed like air. There were grape leaves delicately etched into the glass and, most remarkably, the stems were hollow. They were the most beautiful glasses in the world. John's parents had received them from his mother's sister for their wedding in 1942. On their wedding night, before heading off to the Waldorf for a one-night honeymoon, they'd accidentally thrown the set of six down the garbage chute at 915 West End Avenue, where Grandma Helen lived. They finally found them in the garbage, with just one broken. The other five became the family's most prized possessions, to be taken out only on Thanksgiving. These were the perfect glasses to propose with.

Why hadn't we gotten married until then? That's a good question. As we were writing this book, John left this section blank in his draft, writing a note to Dottie to fill in: "WHY WE HAD NOT GOTTEN MARRIED UNTIL THEN." When he next returned to the book after Dottie had worked on it, there was this: "BECAUSE YOU WERE A JERK."

So there you have it.

In any case, the plan was set. Louis Roederer Cristal Champagne is one of those "prestige cuvées" that cost a fortune, like Moët & Chandon's Dom Pérignon and Perrier-Jouët's "Flower Bottle" (Fleur de Champagne). There's no bottle quite like Cristal. It's clear, unlike the others, and comes in a crinkly gold cellophane wrapping that makes the elegant label look even more elegant. It is a beautiful bottle of wine, both inside and out. This was the bottle Dottie had given to John for Christmas years earlier. She had been venturing into wine shops more and more. Chip at Crown Liquors had made buying wine unintimidating. Plus, she knew much more about wine now. When she saw the Cristal, she knew John would be thrilled to have it and that it was a wine he would never buy himself. We could keep it around for a special occasion. It was the most beautiful bottle in our wine room.

Our one hundred bottles were evenly divided between the two racks, which still left some holes. We had two little chairs in the wine room, and a lecture stand that we used as a book rack.

Dottie had bought that at the Salvation Army, along with most of our other furniture. A new book by Alexis Bespaloff had come out called *The Fireside Book of Wine* that included some great stories. It made wine fun. Few people seemed to have a sense of humor about this subject, but this book proved that someone did. We'd go into the wine room, read, look at our bottles, study the Hugh Johnson atlas, and choose a bottle for dinner. We loved that house, but we especially loved that room. The Cristal seemed to complete it.

John: *On December 27, 1978, immediately after we drove home from Jacksonville, I put my plan into action. I sat Dottie down on a couch in the living room and brought out the glasses. Then I brought over the Cristal in an ice bucket. After being a couple for five years, I was finally going to ask Dottie to marry me, as soon as I popped open the Champagne. By that time, I had opened a lot of bubbly. There had been dozens of bottles of Hanns Kornell and our regular Chandon, and sometimes a good Champagne with friends. Opening a bottle was always filled with a little danger, since I'm a bit of a klutz, but it was never difficult.*

I took the beautiful gold metal off the neck of the bottle, then the wire basket. Dottie waited quietly, with anticipation, looking even more beatific and beautiful than usual. I twisted the bottle and—nothing. The cork didn't budge. I tried again. I twisted until I was starting to sweat. It's a sign, I thought, but I kept trying anyway. I was not going to propose until that goddamn bottle popped open.

Dottie: *This was proof that John was dying. He could pop a Champagne cork in his sleep. But he'd grown quite pale over the past week, which, for him, was quite an accomplishment. Back then, John was one of the whitest people even white people had seen. He rarely left the newsroom, and he wasn't all that fond of the sun anyway. Now, as he fought that cork, he was pale and clammy.*

...

Then the phone rang. The mood was broken. John, frustrated and angry, got up to answer it. On the other end, to his surprise, was his father. He was calling to make sure we'd gotten home safely, which he'd never done before. "Dad," John whispered into the phone, "I'm trying to open a bottle of Champagne so I can propose to Dottie, and I can't get it open."

John's father had opened few bottles of bubbly in his life, pretty much just that bottle of Korbel every Thanksgiving. Not only that, but he never picked up tools. John doesn't remember his father ever fixing anything around the house. The understanding in the Brecher household, in fact, was that there was something in Jewish men's genetic makeup that didn't allow them to use tools successfully. But at that moment, John's father immediately answered: "Use pliers." John knew enough about wine to know that was a terrible idea. "You can't use pliers to open a bottle of Champagne," he said dismissively. "Use pliers," said his father. John hung up and, with no other choice, went to get pliers.

Dottie sat on the couch, sparkling. The elegant glasses were on the table, reflecting the beautiful bottle of Cristal that sat between them. In the midst of this elegant scene, John came out with pliers. He grabbed the bottle and twisted the cork with the pliers. It turned! When the cork finally came out, it was a monster, a massive piece of tree bark that looked like a beach umbrella. John poured the Cristal into his parents' glasses and asked: "Will you marry me?"

John: *Then, after all that, Dottie leaps up without even answering me, runs to the phone, and calls her mother, leaving me there holding a glass of Champagne and wondering what the hell is going on.*

Dottie: *That's not true. I said yes, kissed and hugged John for a long time, then called my mother. You know, my parents have di-*

verging stories about my dad's proposal, too. Dad always insisted
that Mom proposed to him. I think it's one of those weird guy things,
that men create alternate stories of that incredible moment just to
torment their wives.

John took the cork to a plastic factory, where they encased it,
along with an etched Dottie face, in a see-through block of plastic.
To this day, when we look at that cork, we're amazed it ever came
out at all. And as it turned out, John was diagnosed with pneumo-
nia a few days later.

FIVE

Beaulieu Vineyard Georges de Latour Private Reserve 1968

. . .

WE WERE EXCITED ABOUT GETTING MARRIED, OF COURSE, but nervous about it, too. We didn't want anything to change. If someone could have just sprinkled pixie dust on us and said, "You're married," we would have been happy. We weren't looking for a new beginning or the end of anything, but just a continuation of everything we had. We decided to have a very small wedding in Tallahassee. Dottie's mother had been grooming her backyard for a wedding for years. We looked at the calendar to find a good weekend in April to get married and decided on April 14. It didn't strike John at the time, but that was the same day as his parents' anniversary. We drove to each family's home in January to accept congratulations and to start planning.

When we were in Jacksonville, we told John's parents that we needed to get a ring, but were at a loss because we knew nothing about diamonds and were sure we'd get ripped off. John's mother disappeared for a few minutes and came back with a small white box containing a ring with a huge diamond. "Grandpa Dave gave this to me years ago," she said. "I forgot I had it." Through all the lean years when John's family had scraped by, she'd forgotten she had a diamond in her drawer that was worth some real money. It had belonged to John's father's mother. The engagement ring had a large diamond set high in a tiny platinum band with diamonds along the side. The wedding band consisted of several links, each with a fully cut diamond set in it. Amazing rings. John's mom said she had been saving them for Dottie.

We wanted our wedding to be a simple affair. We invited just seventeen people—neighbors on either side of the house, immediate family, and the Gaiters' oldest friend, a very elderly woman who would call Dottie's mother from time to time and teasingly inquire: "Is John still white?" For our own parents, though, race never seemed an issue. We always felt very lucky to have gotten the parents we did. Years later, when we were approaching our second decade together, young women would find their way to Dottie and pour out their anxiety about marrying someone of another race. Calling from other states, they had heard somehow that we were happily married and had loving, supportive families. What was our secret? In our case, our parents weren't supportive of us because they were the world's greatest liberals or the most understanding people in the world or because they saw this as an important social statement. In fact, we're sure that, in bed at night, they worried how the world would accept us and especially our children. But they knew us. We were both middle children and highly independent. We both had left home at eighteen and never really looked back. We were strong-willed and levelheaded, and rarely did anything stupid or impetuous. They were proud of the job they had done raising us. Beyond that, though, our parents were just so damn glad that we'd found someone. And the icing on the cake was that they loved the person we'd found.

Dottie's mother knew a notary public who conducted weddings. Dottie's mother would make her famous lamb for dinner after the ceremony, and the rest of the food would be catered by an old sorority friend of hers.

Dottie's mother's lamb is one of the wonders of the world. John doesn't even like lamb, but he loves hers.

MRS. GAITER'S LEG OF LAMB

Take a 4-lb. leg of lamb, carefully make tiny slits in the skin, and insert slivers of garlic. Place in pan for marinating. Sprinkle salt, pepper, ground ginger, oregano, curry powder, 1 tablespoon of sugar, and 1 tablespoon of vinegar on the lamb. Cover entirely with slices of onions, then foil. Place in the refrigerator overnight. To cook, preheat the oven to 400°F. When the oven is ready, place the uncovered lamb in the oven for an hour. After an hour, turn the oven down to 325°F and cook for another 90 minutes or until fork-tender.

We flew to Tallahassee a couple of days before the wedding to prepare. The only beverage we wanted at our wedding was Champagne, and we knew that we wanted everyone to drink it from the moment they walked in the door until the moment they left. We decided that for seventeen guests, a case and a half—eighteen bottles—would probably be enough. Since that first bottle on our first train trip together, Taittinger had been "our" Champagne, so we knew that's what we'd have to find. It was harder than we expected in Tallahassee, but we finally found a little store near Florida State University that had eighteen bottles, for $17 each, cash only. As we counted out the money to the college kid behind the counter, it was clear that this was the biggest sale this little store had ever made. It was certainly the most we'd ever spent on wine at one time. But the full case actually came in an unopened, straight-from-France box. "TAITTINGER. Reims. La Française. Champagne Brut" it said in big letters on the side.

There were the inevitable glitches along the way to our wedding: A terrible storm the night before delayed John's best friend's flight from New York until the middle of the night, the Jaguar that Dottie's mom owned broke down during our numerous trips to the airport, and—horrors—her mother decided to dye the carpet three days before the wedding even though she had been told that the dye should set four days before the floor could be used. But, as always, Dottie's mom pulled it off. The carpet was fine and the day was sunny when John's family arrived a few hours before the ceremony and met Dottie's mother for the first time. They had talked many times on the phone over the years and felt they knew one another. Before the wedding, John's brother Kris, sitting next to the case of Taittinger, read Dottie a poem he had written about her face, called "Big Cheeks." It began:

> I've always been fascinated
>   with girls with big cheeks.
> Instead of going in, they go out.
> The faces that look like they're
>   stuffed all with food
> Are the faces I'm writing about.

The ceremony was perfect. We met every guest at the door with a glass of Champagne. Dottie's mom suggested we keep all of the bottles chilled in ice in a huge, cement birdbath in her backyard. It was a lovely touch for a garden wedding. John's brother Jim was responsible for making sure that no one's glass was ever empty, and they never were. John's father walked him across the newly cut lawn to the notary public, who was dressed in a nice white robe, and everybody lined up to wait for Dottie. First came her sisters, Juarlyn and Karen. When Dottie walked out, in a lacy, white Mexican wedding dress with flowers in her hair, her golden Dottie necklace shimmering in the sunlight, John thought she'd never looked more lustrous, and he began to cry. When the notary declared us husband and wife, John kissed Dottie on the forehead and then grabbed her head. Then we hugged and both cried. So did everyone else.

When we all sat down at a single long table to eat, Jim kept the Taittinger flowing. When we had to leave at seven—we had to catch a train—there was a single bottle of Taittinger remaining, which we stuffed into our suitcase.

We had decided to take a train trip to San Francisco and Napa Valley for our honeymoon since we loved it so much the last time. John's parents drove us to Jacksonville, where we caught the *Floridian* to Chicago. The *Floridian* was one of the grand old train routes of America, making an arc through the South and into the Midwest. It was discontinued several months after our honeymoon, and was clearly on its last legs even then. But it didn't much matter to us. We crammed into our little cabin—it was late at night, and the bed was already down—and went right to sleep. The next day, we opened the Taittinger for breakfast and, when it was finished, found ourselves without Champagne. The dining car had six half bottles of Almaden "Champagne," a cheap, bulk California bubbly. We bought them all. When we got to Chicago, we bought provisions for the rest of the trip. In other words, we found a wine store near the train station and bought several different Champagnes.

During our entire trip to Chicago, and then on to San Francisco on the *California Zephyr,* we never got out of bed. The porter brought us our meals. We rang for ice, left our empty bottles outside, and otherwise stayed in bed and watched America go by. It was all so scenic during the day: the little towns right out of *The Last Picture Show,* the miles and miles of wheat fields, the beautiful scenery, and the magnificent sunsets. Nighttime brought warm lights illuminating windows of lone houses out in the darkness, cool air surrounding us, and no sound except the click-clack of the tracks. We drank heroic amounts of Champagne, each bottle different. There was Mumm Extra Dry and Piper-Heidsieck and Heidsieck & Co. Monopole and Bollinger. We had never tasted several Champagnes one after another, and it was fascinating. We loved each in its own way, but they were clearly different—some with more taste than others, some a bit sweeter, some with aggressive bubbles, and some with bubbles that were shy.

The *California Zephyr* is a great train covering magnificent landscapes, especially in the West. We stayed in bed, day and night, glued to the window. One sight was more remarkable than the next. But there was no more spectacular sight than the one we saw one night while approaching Denver. The route that leads up and down the Rocky Mountains is one of the greatest parts of the trip, with the train groaning all the way uphill and turns so sharp that if we pressed our faces against the window we could see the back of the train. As we were lying in bed one night, we began to round a mountain headed for Denver. Far in the distance, on a moonless night, the city spread before us like little pinpricks of light. Then we got to the other side of the mountain and the lights disappeared. But in a while we came back around, and there were the pinpricks again, but slightly larger. Around and around we went, the lights disappearing into total darkness, then reappearing suddenly, a little closer, as the city began to come into view. It was magical.

We had made reservations in St. Helena, in Napa Valley, at a new place called the Harvest Inn. When we arrived, we found out how new it was. It was small, and the landscaping had just been planted. It was surrounded on three sides by grapevines.

We looked at our room and immediately rushed out. We had to get to Beaulieu Vineyard. André Tchelistcheff, the legendary Beaulieu winemaker, believed California could produce world-class wines, and he had made believers out of many people. The 1968 and 1974 Beaulieu Georges de Latour Private Reserve Cabernet Sauvignons were among the wines that had established California as one of the world's best winemaking regions. In the years since, as Americans woke up to wine, these wines had become precious. Even in 1979, the 1968 sold for $125 a bottle. The 1974 was almost as expensive. We'd heard that the winery sold ten bottles of each every day, for only $35 a bottle. We had to have one. We rushed to the winery, ran downstairs, and discovered that the '74 was gone for the day, but there was one bottle left of the 1968. We grabbed it and headed back to the Harvest Inn, where we asked the innkeeper if we could borrow a corkscrew and two glasses and walk out among his vines.

Harvest in California takes place mostly in September and October. Not long after that, the vines lose their leaves and look dead. In April in Napa and Sonoma, there is bud break, when the very first hints of greenery appear. Bud break is carefully noted because it gives some idea how long the growing season will be. By late April or early May, the new growth is everywhere—these are vines, after all. It's like the world is being created anew, fresh with promise.

We took our glasses and the corkscrew into a vineyard behind the inn, where we sat down on the very fertile soil and opened our bottle. The sun was just barely above the mountains that make Napa Valley a valley. When we opened that wine, it seemed to fill the entire vineyard with its bouquet. When we tasted it, we couldn't believe our palates. It was simply perfect, like no wine we had ever tasted. It was filled with fruit, but had all sorts of edges and dimensions. It wasn't at all velvety, but instead had so much structure it seemed to take on a solid form. We clinked our glasses. "To your face," said Dottie. "To your bottom," said John. As we sat on the ground, the sun began to set behind the mountains, and the sky turned red and gold. As it did, the wine changed, too. With each sip, it grew and developed. A taste that had been just a hint would become the primary taste. A little cream, a little blackberry, a little cherry. First some power, then some elegance, then a shyness that made us come to it. As the sun went down, finally disappearing, we clinked glasses and finished the last sips. We felt as though we'd tasted a dozen bottles in one.

It was then, and remains, and will always remain, our greatest bottle of wine.

For the next several days, we dropped in on winery after winery. Napa was younger then, far more innocent and a lot less crowded. Winemakers themselves were almost always behind the counter, and they were so thrilled to meet someone who really cared about their craft. We visited Château Montelena, the winery that had made the Chardonnay that beat the French, and Rutherford Cellars, where Bernard Skoda showed us how light a dessert wine could be—airy and ephemeral—when he poured us his Muscat of Alexandria, made from the honey-orange Muscat grape. Bernard Skoda was the first winemaker who specifically studied Dottie's face as she drank to see what she thought. Before she could say anything, Mr. Skoda's face broke out into a smile. He knew the delight that she felt. His Muscat was pure bliss. When we told the Skodas that we were on our honeymoon, Mrs. Skoda went back into her house and came out with a corkscrew with their winery's name on it. "A wedding present from us," she said, pushing it into Dottie's hands. Dottie kept that portable corkscrew in her purse for years—for emergencies—and every time we used it, we could still taste the Skodas' Muscat.

We dropped into Sutter Home again, just as we had on our first trip. The man behind the counter poured us a pink, slightly sweet wine that he was especially proud of. "This is White Zinfandel," he said. "It's getting really popular." Zinfandel, to us, was not only a red wine, but a RED wine—big, bold, and unrestrained. The 1970s were a time of great experimentation in California winemaking, and no grape was more experimented with than Zinfandel. And with good reason. While other fine grapes are associated with other countries—Cabernet Sauvignon and Chardonnay from France, for instance, and Nebbiolo from Italy—Zinfandel is truly American, and grown only in the United States. It's a very peppery, aggressive wine that seems to suit the American character, and especially California winemakers. So they had fun with it. They made big, heavy Zinfandels, even late-harvest Zinfandels with massive tastes and alcohol levels up around 17 percent, compared to 12 percent or so for most table wines.

Wineries had been experimenting, too, of course, with what might score big with the American public. Pink wine seemed like a very good bet. After all, hadn't we all started with Lancers and Mateus? Sebastiani made a pink wine it called "Eye of the Swan," "a wine of light pigmentation produced of the Pinot Noir variety." Simi made "Rosé of Cabernet Sauvignon," "a rosé with personality."

Sutter Home took both of these strains and made a pink wine from Zinfandel (pink wines are made from dark grapes by squeezing the juice out and leaving it in contact with the skins, which provide the color to the clear juice, for just a short time). But the winery did something else, and this was the genius: After two years, when it made White Zinfandel and fermented it to dryness, Sutter Home shifted course, and instead left it slightly sweet. There's an old saying that "Americans talk dry but drink sweet," and the people at Sutter Home clearly understood this. We found out how smart they were that moment, when a man burst into the tasting room. "Can I get two cases of your White Zinfandel?" he asked breathlessly. He had already backed his car up to the tasting room door, trunk open. The man behind the counter looked at us, smiled, and said: "I swear to you I didn't set that up."

When we tasted the White Zinfandel that day, it was really quite good—lively and very refreshing. It was the start of a national sensation. The company says: "During the 1980s, Sutter Home White Zinfandel was the single most popular premium wine in the United States, with sales growing exponentially from 25,000 cases in 1981 to three million in 1990. Not surprisingly, this unprecedented sales success spawned an army of emulative 'blush' wines, many of which became the salvations of the financially-strapped small wineries producing them. (The ultimate cash-flow wine, White Zinfandel is easy to produce, requires very little aging, and begins returning revenue a few scant months after the harvest.)" For years, White Zinfandel was the most popular "varietal" wine in the United States. Sutter Home's White Zinfandel is around 3 percent sugar now.

On the last day of our trip, we drove up a mountain because a guidebook said there was a winery there called Nichelini Vineyard. It was just a house and a barn, and there was no sign of life anywhere. We rang the bell and since there was no answer, we walked around back, figuring maybe the winery and tasting room were there. In back we found a woman sitting alone at a table. We asked if this was Nichelini Vineyard and she said yes and that we should sit down. It was her back porch, right outside the kitchen. There were hummingbird feeders all around, and lots of hummingbirds darting about. The woman took out a bottle of Carnelian from a small cooler.

During this period of experimentation, new grapes seemed to appear all the time—and this really was a new grape, invented in 1972 by crossing various kinds of grapes that included Cabernet Sauvignon, Carignane, and Grenache. She poured all three of us a

big glass—not a taste, but a glass. The woman was Dorothy Nichelini, and she was happy for the company. Her husband, Jim, was in
the hospital for open-heart surgery. Her round face open and
sad, she told us all about Jim. She took out another kind of
wine and told us about how he wouldn't stop smoking, how he
wouldn't slow down. And then her eyes teared up and she stopped
talking and we all just sat there, drinking wine and watching the
hummingbirds.

Jim died in 1985 at the age of fifty-four. The winery, which
was founded in 1890, is still owned and run by Nichelini family
members and it is, according to Marie Antonette Nichelini-Irwin,
Jim's sister and director of marketing, "the oldest, same-family
continuously owned and operated winery in Napa Valley."

La Reserve Dunfey Bordeaux Blanc

. . .

_THE *MIAMI HERALD* HAS ALWAYS BEEN A KIND OF JOURNALIstic farm team. The *Herald* hires bright young kids right out of college and works them hard right from the start. The best of them rise to the top and then often move on to *The New York Times* or *The Washington Post* or the newsweeklies. This was, of course, a matter of great frustration to management, which tried—almost always in vain—to keep its talent in Miami. In 1979, a friend of ours named Steve Strasser was hired by *Newsweek* in New York. A few months later he called John, said there was an opening for a writer in the foreign section, and asked if he'd like to apply.

This was it! We had wanted to live in New York for so long— we'd even sent a few letters over the years to the *Times*—and now we might actually make it there. To be sure, life in Miami continued to be interesting. We loved our house, and the two wine racks were almost filled. Our little tasting group was our social life, and the Les Amis du Vin Miami chapter continued to be active, with tastings of Champagne and wines from the Loire Valley. The news was certainly interesting, too. Ethnic tensions were growing all the time. There had been some wrong-house raids where police had burst into the homes of law-abiding black people and roughed them up. Corruption was rampant. Several members of the Miami police force had been charged with drug dealing. Dade state attorney and future U.S. attorney general Janet Reno—the daughter of a former *Miami Herald* reporter—had her hands full.

On Halloween 1979, John flew to New York to meet with *Newsweek*'s editors. There are only a few days each year when New York's weather is absolutely perfect, and this was one of them. It was crisp and slightly cool. The sky was clear and the sun was shining so brightly that the city seemed almost clean. A few blocks before the cab got to the *Newsweek* building at Fiftieth Street and Madison Avenue, John decided to get out and walk. He was exhilarated. Steve and another old Miami hand took John to lunch, at *Newsweek*'s expense, at a place where they ordered filet mignon. John couldn't believe it. At the *Herald,* where money was always tight, taking anyone out to lunch for any reason was just about forbidden, and here John was at a New York restaurant eating filet mignon for lunch, on the company.

Things seemed to go well in the interview. John would be a writer on the foreign staff. At *Newsweek,* reporters in the field filed notes to a writer in New York, who put the story together and got the first byline. It was a choice, somewhat glamorous job, and it paid well. Not only that, but foreign news was hot at the time. Terrorist groups were on a rampage everywhere, the Mideast was a mess, Libya was acting up, and Ronald Reagan was talking about the Evil Empire. When John returned to Miami, we opened a bottle of Chandon, our house bubbly, the one that we kept in the refrigerator every day. It seemed only a matter of time before we'd move to New York. Then Dottie would find a job. It shouldn't be a problem.

Four days after John's interview, an Iranian mob attacked the U.S. embassy in Tehran and seized sixty-six American hostages, and the people at *Newsweek* forgot about John. Weeks passed, and there was no word. But we were busy anyway. On December 17, Miami police chased a black motorcyclist named Arthur McDuffie, who had run a red light. When they caught up to him, they savagely beat him to death. McDuffie, who was thirty-three years old, was no outlaw—he was an insurance executive—and the incident confirmed the black community's fears about the police.

Christmas that year was an understated affair, since we'd been expecting to spend the holidays in New York. John gave Dottie a Dottie rubber stamp. Dottie gave John a soft-sculpture case of wine that she had made. Each bottle, which she'd sewed and stuffed like a pillow, had a Dottie drawing and a different label with the word "cheek" in it. There was Moulin-a-Cheek, Cheek Cellars, and Château Cheeks. John's mother made a Dottie coffee mug for Dottie's mother and gave John a Dottie ashtray. Fortunately we had a large house, but Dottie ideas were getting harder to come by. Starting in September, John would haunt the newsroom, asking everyone if they had any ideas for Dottie presents. One year, the managing editor took a few moments at deadline to consider this and suggested a Dottie rug, which John then made himself.

Knowing our passion for wine, John's parents gave us a three-ring notebook with a soft brown cover that said *The Cellar Key Wine Diary and Catalog.* Inside were a hundred lined pages, each with space for the name of a wine and tasting notes about it. The year before, we had begun to save the labels of all the bottles we drank starting with the Louis Roederer Cristal that John proposed over, the one with the impossible cork. Soon we realized that every label was a memory, so we saved all of them the way other people save baby pictures.

On January 7, 1980, we recorded our first notes on a wine purchase: Christian Brothers 1974 Cabernet Sauvignon, which we bought for $7.59 at a place in South Miami called the Wine Warehouse. It was part of a growing collection of 1974 Cabernets. It was a great vintage, it was the year of our first official date, and it was close to our hearts because of the 1974 Robert Mondavi we'd had on our very first trip to California together. We focused especially on 1974 Robert Mondavi. We never bought a solid case of anything all at once—it seemed so extravagant—so we bought the Mondavi when we saw it at a price we could afford. We found three bottles once for $8.69 each. We finally found a dozen, from here and there. We decided we'd open one on our anniversary each year. It seemed as if, at that rate, they'd last just about forever. We eventually put together four cases of different 1974 Cabernets. Over the years, we were amazed at how much staying power they had.

Around Christmas that year, Steve Strasser was in Miami and came by the *Herald* to say hello. John went down to the cafeteria with him to talk about the job. Steve said he was sure everything was fine, but he hadn't heard anything yet. When John returned to the fifth floor, and the elevator opened, the city editor was standing there. "Congratulations," he said. "I've promoted you to deputy city editor." It was a nice gesture by a newspaper trying to keep John in Miami, but our sights were set elsewhere. John waited weeks to call *Newsweek*. He figured they were just too busy to talk with him. By early March, he couldn't stand it anymore. He called the foreign editor to find out what was happening with his job. The foreign editor was taken aback. "Didn't I ever get back to you?" he asked. "I meant to call and offer you the job." John was flabbergasted. The foreign editor said John should call the executive editor in the next few days to talk about the job and formally accept it.

Barely able to speak from excitement, John called the executive editor a few days later. "Can I speak to Maynard Jackson?" John asked in his deepest voice. There was a pause. "There is no Maynard Jackson here," said the secretary. Maynard Jackson was the mayor of Atlanta, the city's first black one; the editor of *Newsweek* was Maynard Parker. When John finally got it straight, the secretary put him through. "Hi, this is John Brecher. I just wanted to talk about the job. Is this a good time?" "Well," Maynard said sharply, "I'm watching the president speak on television about the hostage crisis right now. Call back." John felt like such a bonehead. Some foreign writer he'd be.

John formally accepted the *Newsweek* job on March 15. We celebrated with a bottle of Ayala Champagne from the 1970 vintage, one of our treasures. We told our bosses the next day. We had a long round of good-byes, but none as special as our last Les Amis du Vin dinner, which happened to be scheduled for the day before the movers arrived. The dinner was at a lovely restaurant called Vinton's. Our own little tasting group, all of whom were also Les Amis members, figured this could also be turned into a going-away party, and it was a major bash, with massive quantities of food and wine. We can still taste the Corton Bressandes (Prince de Merode), a fine red Burgundy from the very good vintage of 1976. The high point came with dessert: a German wine called Niersteiner Oelberg 1976 Beerenauslese. German wines are rated by ripeness, which usually equates to sweetness. Kabinett is generally the driest, followed by Spätlese and Auslese. Those are the ones you usually see, and the ones that most people can afford. The next step up is Beerenauslese, a luscious, sweet white wine with a "finish" that seems to last forever. For some reason, sweet wines, even though they often have lower alcohol, sometimes give us headaches the way dry wines don't. But this was so absolutely perfect that we just kept drinking it, damn the consequences.

At the end of the evening, waiters came around with massive silver trays piled high with huge cigars, which they offered to all of the men. Dottie and another woman, the only females at the dinner, insisted that they also get cigars and then, having gotten them, figured they had to smoke them, which they did.

John had never seen Dottie sicker. It wasn't the wine. It was the cigar. It's a funny thing about us. We aren't what people would call "serious drinkers." Maybe it seems ironic for wine lovers, or maybe it's perfectly appropriate, but we don't have much capacity for alcohol. If we have even a little too much to drink, we immediately get sick and stay sick for days. That's a powerful incentive never to get drunk. But this cigar was lethal. By the time we got home, Dottie could barely stand, and ran to throw up in the bathroom. The next morning, when the movers were scheduled to arrive, Dottie was actually green—or, as John put it to an unamused Dottie, "You are the cutest shade of brown-green." Years later, Marvin Shanken, publisher of *The Wine Spectator* and *Cigar Aficionado,* told Dottie the correct way to smoke a cigar, but she hasn't tried it yet, and probably never will.

We spent our last night in Miami in an empty house on a mattress loaned to us by a friend. The one thing that had not been packed, the only thing left, aside from stuff we had stowed in our luggage, was one of our best bottles of Champagne: Perrier-Jouët Fleur de Champagne—the flower bottle—which Dottie managed to enjoy as she slowly recovered from the cigar debacle.

The day we flew to New York, our new home, was April 14, 1980—our first anniversary. *Newsweek* was putting us up for a couple of weeks at a hotel near its offices called the Berkshire Place, then owned by the Dunfey hotel company. After we checked in, we called room service and told them to send up a bottle of white wine. What arrived was this: "La Reserve Dunfey Bordeaux Blanc.

Bottled exclusively for Dunfey Family Corporation, New York." It cost $9. When the room service porter brought the wine to the room, he brightened when he saw us. "Hey," he almost shouted, "didn't I get high with you last night?"

While Bordeaux is known for its reds, some great white wines are made there, too, especially around an area called Graves. The wines, made primarily from Sauvignon Blanc and Semillon grapes, have a crisp taste with a hint of melon and an underpinning of the gravelly soil that gave Graves its name. This, however, was not like that. We had our wine notebook with us. "So-so," we wrote. "Hard, young. Very biting and green."

Fortunately, this was just an aperitif. Even in the hysteria of the move, with Dottie green, we had remembered to pack something special in our suitcases: a bottle of 1974 Robert Mondavi Cabernet Sauvignon. For our first anniversary, we drank it at the Berkshire Place, and it was delicious. "Very fruity, light, fiery color. Big, sweetish nose and taste due to huge fruit. Complex, not too oaky. Spicy. Youngish. Long, fruity, big finish. Zesty." We drank that bottle for three full hours while we watched midtown New York go by outside our window. The wine, and our mood, only got better. The next night, we both had drinks with the editors of *Newsweek,* who said they thought they could help get Dottie a job at *The New York Times.* They said she was overqualified for the openings they had at the magazine.

We had heard terrible things about the price of housing in New York, and we were prepared. We were paying $450 for a two-bedroom, two-bath house in Miami, so we calculated what it would take to live well in New York, and what we could afford. It would be a stretch, we decided, but we could pay $800 a month and, for that, surely we could live anywhere we liked. Friends had given us the name of an apartment broker, so we dropped by. Inside a cluttered, depressing little space, we found an odd little woman surrounded by stacks of paper. We told her we were looking for a two-bedroom apartment—one for us, one for the wine. "Most people have a hard time affording a second bedroom for a child," she responded. "And you want one for your wine?" Then she asked how much we were willing to spend. We straightened up, looked at her, and proudly said, "Eight *hundred* dollars a month." She laughed at us—literally, she laughed out loud—and said there was nothing for $800 a month. She said she couldn't help us. We were on our own.

In time, we found an apartment. It was at Twentieth Street and Park Avenue South. The building had been converted from something—maybe a factory, or offices—and the apartments were oddly configured. Ours had an angular living room with a big column in the middle, a cavernous bedroom and a little loft that was big enough for a bed but not high enough to stand up in. The kitchen was a former closet, with only enough room for one person to stand in and lots of really big roaches. The biggest problem was that the apartment got absolutely no light. It had sliding glass doors in the living room and a window in the bedroom, but both looked onto the air shaft, and we were only on the third floor. It was impossible to know what the weather was like outside. All of our plants were dead within a month. But the apartment was in Manhattan, wasn't far from work, and cost only $850 a month.

As far back as John can remember, his father talked about blivits. A *blivit*, he explained, was "five pounds of shit in a three-pound bag." It was an oft-used word, first in John's family and then between the two of us. Well, when we took everything from a house in Miami and tried to put it into an apartment in Manhattan, we got a blivit. The boxes filled the entire apartment, and in some places were stacked to the ceiling. We were overwhelmed. On our very first night in our first apartment in New York, we cleared enough room around the boxes to sit on the floor. With mountains of cardboard surrounding us, we opened—of course—a Taittinger, but this time the really good stuff, the Comtes de Champagne, from 1973, the year we'd met. "To your face," said Dottie. "To your bottom," said John.

The next evening, May 17, as we were unpacking, we watched on television as Miami burned. The white police officers who had been charged in the beating death of Arthur McDuffie had been acquitted by an all-white jury in Tampa. We sat there stunned, and so very happy to be so very far away.

SEVEN

Beaune Cent-Vignes
(Domaine Duchet) 1969

· · ·

*E*ACH DAY THE M1 BUS STOPPED IN FRONT OF OUR BUILDING at Twentieth Street and Park Avenue South, turned left on Twenty-third Street, and then went north up Madison Avenue, right to *Newsweek*. It was a short trip through the most exciting place in the world. John started on Tuesday, which was the beginning of *Newsweek*'s Tuesday–Saturday workweek.

John: *I was so excited I could barely breathe when I walked into the building with the big red neon NEWSWEEK on the top. I showed up promptly and found no one in the foreign department except a secretary, who showed me to my office. I had never had an office before. Not only that, but from my window I could see little angles of famous buildings like St. Patrick's Cathedral and Saks Fifth Avenue. I sat down in the empty department and wondered what to do next. Suddenly, a short man with white hair stopped at my door. I stood up.*

The man didn't step in or extend his hand. He seemed drunk at nine o'clock in the morning. "You the new writer?" he asked. When I introduced myself, the man said, "This is the worst fucking job in the whole fucking world," and then he left.

Dottie, meanwhile, had been hired by *The New York Times* as an editor of the Week in Review section.

Dottie: *On my first day, when I entered the building, I felt a little like kneeling. This was* The New York Times, *the temple of world-class journalism, written and edited by the best. They issued me credit cards for air travel and car rentals and a laminated, wallet-size card that I was to read to officially protest the closing of a meeting to the public. This was serious stuff.*

It was a great time for us. It didn't matter to us that we didn't really have a kitchen because we ate out almost every night. John worked at Fiftieth and Madison, and Dottie worked in Times Square, at Forty-third Street. Since most of *Newsweek*'s work was done on Friday and Saturday, John could almost always leave at five or six on Tuesday, Wednesday, and Thursday to pick Dottie up. On Fridays, when *Newsweek*'s writers broke for dinner, Dottie sometimes walked over to join John. It was a short walk, but the lights, the people speaking different languages, the smells wafting from the open doors of restaurants, were always exciting. We got together most nights with no plans and just decided on the spot what we wanted to do. Sometimes we walked down the street and bought tickets to any Broadway show we could get into. Most nights we went out to dinner. The food was so good, the wine lists so remarkable, that we didn't eat—we *dined*. It was our entertainment, our special time together. Waiters thought our leisurely pace and obvious enthusiasm were charming, and they let us linger for hours.

To celebrate Dottie's job, we went to the fabled Coach House restaurant in Greenwich Village. This place was famous for its black bean soup and corn bread. While we sat looking at the wine list, we noticed that the people sitting at a table next to ours were having something we'd never seen before, a 1978 Chardonnay from Robert Keenan Winery in California. It wasn't on the wine list. When our waiter appeared again, we asked if we could have a bottle of the Keenan. He nodded, hurried away, and reappeared with the wine. It was $18.

For years, California wineries had wondered what would be America's favorite wine. It turned out to be good old Chardonnay, the great grape from Burgundy. In Burgundy, Chardonnay makes a wine of great finesse and an almost soulful earthiness. But in California, well, it's like a tomato that grows to epic proportions in just the right soil. The warm sunshine can create Chardonnays of immense power, so aggressive and big they seem to lumber to the table. Not only that, but in the 1970s and 1980s, when California wineries were experimenting, many of them fermented and aged their Chardonnays in oak—sometimes even new oak—for what seemed like forever, giving the wines a massive, woody, buttery taste. These were not wines of finesse, but their very lack of restraint, their verve, is what made them special to us. Like the late-harvest Zinfandels of the time, we considered these quintessentially American wines. If we wanted a Chardonnay with charm that was great with food, we'd look for a French wine. The American wines we fell in love with weren't imitations. They were originals. This Keenan was certainly an original.

With the journal John's parents had given us, we had started to keep track of every wine we had. Each was such a special memory. Our notes were simple, and while they might not make sense to anyone but us, who else would ever see them? John almost always wrote the notes as Dottie talked about the wines, since she always had the better palate and the better sense of description. As time went on, we realized that we were giving wines ratings: Yech, OK, Good, Very Good, Delicious, and Delicious! We never intended it, but this became our system. To be sure, there were some Yechs, like an Alfred Rothschild Blanc de Blancs ("Like a very cheap California bulk champagne"), a Chateau Esperanza Diamond ("Tastes like a wet dog"), and a Valley of the Moon 1983 Zinfandel ("Dottie finds vegetal, I find clumsy and badly made"). But we found that life was more full of Delicious! than Yech, and this Keenan was a Delicious! "Spectacular! Huge! Much oak, obviously late-picked," we wrote. "Much character, complexity, even a hint of Riesling. Yet great butteriness combined with oak and bigness. Very wonderful."

We had some restaurant missteps, too, of course, but far more often than not, we had a lovely time. Maybe it has something to do with attitude. Whenever we go to a restaurant, we expect that one way or another—maybe because of the wine or the service or the trendy crowd or the food—we will have a memorable time. And we almost always do.

We went to a steak house called the Post House, where they had a 1970 Château Gruaud-Larose—a fine Bordeaux from a fine year, and then a decade old—for $38. It was the greatest steak/wine pairing we ever had. The wine was hard and tough for the first hour, and then—bang!—it suddenly opened up. It was a classic, crisp, complex Bordeaux that was sweet with fruit yet dry at the same time. It was a genuinely exciting bottle of wine. From that moment, Gruaud-Larose became kind of our "house" expensive Bordeaux. We have had more vintages of it than of any other wine.

We went to the famous Four Seasons for its pre-theater special. We sat in the Pool Room, next to the pool. We were the only people there except for the old couple next to us. Dottie kept gesturing over, but John didn't know why. He didn't recognize Hume Cronyn and Jessica Tandy, who were as wrapped up in each other as we were. We saw them years later in *Foxfire* at the Ethel Barrymore Theatre and thought of Clos Blanc de Vougeot. That was the wine we had that night at the Four Seasons. It was $37, and it was very exciting for us to see it. Clos de Vougeot is home to some of the best red wines of Burgundy, but we'd never seen the white. In fact, we didn't even know there was such a thing. We ordered it— "the only white wine produced at famed Vougeot," the label said— and the waiter poured a taste for each of us. It was tight and hard, and our faces must have betrayed our disappointment. The waiter was genuinely concerned. "Is it all right?" he asked. We assured him that it was. "Are you sure?" he asked. He seemed ready to take it back. But we suggested he just leave it on the table to warm up. When it did, it was magnificent, one of the classiest white wines we've ever tasted.

We joined the New York chapter of Les Amis du Vin and continued to go to every tasting we could. The group was a little snootier than the one in Miami even though its members seemed less knowledgeable, but the tastings were still fun and educational. There were also some remarkable dinners, like this one, featuring the wines of Alsace, a region of France that specializes in distinctive white wines, especially Gewürztraminer, the peppery white we'd discovered at Sebastiani during our first trip to California.

LES AMIS DU VIN DINNER

CAFÉ DE FRANCE RESTAURANT

CHEF ROGER BONNET

TUESDAY, NOV. 25, 1980

PÂTÉ BONNET

1978 Riesling, Maître Goustier

TARTE À L'ONION

1978 Tokay D'Alsace, Clos St. Landelin Mure

CHEVREUIL WITH PURÉE MARRON AND SPAETZLE

1976 Gewürztraminer Les Soricieres, Dopff et Irion

SALADE À LA FRANÇAISE

Gewürztraminer Preiss-Henny

LE FROMAGE D'ALSACE

1977 Cabernet Sauvignon, Franciscan Vineyards

SOUFFLÉ GLACE À LA FRAMBOISE

1976 Gewürztraminer, Vendange Tardive, Hugel

We continued to visit Cellar in the Sky whenever we could. That's where we had our first Sauternes, the great white wine from France that really is the standard by which all dessert wines must be judged. A good Sauternes, and most of them we've tried are good, is a remarkable combination of sweetness and light, with a taste of sweet soil underneath that makes it unique throughout the world.

Near the end of 1980, John's parents came to visit. This was special for John's father, because he loved the food in New York, and John's mother, who never stopped missing the city. They spent whole days just riding buses and looking out the windows, amazed at all the changes in the thirty years since they had left. We took them to Windows on the World one night and had a remarkable Château Pichon-Lalande, a great Bordeaux, from the 1970 vintage, for just $30. Alan Lewis, the man who ran the place and sat with us at Cellar, came by to say hello just as the dessert cart appeared. "I can't decide," said John's mother. "I'd like to have every one." Alan Lewis said he would choose for her. A few minutes later, several waiters came by with a small piece of every dessert on the cart.

The area around Park Avenue South and Twentieth Street is now one of the hottest neighborhoods in Manhattan, especially for restaurants. All of the trendiest people eat there at all of the coolest places. Some of the best restaurants in the city are now right next door to our old building. But in the early 1980s, our neighborhood was desolate. Gramercy Park was to the east, a nice little neighborhood with historic brownstones and a tavern where O. Henry wrote "The Gift of the Magi," but there was nothing to the west, especially on weekends, and Park Avenue South was a wasteland. There were some interesting restaurants just north of us, on Lexington Avenue, including a whole string of inexpensive Indian joints, but that area was choked with hookers. We were horrified once when old friends from Miami came to visit us and, walking in that neighborhood, were accosted by a prostitute who tried to entice the husband, yelling in very graphic terms what she would be happy to do to him and for how much.

We were walking on Lexington one day when, to our surprise, we passed a cute little French place called Entre Nous. We walked over to look at its menu and, to our delight, there was a wine list—not a menu—posted outside. This was clearly our kind of place. Dottie's twenty-ninth birthday was right around the corner. The next week, John went into the restaurant on a Monday afternoon and told the chef-owner, a man named Bernard, that he wanted a special dinner for Dottie. The two of them together decided that duck would be a good choice. John told Bernard the wine was up to him.

The next Saturday night, John didn't tell Dottie where we were going. When we walked into Entre Nous, Bernard greeted us. On the table was a bottle of wine—Beaune Cent-Vignes (Domaine Duchet) 1969, a fine red Burgundy.

Burgundy is hard. There are châteaux in Bordeaux that produce a pretty good amount of consistent wine year after year. Since we know we like Château Gruaud-Larose, for instance, we can pretty well count on being able to find it, and enjoy it, year after year. Burgundy is different. Landholdings are all cut up—it goes back to the French Revolution—and it's difficult to find the same wine from the same producer or négociant year after year. Not only that, but Burgundy is made from the Pinot Noir grape, which is far more fickle than the Cabernet Sauvignon of Bordeaux. Burgundy wines also tend to be expensive. So while we were familiar with Burgundy, it was not a passion of ours. Until that night. The wine was magnificent—smooth as velvet, filled with raspberry-cherry fruit and a taste of the soil—and it seemed to grow in our mouths. With the duck, dark and juicy, it was even better. Something about the rich, almost sweet taste of the duck seemed to make the taste of the Burgundy even more vibrant. The earthiness of the crisp skin and the succulent meat seemed perfect with the soulfulness of the wine, and the crackle of the skin combined with the smoothness of the wine was sublime. The wine was $22.50.

Many people who love wine go through various periods. They'll have a great Chardonnay and go through a Chardonnay period, for instance. That was the beginning of our Burgundy period. We became convinced then—as we are now—that Burgundy, when right, is the greatest and most romantic wine in the world. In our Cellar Key book, there are more exclamation points and excited scribbles on the red Burgundy pages than on any others. It all started that night. Unfortunately, the next time we called Entre Nous for reservations, it had become a Chinese restaurant.

Now that we were in the big city, the range of possible Dottie presents for Christmas seemed much broader. We already had Dottie drinking glasses (heavy, crystal mugs with etched Dottie faces on them), a Dottie rug, a Dottie table, Dottie jewelry, Dottie ceramics, a Dottie clock, a stained-glass Dottie, a Dottie copyright, a Dottie Goodyear blimp (it was a toy blimp with messages you could draw yourself), Dottie socks, a Dottie piñata, a Dottie cookie cutter and sandwich maker, a Dottie mirror, Dottie soap, and many more. Dottie had given John one of those corkscrews with the arms that go up as you twist the top, but the part you twist on top had been replaced with a Dottie face. She had taken John's drawing of her face to a metalworks factory and stood there in the heat watching it take shape.

The first New York Dottie present had to be special. John found a neon shop called Let There Be Neon and took his drawing of Dottie's face there. "This is my wife," he said, as he always did when presenting his ideas to artists. Those artists who didn't throw him out of their shops were charmed and got into the project, improving on his ideas. The owner of Let There Be Neon suggested a red outline and bright blue eyes on a black background. On Christmas Day, John presented Dottie with a Dottie neon. Then John opened his present from Dottie. It also was a Dottie neon, as the artist she had commissioned envisioned it. It had a red outline and bright blue eyes on a white background. We were suddenly a two-Dottie-neon household.

Nineteen eighty-one was remarkable. It was the first year we drank so many different wines that we had to use two photo albums to contain all of the labels—255 different wines in all. That probably seems like a lot of alcohol, but consider the context. Each bottle was savored through an entire night. If we were home, we opened the bottle when we arrived, sipped while we cooked, drank with dinner, and probably saved the last glass for right before bed. If we were at restaurants, we sat eating and drinking our bottle of wine forever—and we were at restaurants a lot. The first time it snowed—it was the first time we'd ever been in snow together—we ran over to a neighborhood Italian restaurant with good windows and saw a 1964 Spanna from Cantine Curti on the list for just $17. In the Piedmont region of Italy,

Spanna is the local name for the Nebbiolo grape. Nebbiolo is the basis of some great wines, but this was just a simple Spanna and the restaurant must have been desperate to get rid of a bottle that was probably well past its prime. But, still, $17 for such an old wine? We had to try it. As the snow fell outside, with us warm in the window, it couldn't have been more delicious—muscular and filled with fruit, and still vibrant enough that it was better after thirty minutes, as the snow began to pile up.

Not only were the restaurants in New York special, but the wine stores had so many wines we'd never seen before, wines from all over the world. We were willing to try anything, and we did. We bought a bottle of a cheap Italian white called "Always Elvis," with a picture of Elvis on the front. We could suddenly buy wines from just about every state—Chateau Ste. Michelle Cabernet Sauvignon 1976 from Washington State, Ste. Chapelle Gewürztraminer 1979 from Idaho, Hermann J. Wiemer Johannisberg Riesling 1979 from New York, Montbray Seyve Villard 1978 from Maryland ("Bottle No. 2, Vat No. 113"), Chicāma Vineyards Zinfandel from Massachusetts, South County Vineyards Cabernet Sauvignon from Rhode Island, Boordy "Maryland Vin Gris" 1978 ("a very pale rosé wine"), Sokol Blosser Chardonnay 1978 from Oregon, Sakonnet Aurora from Rhode Island, Nissley Vineyards Susquehanna White 1979 from Pennsylvania, Cagnasso Leon Millot 1977 from New York, and one of our favorites, Maui Blanc from Tedeschi Vineyard and Winery of Hawaii. It was made from pineapples, but it was really quite good, light and just slightly sweet.

Then there was Bully Hill, from New York. Bully Hill was run by Walter Taylor, a colorful member of the family that ran the giant Taylor Wine Company, which it sold to Coca-Cola in 1977. After he started Bully Hill, a federal court banned him from using "Taylor" on his labels. So on our bottle of Bully Hill White Wine, the name had been marked out with Magic Marker wherever it appeared. On the front was a signature: "Walter S. XXXXX, Owner of the Bully Hill Estate." On the back: "Not connected with or a successor to the XXXX Wine Co." Later, Bully Hill labels said: "Our products produced by the employees of Bully Hill Vineyards, Inc. Names by request." Said Walter Taylor: "They have my name and heritage, but they didn't get my goat!"

We also bought the very first Cabernet Sauvignon made by the very first winery on Long Island, New York, a Hargrave Vineyard 1976, Bottle No. 3070.

Dottie bought John a 1959 Château Latour, for $80, for his twenty-ninth birthday. It was a special deal, passed along to her by a fellow wine lover at the *Times*. We bought a third wine rack, able to hold forty bottles. We put our three racks up in the loft, but the temperature was all wrong. The ideal temperature for wine storage is about 55 degrees, but ideal temperatures are for people with a collection of fine wines meant to age for decades. For the rest of us, any dark place with a moderate, fairly constant temperature is fine. Unfortunately, our loft seemed to always hover somewhere above 70 degrees and was subject to dangerous temperature fluctuations, so we moved the wine down to the bedroom. We didn't get any light in there anyway, so it was a good place. We kept the air-conditioning on all the time. Dottie constantly had a cold, but the wine was fine.

Our apartment was within walking distance of a Reform synagogue called the Village Temple. That's where Dottie converted. People sometimes assume that Dottie converted because John was Jewish or so our children could be raised Jewish. But she was thinking about this long before she met John.

Dottie: *As a teenager, I had fallen out with the Presbyterian church that my parents had helped found. Its prosperous members seemed unconcerned with the plight of those less fortunate, even when they lived right across the street from the church. They have since* *changed, but when I began searching for another spiritual home, everything in me pointed to Judaism. In high school, I had become close friends with a Jewish girl. I visited her synagogue, and the more I read about her religion, the more I liked it. The strong emphasis on ethical behavior and the command to work for justice appealed to me. It was also, I guessed, the religion of some of the reporters who had come South to tell the rest of the nation the civil rights story. It occurred to me that their work might be viewed as an exercise of their religion as well as the pursuit of an important story.*

There was another thing: For months during the summer of 1964, my family and millions across the country had waited anxiously for authorities to find the bodies of James Chaney, Andrew Goodman, and Michael Schwerner, three youths—a black and two Jews—who had disappeared in Mississippi while working to register blacks to vote. Jews and blacks had a community of interests.

For several hours, twice a week for six months, I went to classes after work. On many Fridays, because that was when Newsweek *had its marathon day of work, I went to the Village Temple alone, the only black person present. After several Fridays of kindly old ladies asking, "Dear, do you know where you are?" and pointing out the bima and the cantor, and telling me about a congregation of black Jews somewhere, they got to know me. Then, in early December, I was ready. With my temple family looking on, I officially converted to Judaism, taking Ruth, John's mother's name, as my Hebrew name. My family, as usual, took it in stride.*

By that time, Dottie had moved to the metro desk as a reporter. There were so many famous and familiar bylines at the *Times,* but the first reporter Dottie asked to meet was Frank J. Prial, the famous wine writer. He was in France, so it was a long time before they were introduced, but he was a major reason why we enjoyed wine so much. He made it fun and accessible. With all that he knew about wine, his columns were so down-to-earth that reading them was like sitting down and talking to him. He remains an inspiration today.

Because all of the writers at *Newsweek* had to stay late every Friday night, the company paid for their dinner. So on Friday nights when Dottie wasn't at temple, we made a habit of walking over to a restaurant called Bombay Palace, where we ate some Indian comfort food and always had a bottle of a perfectly lovely little Bordeaux called Fort Médoc. It was $9 and offered the simple, creamy fruit that, ever since then, we've preferred with Indian food.

We'd loved Indian food since our first trip to New York together. We'd never had it before then, and a friend at the *Herald* said we must go to a little Indian place on the second floor of a building near Times Square. When we walked in, the aromas alone were so new to us that we were hooked. The menu offered a multicourse meal. It meant to say underneath the price, "Order this and leave the rest to us." But what it said was, "Order this and leave the rest of us." We did, and even though we drank Indian beer—it seemed like the right thing to have with spicy food then—it made us into lifelong Indian-food fans.

We gained twenty pounds each during our first year in New York and, looking back, it's amazing we didn't gain more. The New York *Daily News* recommended a little bistro on the East Side called La Mediterranée, and we were charmed when we walked in. It was very narrow, with a huge bouquet of fresh flowers in the front in a large Lalique vase, and vibrant, rustic paintings of the Mediterranean on the walls. The service was friendly and crisp, with each waiter seemingly responsible for every table, so we were never ignored. There was a scrumptious chilled half-lobster appetizer with a green mayonnaise sauce, and chilled mussels with a mustard sauce. As a main course, there was calves' liver, one of Dottie's favorite foods. She ordered it and the waiter asked, "How would you like it cooked?" It was the first time she'd ever been asked how she wanted her liver cooked.

There was something else about La Mediterranée. There were huge communal ice buckets where they kept open bottles of white wine, but all of the bottles seemed to be the same thing. We asked what it was and they said it was their house white, Meribeau Blanc de Blancs "Réserve des Amiraux." It came in liter bottles, and dozens were situated all around the restaurant. Everyone's glass was constantly filled with Meribeau Blanc, and soon ours were, too. We came to love La Mediterranée, and the Meribeau Blanc had much to do with it. It wasn't just that the wine was cheap and delicious—flinty yet fruity, with just enough lemony acids to be perfect with food, and especially that lobster—but it seemed so perfectly symbolic of this lovely, understated oasis. We later found Meribeau Blanc at stores, for $3.99 a liter. It was our house white for years, and it always reminded us of La Mediterranée and our first year in New York.

EIGHT

De Loach White Zinfandel 1980

. . .

*N*O SINGLE TRAIN IN THE UNITED STATES WENT ALL THE way across the country. Canada, however, was different. There was a train that crossed North America. We could be in bed all the way from the Atlantic to the Pacific. What could be better? For our first vacation since we moved to New York, that's what we decided to do. We'd take the transcontinental train across Canada, and then the *Coast Starlight* down the Pacific Coast to San Francisco. Then we'd return to Wine Country—Sonoma this time—and fly back.

We flew to Montreal, where we stocked up on our train drink of choice, Champagne, including Brights President Canadian Champagne (Champagne Canadien): "A true Canadian Champagne produced by the time-honored method of natural fermentation in the bottle. *Un véritable Champagne canadien fabriqué selon la méthode traditionielle de fermentation naturelle dans la bouteille.*" It wasn't that good, to be honest, but it didn't matter. We lay in bed and watched the entire continent go by—up and down mountains, past lakes and wildlife, into miles of nothing. We were in the train's last car, and the room attendant once opened the back door of the train for us. We stood, in flannel pajamas, at the very end of the train, with the door open, as snow swirled into the car. We watched the track disappear behind us as we sipped Champagne. It was glorious.

One of the very best things about train trips back then was that we couldn't be reached. There were no real stops between Point A and Point B, nowhere to leave a message. And cell phones didn't exist. We'd already been journalists for a long time, and, even though we loved the news, it was a pleasure to be able to ignore it for just a few days each year.

The *Coast Starlight* was spectacular. We had no idea the Pacific Coast was so gorgeous. It seemed that one minute we were on top of a mountain and the next we were on the coast, right next to the ocean, closer to it than cars on the highway. The sunset was stunning. There was just one glitch: We hadn't brought along enough Champagne. We had to have the porter bring us bottles of the only bubbly on the train, Almaden Extra Dry Champagne, the same bulk Champagne we'd had on our other trip, which, under the circumstances, was just fine.

We found Sonoma very different from Napa. It was slower, more spread out, more obviously agricultural, even friendlier. We'd had a little revelation before we left. Since we'd accidentally stumbled upon Sutter Home White Zinfandel on our earlier trip, we'd picked up White Zinfandel whenever we saw it as a lovely picnic wine. It was sweet and simple and fun. But White Zinfandel was still unusual enough for us that we still listed it under "Zinfandel" in our Cellar Key, with a big underlined note that said "White." We haunted all of the lower-end and mid-range wine stores in the city—the fancy East Side stores were so expensive and, in any case, they had plenty of showcase wines but few really unusual wines—and one day, in Greenwich Village, we saw a new

White Zinfandel: De Loach Vineyards White Zinfandel 1980. It cost $5.99—more than others—and the most amazing thing was the label. We've often found that the more information a wine offers on the label, the better the wine. It shows care, concern, and personality. It may or may not really matter to anyone what day the grapes were harvested, when they were crushed and how long they were fermented, but the fact that the winemaker wants you to know these things indicates a sense of sharing in the art that we've always found important. Back then, far more labels gave precise information. "Sonoma Vineyards Johannisberg Riesling. Special Late Harvest Bottling. Harvested October 21, 1974. Bottled January 16, 1975. 1,200 cases." This, then, was made from super-ripe grapes and would be sweet. "Sebastiani Gamay Nouveau. Harvested by hand Sept. 26–Oct. 13, 1979. Bottling started at 8:00 A.M. November 15, 1979." This, as it should, went from the vine to the bottle in, basically, the blink of an eye. It was as new as a nouveau should be.

Still, to find extensive information on the label of a picnic wine was amazing. The front of the De Loach label said that the alcohol was 11.5 percent and residual sugar was 1.1 percent. Most red wines are bone dry, and fine white wines like Chardonnay are, too. But especially for a White Zinfandel, 1.1 percent was low. The label on the back went on: "Our vineyards are in the Russian River Valley of Sonoma County where the warmth of Summer is moderated by cool ocean breezes—an area prized by winemakers for over a century. Our grapes are grown on light soils at moderate yields for maximum wine quality. For optimum varietal character, we harvested our grapes at a precise point of maturity determined by daily personal judgments on October 8, at 22.3 brix and .9% total acid by volume. To assure the full potential of the grapes, this wine was fermented 42 days at an average temperature of 52 F.

"1783 cases were estate bottled." It was signed "Cecil De Loach, Christine De Loach."

We bought it, of course, and we drank it right away. It was fun to know that the very grapes that made this wine were on the vines just months earlier. "Delicious, the best rosé," we wrote. "Orange. Lots of crisp, steely character, but red tannins for backbone. Beautifully made. Smooth yet assertive."

We had never done this before, but we wrote a fan letter. We told Cecil De Loach how much we enjoyed his White Zinfandel. He wrote back to thank us and invite us to visit his winery if we were ever in California. We took him up on that when we arrived in Sonoma County. He was a gentle bear of a man, big with a big smile, eyes that twinkled, and a friendly mustache. He seemed to have all the time in the world for us. He was so thoroughly caught up in winemaking that it was easy being with him, almost like being carried away by his excitement. He explained to us that he used to be a fireman in San Francisco and that he used all of his time off to make wine. At some point, he had to make a choice: either devote full time to the winery or walk away. So he hung up his hose and gave all of his time to De Loach Vineyards, and it was clearly a labor of love. He and his wife lived on the property and outside their bedroom window they had planted Cabernet Sauvignon grapes. Zinfandel was Cecil's passion, but the Cabernet vines looked prettier from their bedroom.

Cecil took us into the winery, gave us each a glass, and then put a long glass suctioning cylinder called a "wine thief" into a barrel. He dropped a small amount of his brand-new Chardonnay into our glasses. It was the first wine we'd ever tasted out of a barrel. It was still quite cloudy, and it didn't taste like anything we'd ever had before. It was totally huge and unrestrained in our mouths. It was very much like what it was, a fizzy beverage that's on its way to becoming something else. There was something remarkably earthy and soul-satisfying about that wine. Cecil watched our faces as we tasted his Chardonnay. We think we understood then better than ever before how a winemaker could be so passionate about his wine. Personality and commitment matter, even with White Zinfandel. It was an important lesson for us. On later visits to the winery, we saw pictures hanging on the walls of the tasting room of him and his employees in Hawaii. Cecil's the big guy in the white suit and the Panama hat. He believed in the good life and once a year took everyone to some great place to relax and appreciate what a life in wine had made possible for them all.

This was, of course, a great trip for us. It seemed that we had half the winemakers in California sign a bottle for us—a Cabernet Blush signed by James and Vera Kreck at Mill Creek, where we tasted wines in the kitchen of their home; a Gamay Beaujolais by Jim Pedroncelli, who got off his forklift to pour us some wine; and a Gamay Beaujolais by David Stare, who later became quite well-known as the winemaker at Dry Creek Vineyard. It's rare to find anything in California called "Gamay Beaujolais" anymore. Beaujolais is the delightfully fruity wine made in the Beaujolais region of France, which is part of Burgundy. It's made from the Gamay grape. It was another example of California adopting various foreign names to make them seem more familiar. Still, in this case at least, the Gamay grape is the same in the United States and in France.

We passed a winery we'd never seen before called Rafanelli, waved to the man outside who was cutting the grass on a tractor, and dropped in. There was no one inside the barn, which seemed to be a tasting room and winery. We waited, and finally the man from the tractor came in. He was Dave Rafanelli and he poured us his Zinfandel. It was unlike any Zinfandel we'd ever had, with far more restraint and structure. It was good old American Zinfandel, of course, so it had plenty of pepper and zest, but it was a fine wine, too, with class and character. As we enthused about it, Dave Rafanelli told us about his father, Americo, who was the second generation of his family to make wine. After Prohibition killed the family business, Americo sold his grapes to other wineries before striking out with a new winemaking venture, the family's second, in 1974. The family had initially made Zinfandel and Gamay Beaujolais, but had ultimately distinguished itself with its awesome Zinfandel. Americo had recently died. Dave told us with great pride that his father thought that all wine should be red, that all red wine should be Zinfandel, and that all Zinfandel should be priced fairly. Americo's pursuit of excellence in the vineyard had made Rafanelli grapes much sought after, and as a dutiful son, he was trying to continue his dad's legacy by continuing to make great Zinfandel. But he also had begun to make a little Cabernet Sauvignon, a grape that his dad never cared for.

When Dottie told him that her father had died and that the older she got, the more she missed him, Dave started to tear up. His dad had been his best friend. To honor him, he said, he was planning to set up a scholarship fund for some bright young person who was interested in winemaking. Then he poured us his Cabernet. It was rich and had so much clarity, so much tightly focused, splendid fruit, that we told him it was a wine that we were sure his dad would be proud of. Later, after we returned to New York, we sent Dave a check, our contribution to the scholarship fund that honored his dad. Rafanelli Zinfandel is now one of the most prized Zinfandels in California, almost impossible to find outside the winery's mailing list. But it is still priced fairly.

After our visit to the Rafanelli Winery, we ate at a restaurant called the Wine Cask, where we sat in wine casks that had been turned into booths. The next day we had a picnic outside V. Sattui, a winery that's popular with tourists and, to this day, is one of our favorite places in Napa Valley. There was just one faux pas during the trip. While John has always been socially awkward, an inherited family trait, Dottie is always charming and socially adept, except about once a year, when something truly inappropriate escapes her lips. It's always a shock when it does.

There is nothing quite as good as a fresh young wine bought from the winery, opened right there and drunk in the winery's own picnic area. It doesn't matter if the winery is in Napa Valley, Tuscany, or Ohio, that wine will taste great, especially if it's a wine that's sold only at the winery. Partly this is because the wine itself has never traveled and been stored by someone less passionate about it, so it's in pristine condition. And also, when you're sitting at a winery on a beautiful day having a picnic lunch surrounded by vineyards, how could it not taste terrific? On our trip to Sonoma, we would find a deli sometime before lunch, then find a winery with picnic tables. We tasted some of the wines—always asking if there was some wine sold only at the winery, and there usually was—then bought a bottle, borrowed two glasses, and had a picnic. One day, we dropped in on Hacienda Winery in Sonoma, picked up a bottle of its brand new Johannisberg Riesling, borrowed a couple of glasses from the man behind the counter, who said he was an owner of the winery, and sat down to enjoy a picnic under the trees.

It was a beautiful day. The picnic of assorted salads and fruit was great and the wine was delicious. But suddenly our idyllic day was interrupted by a large group of very loud women who had descended on the winery. When we returned the glasses, the man behind the counter asked if we had enjoyed our picnic. "It was fine," Dottie replied, "until those loud women arrived." The man recoiled. "That's my wife!" he replied. "And her Junior League!" Dottie froze with embarrassment, flashed him her prettiest smile, then murmured "I'm sorry" before running for the door.

NINE

Louis Martini Pinot Noir 1974

. . .

WE LOVED EVERYTHING ABOUT NEW YORK, BUT NOTHING more than the free concerts in Central Park. Every summer, the Metropolitan Opera and the New York Philharmonic each give a couple of free concerts that tens of thousands of people attend, filling the Great Lawn with blankets, picnic baskets, and wine. Vendors, of a sort, walked among the crowd, hawking "Loose joints. Loose joints." We attended our first opera in the park on June 16, 1980. In case it cooled down at night, we brought along light sweaters and a red wine we thought might warm us up: a Sutter Home Zinfandel—the red kind—from 1977. It was big and chewy. We sat there on our blanket, drinking Sutter Home Zinfandel and listening to the Metropolitan Opera, while the sky grew dark. To the south, all the buildings of New York City were lighting up, and so were the stars.

All around us people were sitting or reclining on blankets,

pulling food out of fancy picnic baskets or paper bags. Some had simply brought cheese and good bread. Others had veritable feasts, multicourse meals on linen tablecloths with sparkling crystal glasses and sweet-smelling cut flowers that looked quite extravagant. We always dine when we're together—we make the food central to the moment and savor each bite—and the fact that we had a lawn for a table was no reason to depart from that tradition. We had gone to the Silver Palate, an outstanding gourmet take-out shop on Columbus Avenue that prepared food that was almost too pretty to eat. We started with liver pâté and a French baguette, then proceeded to a smorgasbord of salads—curried chicken salad with raisins and almond slivers, poached salmon in a creamy dill sauce, and large chunks of fresh fruit. To finish, we nibbled on fruit tarts and an assortment of cheeses. All around us, we heard corks popping or being pulled and wine constantly being poured into glasses. All this with world-class music, too. It was a great evening.

A year later, we were back in the park for a different kind of concert. We'd grown up with Simon and Garfunkel, of course. Everyone in college related to "I am a rock, I am an island," everyone knew the words to "Mrs. Robinson," and John had made a special trip to the Fifty-ninth Street Bridge during college just to walk across it. Simon and Garfunkel had broken up in 1970, but on September 19, 1981, they were getting together again for a free concert in Central Park. We got there early, but with the crowd estimated at 500,000 people, we sat far back and to the side. It really didn't matter. We could still hear from the big loudspeakers, we had our picnic, and we had our wine.

This reunion concert required something special, something that would be up to the occasion. Our "cellar" was still small. But there were, in our small cache, a couple of bottles we were absolutely dying to try.

Louis Martini was yet another of those winemakers who had

come from Italy, started making wine in California, survived Prohibition, and helped build America's wine industry. Or, as it said on the back of the old-fashioned, block-letter labels back then: "The Louis M. Martini winery is a company wholly owned by the Martini family. Louis M. Martini, the founder, immigrated from Italy in 1900. In 1922, he started the L. M. Martini Grape Products Co. in Kingsburg, California. The winery in the Napa Valley was completed in 1934, enabling him to sell the Kingsburg plant and move to St. Helena, where he specialized in table wine production." Pioneers like him were men of strong opinions. Winemaking was not just a job but a passion and a link to history. In a 1948 book called *California's Best Wines,* Robert Lawrence Balzer writes of the first time he met Louis Martini, in 1940: "From other sources I learned that the indomitable Mr. Martini not only refused to sell his wines to many comers, but stood guard over them like an anxious parent."

His wines, to us, had always been special—not elegant, not wines for special guests, but honest, solid, reliable, earthy, and inexpensive. He made some wines from traditionally Italian grapes, such as Barbera, but even his other wines tasted Italian, especially his deep-flavored Zinfandel (Zinfandel probably originated in Italy). Martini wines were like meat loaf—homey, comforting. At $3 to $4 a bottle, they were meant to be bought, opened, and enjoyed. We had a couple in our racks with some age on them, but only because we hadn't gotten around to drinking them. Now, with a special event coming up, we thought it might be fun to taste what an old Louis Martini wine tasted like. We brought along a 1977 Zinfandel and a 1974 Pinot Noir.

We knew the Pinot was a risk. Pinot Noir is the grape of the great red Burgundies of France that we loved so much. But it's finicky even in France, and does better in cooler climates. The hot weather of California seemed unsuited to petulant Pinot Noir, not to mention the heavy-handed winemaking style of many California winemakers. Experts said that Pinot Noir, unfortunately, could never really be made well in California. The Martini label said: "Essentially the Pinot Noir is a cool country grape, and the few small plantings that exist in this country are in the North Coast Counties of California." On top of all that, our Pinot was a $4, seven-year-old wine from a winery not known for its elegance.

As Simon and Garfunkel began with "Mrs. Robinson," we opened the Pinot. We figured it would be much lighter than the Zinfandel, and therefore a better first wine. In any case, if it was really terrible, we could always immediately open the Zin and save the day.

What we uncorked was incredible. When we first tasted the wine, it was so huge that it tasted to us like a Petite Sirah—a re-markable, big, almost black red wine that California vintners were excited about at the time, the grape that made many of those early California "Burgundies." A little later, as the concert wore on, the wine tasted like a Cabernet Sauvignon, which means it tightened, developed some structure, some layers of flavor. Then Paul Simon spoke to the audience. "Well, it's great to do a neighborhood con-cert," he said to a roar, and then he thanked "people that never get recognized for doing good deeds for the city, a group of people that have donated half of their proceeds they're making tonight— the guys who are selling loose joints!" Soon after he spoke, the wine developed some pepper and spice, and began to taste a little like a Zinfandel. Yet, through it all, the wine never lost its Pinot Noir elegance, a kind of feminine majesty that was genuinely ex-citing. Remarkably, at seven years old, it was still young.

As Simon and Garfunkel sang "Slip Slidin' Away" halfway through the concert, we opened the Zinfandel, and it was a sur-prise in its own way. This was a wine we knew well. We'd had many bottles of Louis Martini Zinfandel over the years. It was a great red sauce kind of wine. When we walked over to Pete's Tavern near Gramercy Park for dinner, we'd have a very rustic lasagna and an

$8 bottle of Louis Martini Zinfandel. Maybe because it was so easy to drink, or maybe just because it was cheap, we'd never thought to cellar one, to "lay one down." That was something we'd do with great, expensive wines, like fine Bordeaux.

That Zinfandel, though only four years old, was a thoroughly different wine. Its tannins had softened, the aggressive, dark fruit had gotten rounder, and that taste of the earth had mellowed into a kind of dusty memory that tasted like wisdom. We were drinking a $4 bottle of wine that tasted remarkably expensive, and all we'd had to do was forget we had it for a couple of years. This was the first time we really understood that price and ageability don't necessarily go hand in hand, that even an inexpensive wine's whole character can change with age and that even we, with the wines sitting in the bedroom, could age our own wines—and they would get better. With some patience, we could turn inexpensive wines into expensive-tasting wines, like magic, and it didn't require anything more special than a wine rack.

Thanks to that remarkable Louis Martini, we went into a Pinot Noir period. It wasn't just that the wine was delicious, though it was. It was also that we loved the idea that the "experts" were wrong about this wine. Everybody "knew" that California couldn't make a great Pinot Noir—and we knew different.

Raymond Vineyard 1978 Pinot Noir ($9.99). Delicious! Fantastic! Chocolate liqueur nose. Big, luscious, rich. Very much American (bold, assertive, brash), but not at all a Cabernet or a Zin. Definitely a Pinot, fruity and "sweet" and flat and full instead of delicate and glassy. Very young, many years ahead of it.

Hanzell Vineyards 1977 ($22.00). Fantastic! One of the all-time greats. Huge and rich and woody. Big, big red nose. Classy and glassy. Got bigger and bigger, so much so that we took smaller and smaller sips until we were barely sipping any. Chewy but perfectly balanced. Even minty at the end. Ready now and for 20 years, at least.

During this same time John had moved up to some major

cover stories, including one on Israeli prime minister Menachem Begin, and Dottie was getting her share of front-page stories, including an exclusive about a pair of young ballet dancers, Li Cunxin and Elizabeth Mackey, who had overcome international politics to find love.

We knew that we were never going to leave New York and that it was time to buy a home. We had never saved any money. We didn't make a lot anyway, and what we made we spent on wine, restaurants, and Broadway shows—the important stuff. But for all the years we were in Miami, we had bought stock in Knight-Ridder, the *Herald*'s parent company, through a payroll-deduction plan, and we'd never sold any. Dottie had also received stock through the *Times*'s plan. Our combined stock was now worth $27,500. If we could put 25 percent down on a co-op, we could afford an apartment that cost around $110,000. We called an agent and began to look. We loved Central Park, and we liked the Upper West Side, so we had a pretty good idea where we wanted to live.

We wanted lots of sunlight, hardwood floors, high ceilings, and large windows we could sit in front of for hours to watch the parade of people below us. There was something wrong with everything the agent showed us, and there seemed to be little we could afford anyway. One Sunday as John was reading the classified ads in the *Times,* he saw an ad for a one-bedroom apartment off Central Park West, in a modern, full-service building, for $125,000. It turned out to be in a high-rise just off Central Park West at Seventy-second Street, a rare modern building in the area, because for many years the land it was built on had been the tennis courts and rose garden for the Dakota, the famous building next door. The apartment was small and seemed even smaller with its depressing midnight-blue walls. But it looked right out onto Seventy-second Street. Another window, from the kitchen, looked into the Dakota, and, best of all, the apartment had a small balcony. It was perfect.

It was an estate sale. The young woman who had lived there had died mysteriously in her hotel room at Walt Disney World. Her family wanted to sell it, fast. They weren't pleased with our offer, but it was, quite literally, all we could afford even with a small loan from Dottie's mother. Interest rates at the time had gone haywire, and mortgage rates were close to 17 percent. The housing market was dead. We had a deal.

The closing was scheduled on March 22, 1982. We put a bottle of Taittinger in the refrigerator so we could celebrate when we got home. This time it was the Taittinger Comtes de Champagne Brut Rosé, from 1973, the year we met. Dottie had given John the bottle the year before, in 1981, on his birthday, and it was special and rare. Rosé Champagne is one of the world's more romantic things, but little is made. While rosé still wine is made by leaving the clear juice in contact with the grapes for a short time, most rosé Champagnes, even the great ones, are made by adding a little red wine—usually Pinot Noir from areas in the Champagne region like the appropriately named Bouzy. This gives the bubbly a lovely color, of course, but also a little bit of extra backbone that makes it especially complex. Only such a special occasion could be appropriate to such a special wine.

We'd never owned a home before, and we couldn't believe the hassle—the papers, the records, the references. John's cousin Peter, a lawyer, offered to handle the closing, which was scheduled at the midtown offices of the bank's attorneys. Everything was set. Peter arrived with his wife because we had promised to take them to lunch at La Mediterranée after the closing. We all sat down and cooled our heels as we waited for the bank's lawyer to appear.

Finally, the lawyer swept through the door and sat down. He put his papers out in front of him. The very first thing he said was

"Do you realize that there's a lien on this property?" We were crestfallen. Peter grabbed the papers from the other lawyer and began to review them. Without looking up, he asked, "Who are the Smiths?" The lawyer looked around. "Isn't this the Smith closing?" We all looked at him like he was crazy. "I'm in the wrong office!" he said as he ran for the door. The right lawyer—with the right papers—finally arrived a few minutes later, and we were soon homeowners, poor but happy.

Late that afternoon, after lunch at La Mediterranée, we took a cab to Twentieth Street and Park Avenue South, picked up the Taittinger, took a cab to 15 West Seventy-second Street, and, as the sky grew dark outside, sat on our floor and drank the Taittinger, our very first wine in our very first home together.

Delicious! Cream on the nose and taste but very fine and delicate. Extremely delicate, perfumed and lightly fruity. Completely unaggressive, laid-back. Pinpoint bubbles. Elegant. Bubbles ever-so-gentle.

Soon it was dark outside, and we fell asleep on the floor in each other's arms.

TEN

The Red Hills Vineyard Sparkling Chardonnay (Yamhill County) 1979

. . .

IT WAS A GREAT TIME TO LIVE ON THE UPPER WEST SIDE OF New York City. New York was the center of the universe, and Columbus Avenue was the most happening place in it. Our apartment building was on West Seventy-second Street between Central Park West and Columbus, and it was right next door to the famous Dakota. When the Dakota was built, in 1884, it was so far away from anything else that they called it the Dakota for laughs. The building had been home to well-heeled people for many years. Boris Karloff lived there. He left candy for kids at Halloween, but they were too afraid to take it, according to Stephen Birmingham in *Life at the Dakota*. It was the scary location used in the movie *Rosemary's Baby*. But it really became famous in 1980, when John Lennon was shot outside as he was coming home with his wife, Yoko Ono.

Our little apartment next door had wooden floors, and for

once, no shag carpeting. It was the first place that was really ours, the first place Dottie could decorate herself. In the kitchen, we removed the doors from the cabinets, painted the insides bright white and the outside rims China red. The packaged foods and Dottie's pretty dishes—the Fiesta plates, the Art Deco salt and pepper shakers, even the dark green Depression glass plates she had collected at flea markets for years—added a riot of colors. We laid plain white tiles in the kitchen ourselves. We painted the living room white and bought some pretty wallpaper for the bedroom and the bathroom. The wine racks, the same ones we'd had years ago in Miami, sat in a corner in the bedroom. We bought green AstroTurf for the balcony, painted its ceiling white, and furnished it with two plastic chairs and a little plastic table. This became, to us, the most important room in the house, though it was only ten feet long and seven feet wide.

This balcony was where we spent much of our lives. Busy West Seventy-second Street was right below. If we bent over a little to the left, we could see Central Park as it changed through the seasons. Immediately to our left we looked right into the awesome apartments of the rich people in the Dakota. They were huge and filled with deep, dark wood panels, big picture windows, and the most beautiful curtains. We'd see Yoko Ono walking, with her bodyguards, below us, and sometimes Roberta Flack or John Madden, the sports commentator, who apparently was banned from smoking in his Dakota apartment. From our balcony, we could see the spot where John Lennon was shot. Every year on his birthday, crowds gathered, lit candles, and sang "Happy Birthday, John." Every year, John went out and waved. No one waved back.

Across the street was a trendy Chinese restaurant where actors and models ate. Tommy Tune was there for the cast party after he opened his show *My One and Only* on Broadway with Twiggy. Most days, we came home from work, rushed to open a bottle of wine, and then just stood there, for hours, watching New York go by. When Dottie's mom visited she always marveled at how at some point, Dottie would sense John's presence and go out to the balcony just in time to see him walk onto Seventy-second Street from the subway. On some weekends, we bought lox and bagels and made Bloody Marys—extra horseradish and probably more Worcestershire than vodka—and stood on our little balcony, watching the crowds of tourists and trendy New Yorkers. At night, we went to sleep to the sound of the clip-clopping of horse-drawn carriages, figuring we were just about the luckiest people alive.

Every day seemed a reason for a celebratory bottle of wine. We celebrated the last show of *M*A*S*H* with a bottle of Château Chasse-Spleen 1976 from Bordeaux, our first dinner on the balcony with a Harbor Winery Cabernet Sauvignon from California, and our very first snowstorm in our Seventy-second Street apartment with a Croft Port from the 1963 vintage. It was the first Port we'd ever tasted—real Port, from Portugal. It was from a great year and was almost twenty years old, and it was magnificent. We have never had a better bottle of Port. For Christmas Eve 1983, we opened a bottle of 1964 Pichon-Lalande, a fine Bordeaux château.

Delicious! Very, very special. Extremely dark ruby red, looks old. Brown-tinged edges. Acid nose. Edges lighter than you'd expect. Light in front of mouth, not much taste on tongue. Not much taste at all, but incredibly fine. The tannin and fruit have broken down—this is old—but they've come together into an incredibly delicate old age that makes you come to it. So ephemeral. Dottie says: "It's so incredibly still and fine and clear. There's a strange serenity. It's seamless, beautiful." With filets it got bigger, almost gutsy, with more years left. THE SEDIMENT IS INCREDIBLE, huge and long finish. Powerful. (The sediment didn't taste at all dirty or gritty. With eyes closed, you wouldn't know it was sediment.)

Pichon-Lalande quickly became one of our favorite Bordeaux wines, until it became well known and too expensive for us to afford.

On some Sundays, we went rowing in Central Park. There were old rowboats for rent at just $4 an hour (and a graffiti artist had spray-painted "Clyde" on every one of them). We would row to the middle of the lake, surrounded by Central Park and, beyond it, all of Manhattan, and read *The New York Times* for hours, while drinking white wine in the summer, red wine in colder weather. The very first bottle we opened in a Central Park rowboat was a 1978 Chardonnay from Chalone, one of California's classiest wineries. Even then, some California wineries were deciding that "American-style" Chardonnay—powerful, rich, buttery, and oaky—was far too heavy and not really drinkable with food. The Chalone we had that day was on the leading edge. "Very good and beautifully made," we wrote. "Not big and rich and buttery, but instead earthy and much taste of the earth and very French. Classy and elegant and nice, but more French than California."

With an actual kitchen for the first time, we began to cook more. Shopping for dinner was as much fun as cooking and eating it. We walked all around the Upper West Side of Manhattan for the freshest everything—fish at Citarella, vegetables at Fairway, meat at Nevada, even dessert (we were young) at Miss Grimble's. Then we came home and cooked and drank wine for hours. We were hardly accomplished cooks—we still referred regularly to Craig Claiborne's *Kitchen Primer*—but we enjoyed it so. Dottie's specialty became roast duck, which was far better than anything we could get at restaurants. Her duck was not only delicious, but had the advantage of being perfect with good red Burgundy, good Bordeaux, and good Cabernet Sauvignon.

DOTTIE'S FAMOUS DUCK

This recipe will feed four easily. If there's any duck left over, it's delicious the next day cold, either in sandwiches or sliced over a simple green salad.

One 4½- to 5-lb. duck
Salt and pepper to taste (don't be timid—I use a little less than
1 teaspoon each inside the cavity and sprinkle liberally on the outside)
1 garlic clove
1 bay leaf, some sage, or whatever herb I have handy
1 medium onion, halved
1 roasting pan and 1 rack

1. *Preheat oven to 425°F.*
2. *Prick duck skin all over with a fork and rub the outside with salt and pepper. Rub garlic clove all over the cavity and leave inside. Add salt and pepper, herbs, and then the two halves of onion to the cavity.*
3. *We like duck with crispy skin and little fat. So what makes this work is the high heat and the constant rotating of the bird and pouring off of the fat. Roast the bird on the rack on its side for about 30 minutes, take it out of the oven using seriously protective mitts, and pour off the fat. Turn the bird on the other side and repeat the process. After an hour or so, turn the oven down to 350 and turn the bird breast side down for 30 minutes. Take it out and pour off the fat. For the final 30 minutes or so, place the duck on its back. Total cooking time is about 2 hours for a well-done bird; cut the time down if you like a rarer bird. Test the doneness by pricking the bird*

inside the leg to draw juices. If the juices run clear, it's well done; if pink, it's rarer. Let the duck sit for 10 to 15 minutes before serving. After years of using a sharp knife as John looked away in fear, I've found that it's easier to quarter a duck using kitchen shears.

The downside of preparing duck is that the cooking fat creates a great deal of smoke. One night, as Dottie was making duck, there was a loud pounding on the door. When we opened it, three men from our building—a maintenance man, a doorman, and the superintendent—were standing there. "We heard there's a fire here," they said. "Oh, that's just my wife cooking," said John. Dottie was not amused.

In the summer of 1983, we were finally able to walk to and from the free concerts in Central Park. No need to take a taxi anymore. We'd never felt more like real New Yorkers. For the last concert of the season, we shot the works and brought along a Château Les Tabernottes Bordeaux 1975. We had bought it years earlier in Miami and had moved it to New York with us, first to Park Avenue South and then to West Seventy-second Street. Bordeaux produces a great deal of wine, and only a small amount is made by the famous, great châteaux. Most of it is produced by smaller properties that make good, reliable wines that sell for reasonable prices because nobody has ever heard of them. This was one of them. We had never seen it before, and we have never seen it since. But that night, on the Great Lawn, looking out at New York City and being able to see the building we lived in right next to the park, this bottle was pure magic.

Delicious! Old and brown, but still so fruity and full of life. Aggressively plump. Long finish. Warm and sweet in mouth, a bit watery in middle, then big finish.

There wasn't a more famous restaurant in New York at the time than Lutéce, the classic French restaurant run by André Soltner, and, as real New Yorkers, we had to go. We didn't really know enough about New York then to know that we were supposed to be afraid of such fancy restaurants and approach them with trepidation. We just called, made reservations, and showed up. Dottie looked luminous in her vintage midnight-blue satin dress. We were seated at an excellent table and handed the menu and the wine list. The menu was entirely in French, but the wine list was understandable, and rich in fairly priced Burgundies. As we studied them both, the man at the table next to us bent over and said, "You have to have the veal tonight. It's really great." We clearly must have looked taken aback, so he added, with a laugh, "Everybody talks to everybody else here." It turned out he was a regular, and quite tight with the maître d'. With his imprimatur, we were accepted into the party.

We ordered a Chassagne-Montrachet 1979, from Louis Latour. It was $35, which was a pretty reasonable price for such a fine white Burgundy. John had the veal, and as promised, it was tender and sweet. Dottie had the sweetbreads, gently sautéed in lots of butter.

Nose is creamy, thick, with vanilla, banana and a real sweetness. Nose is huge and spicy. Taste is huge, thick, sweet with fruit. A real backbone of nutmeg, cinnamon, slate, wood. Powerful, awesome, incredible, complex. Smoky. Big, round, sensuous, a touch of sourness.

To this day, if we were going to try to describe a great white Burgundy to someone, we couldn't do better than that. But that's not the drink we remember best from that night.

Sometime toward the end of our neighbor's dinner, the waiter came out with a huge glass. He filled the glass with crushed ice and then sloshed the ice around in the glass several times. Finally he emptied the glass and picked up a bottle of something we'd never seen before, something clear. The ritual itself was amazing to us, so we asked him, even as he was pouring the liquid, what it was. "It's eau-de-vie," he replied. "I'll get you some after dinner. Do you prefer pears, cherries, or raspberries?" We had no idea what he was talking about, but we told him that Dottie preferred raspberries and John preferred pears. When our dinner was over, it was our turn. As he chilled the glasses, he explained that eau-de-vie was distilled from various fruits, like pears and cherries. It was totally clear. When we smelled it, we couldn't believe the purity of the fruit smells. The taste was far more alcoholic than we were used to, but so clean and fresh that it made a perfect drink for the end of the memorable meal.

Later that year, we visited Café Carlyle to see the great Bobby Short play the piano and sing some of our parents' favorite songs, and ours. We couldn't afford dinner—the cover charge alone was steep—but John did look at the wine list. There was a sparkling wine on it that we'd never seen before, and he surprised Dottie with it. It was a California bubbly called Scharffenberger. It was even vintage-dated—1981—and it cost $30. It was crisp, a little chalky, and almost as elegant as Bobby Short himself. Many years later, in a blind tasting of California sparklers, Scharffenberger came out on top. Unfortunately, we recommended it just as the company was sold and the name of the wine was changed to Pacific Echo.

While we ate out constantly, we rarely ate at fancy, expensive places. We specialized in finding little places where we could bring our own wine. Our favorite was a spot in Greenwich Village called the Grove Street Café, where a couple named Jim and Gerald, and their trusty waiter Sluggo, presided over about a dozen tables at one of the cutest little places in New York. At least once a month, we'd choose a special bottle or two and head to Grove Street. Since we weren't paying restaurant prices for wine, we could afford to open some of our own better stuff. We could even have tastings, like the 1979 Pinot Blanc from Domaine Weinbach in Alsace versus the Cordon d'Alsace Willm Pinot Blanc from 1981.

We'd been dabbling in Alsatian wines for a while. We'd been introduced to Gewürztraminer, of course, at Sebastiani years before. But the natural home of "Gewurz" is Alsace, the beautiful region on the French border with Germany whose wines seem a little French and a little German. They're mostly white, like German wines, and come in those long, pretty bottles, like German wines. But they're quite dry, with a distinctive prickliness, and—to make matters more confusing—are identified by their grape type, like American wines. They're unusual and generally unknown in America, so they can be great buys—certainly a great enough buy for us to take two to Grove Street. The Willm, which cost $3.49, fell by the wayside. "Good," we wrote, "but a bit too soft. Not dramatic enough for an Alsatian." The Domaine Weinbach, on the other hand: "Very Good. Very Alsatian, with lots of finesse. Classy. Complex, restrained, long finish."

We continued to attend tastings with our Les Amis du Vin New York chapter. We attended one with a winemaker we'd admired from afar for years for his big, unrestrained California wines. We so looked forward to meeting him. He stood at the podium as his wines were poured. Then he smelled a wine and said, "What does this smell like to you?" Someone said, "Plums," and he said, "No! Wrong!" This went on and on, with people desperately searching for the "right" answer and the winemaker getting increasingly angry that our "nose" didn't match his. He was, in fact, the most unpleasant winemaker we'd ever met. What we had found, time and again, was that winemakers were passionate and sometimes irritating in their strong beliefs about the best way to make wine, but few were unpleasant or snobbish. He was the exception. We still had him sign a bottle of his 1978 Late-Harvest Zinfandel, though. We also met the owner of Château Giscours in Bordeaux, who brought over a barrel sample of his 1982 wine. "*Degustée avec Dorothy,*" he wrote on the label we asked him to sign.

Except for showing up at tastings, we weren't active members. Neither one of us ever raised our hand in class much. Some people at the Les Amis tastings and dinners seemed to want to show off their knowledge, or at least make new friends. We just wanted to be alone and taste some wines. At one tasting, though, we happened to be seated next to a nice young couple named Cathy and David Chirls, who became close friends and wine-tasting companions. John also met someone at *Newsweek,* the dashing James LeMoyne, who enjoyed wine and knew far more about it than we did. All of this meant we could have our own little wine-tasting dinners and parties, and we could share more and better stuff than we could ever drink on our own. James, for instance, once brought over two old Bordeaux: a 1953 Château Malartic-Lagravière and a 1955 Château Haut-Brion, one of those great "first growths" we'd read so much about but, even then, had rarely had. And we'd certainly never had one with so much age on it.

The '53 is delicious, assertive and big and fruity and woody despite its years. Almost spritzy in its assertiveness. But it is completely outshone by the '55, which is red-gold, fruity, "feminine," with a long finish. Utterly elegant, with a backbone to boot. The '53 is beautiful, like black smoke, but clumsy compared to the '55, not as elegant.

We had traveled all the way to California to meet winemakers. It seemed as if we should meet some in our own backyard. We rented a car and drove to Pennsylvania, where we stayed in a place called the Black Bass Inn in Bucks County. It was fall, and the leaves were changing. It could not have been more beautiful. The real surprise was the wine, things like Bucks Country Vineyards Country White Wine. It's not that the wines were great, because they were far more charming than great. But we were amazed by the people we met at these wineries. They were so passionate. They could talk forever about the challenges their weather brought them and which grapes grew best where.

While driving around one night, we spotted a good place for dinner and went inside to see if they could take us. The Pig 'n Thistle was warm and charming, but it served no wine. So we dashed to our inn to retrieve one of those lovely, fresh wines we'd bought at a winery earlier in the day. We have never since thought about the glorious changing of the seasons and the colorful pageantry of the leaves without remembering those Bucks Country wines.

For our big vacation that year, we decided the time had come to take the ultimate train trip: an entire circuit of the country on Amtrak. This would require planning with military precision. We had only two weeks of vacation, after all. We needed scarce bedroom space on every train. There was something called the All Aboard America fare that allowed us to travel as much as we wanted for a set fee (plus the cost of the bedroom), but we could have only two "layovers." So we had to plan early, had to move fast, and had to figure out a way to get from train to train without more overnight stays than we were allowed. Of course, we wanted to stay on every train from the beginning of its run to its final stop, so we'd have to get out of bed as little as possible. This was something John had to do himself. No travel agent—indeed, no one even at Amtrak—could figure this out.

Miraculously, John had mapped out a plan. We'd take the *Lake Shore Limited* to Chicago, then the *Empire Builder* across the top of the country to Portland, then the *Coast Starlight* to Los Angeles, the *Sunset Limited* to New Orleans, and the *Crescent* home. Five trains, eight thousand miles, and who knows how many bottles of Champagne. We set out with a full case of Taittinger. We figured that would at least get us to New Orleans.

It was a magnificent trip. The scenery from the *Empire Builder*—North Dakota, Montana, Idaho, and so many more states we'd never seen—was more spectacular than we could have imagined. Days were great, nights were even better. Amtrak was using a new sleeper car west of Chicago by then that was somewhat more luxurious and even had a shower. We missed the stylish old all-metal sardine cans, but the view from the window was just as special. We stayed in bed the entire time. The porter, who asked if we were on our honeymoon, took away the empty Champagne bottles, left more ice outside the door, and brought us our meals. Time passed so quickly.

One of our overnights was in Portland, and we liked the city the moment we saw it. It was so pretty, and everyone seemed so friendly. Having barely set a single foot on a busy roadway, we noticed that cars going both ways would immediately stop to let us walk across. Drivers in New York or Miami probably would have made sport of us. As we kept walking, we happened upon a small wine shop. It had maybe three hundred different bottles, all carefully chosen. The amazing thing, to us, was that so many of the wines were from Oregon. We'd rarely had a wine from Oregon. When we expressed interest, the man behind the counter acted as though he'd been waiting for us his whole life. He talked passionately about how Oregon could be a great place for winemaking, about all of the exciting things that were happening, about how energized the whole state was about this. We were amazed. Sure, people in California were excited about their wine. But everywhere else we'd been, everyone except winemakers themselves seemed embarrassed about their homegrown wines. New York State wines were always consigned to the dusty back of New York stores. People laughed at us when we told them we'd had a wine from Florida. When we were in Pennsylvania, no one even seemed to know that wine was made there. Ditto for the folks in Connecticut.

We knew that day in Oregon, in that wine shop, that something exciting was happening. When we left, the man handed us a bottle. "Oregon's 1st Sparkling Wine," the label on the neck read. It was The Red Hills Vineyard 1979 Yamhill County Sparkling Chardonnay. The label said it was "fermented in this bottle," just like Hanns Kornell's did. The label also said: "Produced and bottled by Arterberry Ltd., McMinnville, Oregon. Grapes were grown by Jim and Lois Maresh of Dundee, Ore." Over the next twenty years, Oregon became one of America's hottest wine-growing areas. Its wineries are famous now for their Pinot Noir—the difficult grape that thrives in cooler climates—though our personal favorite is a white called Pinot Gris that a friend once described as "like drinking the cold."

Of course, one thing we've learned over the years is that wineries come and go with frightening speed in the United States. In a book called *The New Connoisseurs' Handbook of California Wines,* Norman S. Roby and Charles E. Olken later wrote: "Arterberry Winery. Willamette Valley, Oregon 1979. With a degree in enology from U.C. Davis in hand, Fred Arterberry moved to Oregon intending to make only sparkling wine. While he was renovating and enlarging his winery in downtown McMinnville, he produced sparkling cider to help finance the project, and for several years his cider was coveted in the local market. It is generally agreed that in '79 Arterberry made the first traditional *méthode champenoise* Oregon wine. He remained an advocate of Oregon sparkling wine, but in '82 he began producing a line of table wines that has steadily increased in importance. . . . But in 1990 Fred Arterberry died, and thereafter the winery was operated by his family. After producing wines in '91, the family decided to quit the wine business."

We drank that wine on the *Coast Starlight* as the sun set over the Pacific. It was excellent, of course, but what we learned was more important: In a very short time, the United States had gone from a country that didn't make much fine wine to a country where fine wine was being made, with passion, in wholly unexpected places.

The *Sunset Limited* was a spectacular train, with great scenery and attentive service. The West looked just the way we had always imagined it would look. Big, sprawling, wild. It seemed as if we were in Texas for days. Finally, we entered New Orleans on a six-mile trestle over Lake Pontchartrain, one of the most scenic approaches we ever found on Amtrak.

We'd heard about New Orleans forever. It is, after all, a mecca of good food and drink. John's brother Jim had once spent several months there and never stopped talking about it. We arrived in early afternoon after a bottle of bubbly, checked into our hotel, and had dinner that night, at Jim's suggestion, at Galatoire's. There, the waiter said everyone starts dinner with Galatoire's Special Cocktail, so we did. It was refreshing—it had sugar, water, and a lemon peel—and seemed light enough. With our dinner, we had a light white wine. Jim had told us we just had to go to a bar and restaurant called Pat O'Brien's and have a drink called a Hurricane. We ordered one, and it came in a tall, touristy glass. It was sweet and tasted just like fruit punch. It was a perfect, simple after-dinner drink, we thought. So we had another.

Not being big drinkers, we were in trouble and we didn't even know it. We've rarely had real, man-size drinks and rarely had too much to drink. What we didn't know about the Hurricanes was that the fruit juice was disguising a brain-numbing amount of alcohol. At that point in the day, we had had a bottle of Champagne, a bottle of white wine, a drink before dinner—it turns out that Galatoire's Special Cocktail is made with rye, which we're not sure we've ever tasted before or since—and two Hurricanes.

Jim also told us that, after dinner, we had to go to Café du Monde for beignets, those little fried dough-and-sugar concoctions. As we headed for the café, all of the alcohol suddenly hit us. Weaving now, we found ourselves right on the bank of the Mississippi River. "It's the Mighty Mississip!" John cried.

At that point, Dottie—John's quiet, understated wife, always cautious in public and always proper—walked over to the riverbank, spread her arms wide, and began to belt out a song in her best Paul Robeson voice: "OLD MAN RIVER. THAT OLD MAN RIVER. HE JUST KEEPS ROLLING AAAAAAAAALLLOOOOOOONG."

When Dottie woke up the next morning, she asked John to shoot her.

Gevrey-Chambertin
(Gérard Quivy) 1982

. . .

*E*XCITING THINGS WERE HAPPENING DOWNTOWN AT *THE Wall Street Journal.* John had always loved that paper. He still read it every day and admired it from afar. A forty-year-old wunderkind named Norman Pearlstine had just been named managing editor of the paper—the top editorial job—and all of New York was abuzz. Norm seemed to be hiring everyone in town. The old, gray *Wall Street Journal* was suddenly a sexy place to be. The paper had gone from one section to two in 1980, and the editor of the "second front," Fred Zimmerman, was looking for people. Things were going fine at *Newsweek*—John had moved to the business desk, and really liked his editor—but now seemed like the right time to finally get back to the *Journal.* With the help of a mutual friend, John called and set up a meeting with Fred, and with Norm.

Norm is a mythic figure among those who know him. He

seems to know everything there is to know, including what you're thinking. His charisma fills rooms. The stories of his exploits are legendary. Whenever anyone is with him, he or she is certain there is no one in the entire world Norm loves more. Much later, when Dottie and the wife of a friend came to the *Journal* to meet their husbands for lunch, Norm happened to be waiting for the elevator with the two women.

Dottie: *The three of us got in and no one said a word. Jan and I just stared at him as he leaned against the wall of the elevator, eyes closed, holding his black umbrella. He was wearing a black coat and there was something almost feline about him. The raw energy emanating from his corner of the elevator was enough to make us swoon. After he stepped out, Jan turned to me and said, "That is a very dangerous man," and I knew just what she meant.*

Even though John had worked for the *Journal* for only three months a decade earlier, everyone treated him like long-lost family when he came in for his interview. When he sat in Norm's office, he was sure that Norm loved him more than any job applicant who had ever walked in the door. He left the building desperate to be hired, and sure he would be. Two weeks passed with no word. Finally, John called Fred Zimmerman and asked what was happening. "Well," Fred said, "I just don't think I can afford your salary." John burst out laughing. He said he didn't care what he earned, he just wanted the job. Fred, pleased, matched his salary. John started work as an editor for the second section a few weeks later.

John: *What a time it was. Norm had cast his net and picked off the best journalists from everywhere. Here I was in New York, where I'd always wanted to be, and at* The Wall Street Journal, *where I'd always wanted to work, working for the smartest man I'd ever met.*

Sitting right there next to me on the second front, just copyediting stories that weren't good enough for the famous Page One, were the former Style editor of The Washington Post, *the former managing editor of* The Village Voice, *the former managing editor of* Harper's, *the former deputy managing editor of the Lexington, Kentucky, newspaper, and more. People were coming from everywhere, including the former executive editor of* American Lawyer, *James B. Stewart, who had just written a best-selling book called* The Partners. *He was famous, and I was editing his copy. Not only that, but he loved wine.*

It was chaos, but it was so exciting. Norm had hinted to all of us that we'd run the paper someday, and we all believed him. But beyond that, everything was fair game. Norm wasn't afraid of anything. If stories were unpopular, if people were pissed off, he didn't care. This was real journalism. Everybody seemed to be having a good time. A brand-new reporter named Joanne Lipman, fresh out of Yale, played the viola on the street in several areas of New York, and wrote a first-person Page One story about it. She reported that she made more per hour in tips than she made as a reporter. She said she received the smallest tips when she played on Wall Street.

The *Journal* thought John was really good, from the very first day. He quickly became a star. In fact, the editors asked him to put together some Page One stories, even though he was just a second-front editor. They thought he had a special knack. One day, as John was writing a "roundup" story about insider trading, Norm came over with a paragraph he asked John to insert. "It was learned yesterday, for example, that the SEC is informally investigating allegations that a stock trader had advance knowledge of certain articles that have appeared in *The Wall Street Journal*." John had no idea that he'd just inserted the first hint of the Foster Winans case, which soon became the *Journal*'s biggest black eye.

We decided to celebrate John's return to the *Journal* with a romantic weekend. John's office was right next door to the World Trade Center, and the World Trade Center had a hotel called the Vista. The Vista was so empty on weekends—there was nothing happening near Wall Street on weekends back then—that it was practically giving away rooms to get people into the hotel. Dottie, who had written about the hotel's opening for the *Times,* met John downtown Friday night with a little suitcase. We checked in, changed clothes, went back downstairs, walked a few feet to the elevator banks, and went up to our old favorite, Cellar in the Sky. We could actually walk to and from our favorite restaurant in the world. It was heaven.

CELLAR IN THE SKY

CHEF'S CANAPÉS

Cellar Aperitifs

SALAD WITH MARINATED FRESH TUNA

CHICKEN CONSOMMÉ WITH WILD MUSHROOMS

SAUTÉED SOFT-SHELLED CRABS WITH SWEET PIMENTO SAUCE

Puligny-Montrachet Folatieres Caillot 1982

TOURNEDOS OF BEEF WITH SUMMER VEGETABLES

Volnay Clos des Chênes Ponnell 1978

SELECTION OF CHEESE

Freemark Abbey Cabernet Sauvignon 1975

FIG TART

Château Doisy Daëne Sauternes 1971

COLOMBIAN COFFEE

CHOCOLATE TRUFFLES

There was a restaurant in the Vista called the American Harvest, which featured high-class American food and wine that changed with the seasons. It was a lovely place, and largely empty when we walked downstairs the next night. It didn't start out well. We began with a Raymond Cabernet Sauvignon 1979 from California ($22). We had loved Raymond's Pinot Noir and we didn't often see its wines, so we were pleased to have this. But it was thin and unmemorable. We thought maybe it was just too young, or maybe it just wasn't very good. Still, the sommelier was impressed that we'd ordered such an interesting bottle, and came by to talk. We didn't let on that we were disappointed—we never do—and we got to talking about wine. There really wasn't anyone else there for him to talk to. "So," we said, "got anything special that you're hiding under the counter?" The sommelier straightened up so suddenly that we were both a bit shocked. He stared at us for a few moments and then a story just spilled out of his mouth. His eyes grew wide and he seemed to be in a trance as he told it.

When Robert Mondavi began making Sauvignon Blanc, he thought it needed a trendier name, so he invented the name Fumé Blanc. It's the same wine and the same grape, but a more fetching name. His Fumé Blanc was quite good. It was the wine we had at Imperial Palace with lobster and shrimp in rice paper during our first trip to San Francisco, and that we drank at Commander's Palace in New Orleans. But, the sommelier told us, there was a special, secret Robert Mondavi Sauvignon Blanc that was called Sauvignon Blanc. It was a dessert wine. Its grapes had been attacked by botrytis, the "noble rot" that makes the wines of Sauternes so sweet and concentrated. Botrytis is rare in California. Robert Mondavi made some of this for himself, the sommelier said, but had allowed the sommelier to taste some when he was at the winery. It was never sold to the public. Months later, when the sommelier was telling this story to a Mondavi salesman, the salesman said, "Would you like a case?" The sommelier had the case of half bottles in a room, somewhere in the hotel. "I paid sixteen dollars a bottle for it," he said. "I'll sell it to you for thirty-two dollars. But you have to tell me now so I can go get it."

We said yes, of course, and he disappeared for a long time. When he finally returned, he was sweating and slightly out of breath, perhaps because he had to run to get it or perhaps just from anticipation. He put the bottle—from the 1978 vintage—in an ice bucket. Our notes, typed the next morning when we got home, start with this word: "UNBELIEVABLE!"

Spectacular. Nose was pure nectar, with every imaginable fruit. Bright gold. So incredibly rich that we took very small sips, then let it linger for several minutes; the half-bottle lasted forever. The amazing thing was that it was not thick at all; it smelled thick and from nectar-like description you'd expect it, but it was clean and no less crisp than a non-dessert fine wine. Unbelievably clean. Seemed to coat mouth with pure taste, not so much with pure thickness.

As we watched the sun set over the Statue of Liberty from our hotel room that weekend, we made a couple of important decisions. One was that we should go to France to visit wineries there. The other was that we should try to conceive Media.

Media was our daughter. Sometime way back, probably in 1974, we decided that we'd have a daughter and we'd call her Media. From that time on, Media was very much a real person to us. We'd talk about things that Media would like and how much Media would enjoy this or that. Long before she was real, she was our daughter. We now decided that we were old enough, and secure enough, and settled enough, that it was time to make Media. We figured there wasn't much more to it than that.

We didn't do much homework when it came to planning our trip to France. We'd fly to London—because we could take People Express for $99 each way—spend a couple of days there, then fly over to Paris, spend a night in Paris, and head over to Champagne.

Then we'd just drive south through Burgundy and down to the Rhône Valley. We chose Burgundy over Bordeaux because it looked like an easier trip. We'd drop off the car, take a train back to Paris, spend another couple of days in London, and return home. We made hotel reservations in London, Paris, and Champagne, but figured we'd leave everything open after that so we could let our palates be our guide. Even though John spoke no French and Dottie remembered just a little, we figured we'd get by.

We arrived in London in the morning, so we ate breakfast while we waited for our room to be prepared. John ordered kippers and eggs because that sounded so British. It was awful, and the coffee was virtually undrinkable. The hotel was near Hyde Park, so we went into a wine shop to get a bottle of wine to have in the park. We left with a bottle of Lamberhurst Reichensteiner "White English Table Wine (Medium Dry)." The label said it was "Bottled by the producer, Kenneth McAlpine." As we were drinking our wine, which was simple and slightly sweet, it started to rain. We hadn't brought an umbrella—amazing when you think about it—so we ran to a nearby bandshell for cover. As we were sitting there, drinking wine, John said he knew this sounded weird, but there was something very familiar about this spot. When the rain stopped, we look around and found a plaque. This was the bandshell that had been blown up by the Irish Republican Army in 1982, killing four soldiers and seven horses. John had written the story for *Newsweek*.

Friends had told us two things about London. First, eat Indian. We did that the first night, at a place called Last Days of the Raj. We couldn't resist having its house wine: "Last Days of the Raj. Rouge de France. Vin de Table." It was fruity and fun, and the Indian food was, indeed, the best we'd ever had.

(In fact, the Indian food was so delicious that we decided to take some back with us on our return flight. We bought some at a take-out place. The hotel's doorman was Indian and he stopped us as we were putting it in the refrigerator in the lobby. "Just keep it out," he told us. "Trust me. I know something about this." When we unwrapped the food on the plane, the warm aromas almost started a riot as they wafted throughout the cabin. The airline hadn't stocked enough fruit and cracker baskets for sale, and there we were eating a feast. A woman nearby told a flight attendant, "I'll have what they're eating," pointing to us. A little girl in front of us stood in her seat and watched us eat. It was so delicious. And the doorman was right. It was perfect at room temperature.)

The second thing friends had told us was that we had to go to the Tate Gallery to have its great wines. Most people go to the Tate Gallery for art. We went for the wine. Maybe that's why the security guard at the front door looked at us funny when we asked where the restaurant was. When we found it, we were sure we were in the wrong place. It looked like a snack bar. We asked where the better restaurant was. They said this was the only one. We couldn't understand how we'd gotten this confused.

Then they brought us the wine list.

The British love "claret," as they call red Bordeaux, and they have for centuries. Good claret used to be shipped in barrels from France and then bottled in London. So many of the world's great wine writers, and Bordeaux experts, are British. Here, on this list, was the most extraordinary collection of Bordeaux wines we'd ever seen, and the prices were shockingly reasonable. We were speechless, which our waiter, Christopher, thought was charming. Finally, we settled on a Château Baret from Graves. It was from the great 1959 vintage—we'd never even imagined drinking a '59—and it was $26.22. We had never ever seen Château Baret and, in fact, we have never seen it since. Here are our contemporaneous notes:

Very dark, but with a light nose with a hint of decay. Very light taste, very delicate with touch of vinegar, but with air in mouth, much bigger, fruitier. Surprisingly long, red, delicate finish. Needs some air. Opening up. More fruit. Round and soft and very fine, very feminine. Long, light-fruit finish. Really tastes like an old claret. Bigger with every sip. After 30 minutes, actually pretty big, with lots of fruit, big and dark red in mouth. Taste is mostly in back of mouth and in finish, very big and red and fruity. After 1 hour, another change: deeper, darker, browner, not as aggressively fruity and really tasting older.

Right there, at the Tate Gallery, over the period of an hour, we had witnessed the entire life cycle of a fine old claret. It was one of the most remarkable experiences we'd ever had. We couldn't stop now. We looked at the list for something else. There was a Château Pichon-Lalande from 1964, a Pauillac, for $33.12. This is a far better-known wine from a year that wasn't quite as good. It was almost twenty years old. This was the same wine we'd had on Christmas Eve the year before. How would this one, which was probably cellared better, taste now?

Brighter red, crisper-looking than the Baret. Rich, fruity, red nose, not as brown around the edges as expected. Exceptionally pretty and clear. Much bigger, fruitier, though lightish in color. Dry. A bit harsher and definitely younger than the Baret. After 15 minutes, almost sweet. Almost candy-like in mouth, but no finish. Lightish yet very fruity. Still has years left, but it's not clear what it will be because it's mainly fruit now. Overwhelming taste of fruit and "sweet" without much else behind it. Very fine and fruity, but no real depth.

We'd finished lunch, so we ordered a plate of cheese and sat there, drinking our wines. We spent three hours at lunch, the greatest lunch we'd ever had. Of course, always being effusive, we oohed and aahed and looked into each other's eyes a lot. We were in heaven. An older couple with big smiles on their faces walked up to our table on their way out and asked, "You enjoyed your lunch?" We had been so excited and enveloped in our own little world that we hadn't noticed the other diners taking notice of us. We were the last to leave the restaurant. We said good-bye to the security guard at the entrance and left. We never saw the art.

We flew to Paris and checked into the Hôtel Raphael, which had a view of the Eiffel Tower outside our French windows. On the first night, *Newsweek*'s Paris bureau chief took us to a very informal bistro called Chez Pauline. We had a warm salad of frisée and bacon, and a simple roasted chicken, while everyone around us talked, drank wine, and smoked. We had an unpretentious wine from the Fleurie area of Beaujolais that was made for the bistro by a winemaker named Georges Duboeuf, who later became famous as a kind of French Robert Mondavi, a brilliant marketer who also made good wine. We were taken with the informality of the wine at the restaurant. Every table had a bottle and no waiters were pouring it. Diners were just helping themselves to it. There wasn't an ice bucket in sight. No one seemed to be paying much attention to the wine, either. They were just drinking it. We'd never seen wine enjoyed quite so effortlessly.

That night, filled with Beaujolais and with the Eiffel Tower lit up outside, we made our first attempt to conceive Media. The next day, we left for Champagne.

We all grow up hearing names like Champagne. It's hard to imagine it as a real place, but Champagne is indeed the home of real Champagne, and there is nothing in the world like the real thing. There are many reasons for that, but geography is a large part of it. Champagne is a very northerly region for winemaking. Grapes have acid. Sunshine makes the acid break down into sugar, which in turn breaks down into alcohol and carbon dioxide (about 55 percent to 45 percent). In a northerly climate like Champagne, the grapes don't get very ripe, which is bad for most still wines but great for sparkling wines, which need plenty of acids to give them the perfect balance of tastes. This is the same reason German wines tend to be high in acids and low in alcohol. Not only that, but in Champagne the soil is chalky and filled with limestone, which is bad for most crops but great for wine grapes, which tend to take on the characteristics of the soil they're grown in.

We had reservations in Champagne, at a place in Reims called Boyer les Crayères. We'd read that it had a fine restaurant, so we figured we'd stay there. It was a short drive from Paris to Reims—we didn't even get lost—and we were amazed at how small, rural, and pleasant Champagne seemed. It looked so—well, French, like we'd imagined it. It even looked a little like the French villages they always fought through in the old TV show *Combat*. The stone-walled houses looked ancient and the narrow streets really did wind. We passed Champagne house after Champagne house that we'd never heard of, tiny places that seemed to be entirely located in garages. We didn't know until then that there are scores of small Champagne makers who make so little wine that it never reaches the United States.

When we drove up to the Boyers', we were stunned. It was like a palace surrounded by lush gardens—the most gorgeous place imaginable. We checked in and they assigned us to the most luxurious room we'd ever seen. It had a high ceiling and beautiful, heavy blue draperies that opened onto a view of the inn's grounds. In the distance was another château. The bed was humongous, with great soft pillows, and the bathtub was big enough for both of us, and then some. After taking it all in, we drove out to visit some Champagne houses. Our first stop: Taittinger. It wasn't a particularly intimate stop—they seemed weary of tourists, and there didn't seem to be anything we could do to cut through that—but we did pick up an amazing bottle: Taittinger Brut Absolu.

When Champagne is "disgorged"—when the sediment is finally blown out of it—winemakers pour a little bit of "dosage" in to replace the small amount that's missing. The dosage contains at least a little bit of sugar. Even wines that are called "Brut" in fact have a bit of sweetness, because Champagne's high acidity makes it hard to drink completely dry. Sometimes, rarely, we see a Champagne made with no dosage at all, like this Taittinger. It's risky because if the wine has any flaws they will be easy to taste without the tiny bit of sugar that provides cover. And it's risky because the market for a Champagne that's so stark probably isn't very big. It's truly a connoisseurs' wine.

We had never had a no-dosage wine, so we bought it and headed back to the Boyers' for dinner. After dressing for dinner—Dottie in a full, floor-length silk skirt and one of those beaded vintage sweaters she collects—we asked if they'd mind if we walked around the grounds while drinking this bottle. They smiled, nodded, and handed us two Champagne flutes. Soon we were outside walking through perfectly tended gardens that looked straight out of some book about palaces from another century, drinking a rare Champagne, in Champagne. Dottie said she felt like royalty, as her swooping skirt floated over the perfectly manicured grass. The flowers, the grass, the smells of the garden, all seemed especially sharp—and so did the wine, which was not as pleasant as it was fascinating. We were having such a grand time that we asked if we could delay dinner for a little while to take in the sunset. They were charmed and said of course.

With dinner, at a table overlooking the beautiful grounds, we tried a Champagne we'd never seen before then, Jacquart, from the 1978 vintage. It was flowery compared to the no-dosage Taittinger, with layers of rich tastes and the most exquisite bubbles. When we'd gotten down to the last glass of it, our waiter ushered us into a lovely small green room off to the side, where after-dinner drinks were served. We had a touch of Grand Marnier. How sophisticated! When we woke the next morning and ordered petit déjeuner, it wasn't just that the croissant was the best we'd ever tasted. Even the butter was the best we'd ever had. And the coffee with real cream made us moan. The French really know how to eat.

It was a good thing we'd had some breakfast. When we left that day, traveling south toward Chablis—the first stop in Burgundy—we figured we'd stop somewhere for lunch. We passed town after town. Nothing was open. There was no one on the streets. We kept thinking about *Combat* and wondered where all of the people had gone. Finally, we saw a roadhouse that appeared to be open and we stumbled in. We tried to explain that we were starving and that we had to have something to eat. The young woman looked at us quizzically and, after a long pause, simply said, "San-WEECH?" We said yes and she brought out pâté on French bread with crisp little cornichon pickles on the side. We never knew something so simple could taste so marvelous.

For the next week, we let our stomachs lead the way. No, make that our tongues. We stopped at every winery we saw that looked inviting. Sometimes the invitation to visit was simple, an empty bottle of wine on a low wall. It was a journey into the heart of darker wine. To the north, there was Chablis, which is steely and acidic for the same reasons Champagne is. Then, as we went south, we ran into the great whites and reds of Burgundy, the ones made from the Chardonnay and Pinot Noir grapes. Then there were the villages of Beaujolais, one after another—Saint-Amour and Fleurie and Morgon and others we'd never imagined as real places. Then Burgundy ended and we were in the Rhône Valley, where even the white wines are big and the red wines are massive.

People were welcoming everywhere we went, though they generally spoke no more English than we spoke French. It had been a long time since Dottie had studied French. But we discovered that wine is a universal language. "Pinot Noir" is French, after all, and "yum" is the same everywhere. We ate at a restaurant with a cheese cart for the first time, and the waiter delighted in John's excitement. The cheese cart had two tiers and on each was a magnificent array of hard, aged cheeses, blues, herb-scented cheeses, soft, gooey Brie, and cheeses made with goat's milk. They were dreamy-looking, from a soft off-white to golden, and John was in heaven. One was so particularly delicious that we found the farm where it was made and bought a small wheel of it. For years, Dottie kept her favorite jewelry in the little round wooden box that it came in.

We met a young couple in Monthélie who seemed to love making wine as much as they loved each other. We bought a bottle here and a bottle there, all remarkably cheap, and had the wine-makers sign them. We stayed in a castle in Châteauneuf-du-Pape—right in the tower of it, which had a round bed—near the ancient castle of the popes that gave the town its name. We walked on the roasted, gravelly soil of the Rhône and understood why the wines taste the way they do. During a thunderstorm, we dashed into a restaurant for lunch that was completely empty. We couldn't make any sense of the menu, so we just ordered the "Chef's surprise."

The big surprise was that the appetizer appeared to be an en-tire foie gras, a massive mound of the most luscious food we could have imagined. As we devoured it, we could almost feel our arter-ies clogging. We figured that the chef was sure he'd have no more diners on that dreary day and could afford to be over-the-top gen-erous. Wine was included in the price of the meal. It was Bour-gogne Passetoutgrains, an unusual local thirst-quencher, made from Pinot Noir and Gamay grapes, that rarely leaves the region. It's not a fine wine, but it couldn't have been better under the circumstances.

We passed by the Hospices de Beaune, site of the famous charity auction that helps set the price of the new vintage of Bur-gundy, and we dined one night at a restaurant that was owned by relatives of Pierre Franey, the great food writer for the *Times*, who called ahead to make reservations for us. We were welcomed like family.

With our limited French, we had a few menu missteps. Dottie ordered a fish dish with beef marrow that tasted odd. Then she or-dered some sort of kidney dish for John, who was fairly horrified.

At one charming restaurant, John ordered pigeon in a pastry shell, and they brought out a platter with three of them—covered in pastry—and asked if they were okay. How could he tell? The dish was delicious, basically a very, very fancy chicken pot pie.

In Gevrey-Chambertin, home to some of the world's greatest wines, we knocked on doors and Dottie asked if we could taste. We tasted old wines and young wines, and everyone seemed so happy to taste with us that they didn't care if we bought anything. We ate at a restaurant called La Rôtisserie du Chambertin that seemed part restaurant and part wine museum. We ordered a bottle of Gevrey-Chambertin from 1961, a great year, for $40. It didn't even have a label, just some chalk writing covered in dust.

Almost orange, persimmon looking, very orange at the edge. Big, fruity nose—massive. Taste at 9:10 P.M. a bit too "sweet" and muscular, better at the back of the throat. Needs air. Almost jam-like sweetness. No real hint of age at 9:15. Years left, very fruity and young-tasting. No dusty taste or brown in look or taste. Really dries mouth. Lots of tannins left. Dry, fruity, very Pinot, no wood taste, just fruit, but best at back. 9:30: Richer, bigger, almost like cherry wine. Still a long finish, but fruitier. 9:35: Pepper comes in. 9:45: Nose is unbelievable. Not "deep red" like a claret or California, but big. Austere yet fruity, very dignified, stately, not at all plump. Regal. 10:15: Dusty nose, finally. 11: Huge, lots of fruit, almost sweet yet austere at the same time. 11:30: Still lots of fruit, long, red finish. Terrifically elegant, great character. Rich and austere at the same time. Great finish, long and red and hot and Pinot.

Then, close to midnight, we ordered a '57 Chambertin, for the awesome sum of $90. It didn't have a label, either. Was it worth it?

Oaky, rich, round, red. Chewier, redder, not the same aggressiveness, much more laid back. Very Pinot, yet rich. Color is perfect Burgundy, gorgeous, much more accessible nose, friendlier, redder. "Sweet" nose, almost chocolaty, but also very red. Taste: almost like dessert it's so big and fruity. Gorgeous, soft finish,

not as long as the '61, but much more velvety. Candylike, plump, not as much
backbone as the '61. Tastes more and more like dessert, almost Italian in its
chocolate fruit but with terrific finesse.

Then there was L'Espérance. One night we found ourselves
somewhere near Dijon. We weren't really sure where we were, in
fact, but we saw a hotel and checked in despite some language
problems. Looking at guidebooks in the office, we noticed that
there was a three-star restaurant called L'Espérance nearby. We
didn't know it was famous. We didn't know that you just can't call
a three-star restaurant and show up. So we asked our innkeeper to
make a reservation for us, and she did. The dining room was like a
garden, with windows all around it. When we walked in, the other
diners stared for a second. When we smiled, they smiled back and
returned to their dinners.

We started with a simple Chablis. Our waiter spoke some English and helped us through the menu. We ended up with lamb
cooked with its own sweetbreads. The service was amazing. It was
as though the waiters were reading our minds. Before we could
ask for anything, they brought it. Waiters came and went and we
were totally unaware of them. We finished the white just as the
main course appeared. The waiter decanted the 1978 Ladoix, a
lovely red Burgundy that we'd never tasted before, and poured it
as the plates were being set down. It was a magical pairing and we
ooed and aahed, much to the amusement of the waiters. For
dessert, they suggested flourless hazelnut cake, which was like eating heavenly scented air.

Maybe the French are used to eating like this and are noncha-
lant, but we couldn't hide our feelings. We were totally involved in
the food and each other, utterly unaware of our surroundings. Just
as we were finishing our cake, when the restaurant was virtually
empty, Dottie looked up, and then motioned to John to look
around him. Waiters and people from the kitchen had pretty much

surrounded our table. They were watching us eat. Then they escorted us into a sitting room where they served us madeleines as the house dog slept at our feet in front of a fireplace. It was the greatest meal we had ever had.

On the way back, we were in London for just one night. We went back to Hyde Park and this time rented a rowboat, just as we did in Central Park. When we were in Gevrey-Chambertin, we had knocked on the door of a little shop that looked like it might be a winery. A wiry old man with stubble, a beret, and a cigarette—yes, a man who looked just like what an old French winemaker should look like—greeted us. He didn't speak a word of English, and didn't try. We did our best to explain why we were there. He smiled and motioned for us to follow him. He opened a trapdoor in the floor and led us down a ladder. There, in the basement, was a small cave of his wines. It was cold down there, and very dark. He motioned for us to sit. He took out a bottle of his wine—it had a black label, "Gérard Quivy"—opened, and poured. It was magnificent, with the fruit, chocolate, tobacco, and charm of Pinot Noir, and with great structure and a majestic sense about it. He was clearly pleased by our reaction, and we all began to speak to one another. It was the damnedest thing. We were having a conversation. We knew what we were saying to one another, but we were speaking different languages. It was then we knew: Wine and winemakers are universal. The intensity, the passion, the almost mystical sense of bottled personality—we'd seen it in California, in Pennsylvania, in France. Even more than we'd ever realized, we were part of something that transcended borders and everyday life.

We bought a bottle of the old man's wine, and we opened it in our rowboat in Hyde Park that day. Ducks were all around the boat, and one family of them caught our attention. The father or mother kept coming close to get bits of bread from us to take back to the babies. We had had fun trying to make Media. Had we succeeded? The ducks were all around us, the sun was bright, and the park's grounds were perfect. We opened the bottle and we poured and we were overwhelmed. The wine was monumental, sublime. It seemed impossible to even grasp its tastes. It was beyond words.

We took no notes.

Martin Ray "California Champagne" Cuvée 77

W E'D ALWAYS SAID THAT WE'D GO ANYWHERE TO DO good journalism. If a publisher anywhere told us that he needed us to come help a city, we always said, we'd be there. After all, we couldn't change the world if we were worried only about our own sweet lives. Our job was to comfort the afflicted and afflict the comfortable. In the middle of 1984, *The Miami Herald* called our bluff.

Miami had been torn apart since we left. The McDuffie riots. The Mariel boatlift. Rampant drugs. Corrupt cops. Out-of-control crime. Hate everywhere. John would be city editor, in charge of all news coverage of Dade County, which includes Miami. Dottie would join the editorial board, as an editorial writer and columnist, the first black woman to have those positions at the paper. She would have a weekly column, with a picture and a voice. Between the two of us, news and editorial, we would surely have a large impact on bringing the community together. We were just thirty-two years old, and this was heady stuff.

The timing could not have been worse, though. We loved our little apartment, which was now beginning to look like the bargain of the century as the housing market recovered. We were comfortable in New York. We'd just started trying to have Media, so far without success. John was quite happy at the *Journal,* and Dottie had moved to the Style section of the *Times,* where she was quite content. But we decided that, at the very least, we had to fly to Miami to hear them out.

Just days later, we checked into a suite at the Hilton near Miami International Airport. The *Herald* always hated spending money, so our big top-floor suite was a surprise. Miami is a beautiful place, with blue water, palm trees, and green grass everywhere, and it looked great from our picture windows. When we arrived, we told the desk to send up a bottle of Champagne. It was Hilton Champagne from California, "naturally fermented in the bottle," and it was not good. This should have been a sign, but the editors who came to see us really seemed to need us. We could make a difference, they kept saying. Being there in the city itself, so beautiful and so full of promise, made us believe we really could.

By the time we returned to New York, our decision had been made. We didn't want to go to Miami, but we had to. Our bosses at the *Journal* and the *Times* said they understood. The *Times* even gave Dottie a good-bye party and the same top editors who had dropped by her desk to officially welcome her came to say good-bye and that she had done a good job. The Style section's going-away present was a book of labels from Château Mouton-Rothschild. Most great wines have the same label year after year. But Château Mouton-Rothschild is different. Every year, a famous artist is asked to design the label. It is a rare honor. The pay: a case of the wine.

Looking back, the story Dottie is most proud of is one that doesn't even have her name on it.

Dottie: *Back then, the* Times *had a policy of putting a reporter's name on only one story per edition. If the reporter wrote two, only one would have a byline. One day I was assigned to do a story about elderly, homebound people who were fed by the city, but not every day. I arrived early near the apartment of one such elderly couple and the apartment of a woman who lived alone, and I bought two bags of food. After the interview, I just left the bags in their kitchens. The old couple cried. The single woman, Roberta Garvey, grabbed my hand and kissed it. By the time I got back to the paper, my eyes had dried and my head was clear. I knew that another story of mine, a routine piece about the Board of Regents, was scheduled to run the same day, but I assumed the desk would put the byline on the new story. I was shocked to pick up the paper the next morning and find no byline on the story about hunger and the elderly.*

As it happened, Gael Greene, the food writer, was touched by the piece and called the great chef James Beard, who with her called some other friends in the food and restaurant business. The result of their efforts was the Citymeals on Wheels program, which, to this day, feeds elderly and homebound people. When it was discovered that the story was mine, I was invited by Mayor Koch to Gracie Mansion to celebrate the program's success. The reception was held after we had moved back to Miami. I missed it.

Our friends in New York told us we should have our heads examined. Leave New York? What? They may have been right, but nevertheless, we called a real estate agent to sell our apartment. Later that same day, she called back to tell us she already had a buyer. We opened a bottle of Haywood 1980 Chardonnay, from the year we had arrived in New York, to mark the occasion. It was austere yet huge, with lots of lemon and smoke. "Like sucking charred wood," we wrote—a real California Chardonnay. Our apartment was never officially listed. Less than two years after we bought it for $110,000, we sold it for $195,000. It was sold so quickly that we never really had a chance to consider whether we were making a big mistake.

Our wine-drinking buddies, the Chirlses, came by to say farewell and brought a 1976 Dom Pérignon that we shared. We'd had dinner with Bryan Miller, a *Times* restaurant reviewer, and his then-wife a couple of times, so Dottie asked him where we should go for our farewell–to–New York dinner. He said he'd make some plans and he did. Bryan made reservations for us, for our last night in New York, at the Quilted Giraffe, then one of the hottest restaurants in the city. When we got there, Bryan had ordered a rosé Champagne, Ayala, which was waiting for us at our table. How ironic: Ayala was the Champagne we opened in Miami the night John accepted his job at *Newsweek* in 1980. The restaurant said it would take care of ordering dinner for us. We had rare duck with a marvelous red Burgundy—a 1971 Nuits-Saint-Georges Les Brulées. When dessert came, they'd spelled out "The New York Times" in chocolate on the plate. When it was time to leave, they told us transportation had been taken care of. A white Rolls-Royce pulled up, and a man in a white tuxedo and top hat drove us home through Central Park while Billie Holiday played on the radio. We left New York the next morning.

The *Herald* put us up at a hotel for a few weeks. Miami is not New York, but it has much going for it, at least in principle. When we were there in the 1970s, there was a restaurant right on Biscayne Bay called Miamarina. It was still there when we returned in 1984, and we figured it would be a good place to go to appreciate what was good about Miami. There were stone crabs on the menu. These are one of Miami's most luscious foods, but we'd never had them. We decided we'd order them, despite the awesome price. The wine? When we looked at the wine list, we were agog.

Right there, like any normal bottle, was Martin Ray "California Champagne" Cuvée 77. And it was only $17.

Martin Ray had been a hero of ours for years. Long before most people believed that California could produce great wines, he did. A onetime protégé of Paul Masson, he made wines that he said were the greatest in the world, put them into expensive, heavy bottles, and charged outrageous prices for them. He charged $50 for a wine in 1970, when even Château Lafite-Rothschild cost a fraction of that. He was also a notoriously difficult person. The combination of his personality, his apparent arrogance, and his prices made him a highly controversial figure in the wine world. Many experts felt his wines would never be ready to drink. E. Frank Henriques, in our old favorite *The Signet Encyclopedia of Wine,* said of his 1964 Cabernet Sauvignon, for instance: "Not recommended. At around $25 when first released, this had to be one of the worst wine values in all the world."

We had never had one of Martin Ray's wines, and we had never seen his sparkling wine, which was rare. Not only that, but "Cuvée 77" probably meant that this was made in 1977—the year after his death. This was probably the last sparkling wine that the great Martin Ray had anything to do with. And it was $17! With the cold, briny, juicy, and sweet stone crabs, the crisp yet slightly musty bubbly was just great. Maybe Miami would be okay after all.

We went house-hunting in Miami in July, which we wouldn't recommend to anyone. Most of the houses were empty and therefore not air-conditioned. As oppressive as the heat was outside, it was worse inside. We were hot, sweaty, and miserable as we looked around, and we weren't having any luck anyway. We knew what we were looking for: charm, and a wine cellar. Our feeling was that we were giving up a lot to live in Miami, but a big house would be a serious consolation prize. An actual wine cellar, or at least a wine room, would make a big difference in our lives.

Coral Gables is a charming part of Dade County. A little bit south of downtown Miami, it had strict zoning laws for decades, so while much of the rest of Dade County was ruined by overdevelopment, Coral Gables remained an oasis of lovely houses, many of them in Old Spanish style. The town even regulated the color of houses, which sounds terrible until you see the monstrosities in the communities surrounding it. When the real estate agent showed us an Old Spanish house on San Esteban Avenue, we immediately fell in love—and not just because the owner had been clever enough to leave on the air-conditioning. It was two stories high, but small, with a tiny yard. Its walls were so thick it seemed like it could survive anything—and indeed it had. It had been built in 1926 and was one of the few structures to survive the Great Hurricane of that year.

It even had an exceptionally tall fireplace in the living room. We had always wanted a home with a fireplace but couldn't afford one in New York. There were two regular bedrooms upstairs, for Media and her sister or brother, a bathroom, and then, as we kept walking, a palace for our bedroom. Two stairs led up to it. The room jutted out at the back of the house. That meant it had windows on three sides, and a cathedral ceiling. It was, truly, a Master Bedroom.

As we kept walking on the first floor toward the back, past the washer and dryer, we got to the maid's room. It had its own separate air-conditioning unit, a single window, and its own bathroom. In other words, it was perfect for a wine room. The current owner had clearly fixed the house to sell, even adding a flag on top of the chimney. "Paradise Cottage," it said. We bought the house. Then we spent three months fixing it up. We cut a door through a back room—"the TV room"—and added a deck with a hot tub outside. The man who built it said it could be formed into any shape we wanted. John brightened and started to open his mouth, but before he could say a word about a Dottie face, Dottie snapped, "Don't even think about it."

We made our bedroom even more special, a real pleasure dome. Dottie insisted that the ceiling be painted white and that a single beam be painted sky blue. We had a handyman named Tom Miranda build us a wine cellar. Week after week, he cut pieces of wood, then glued and nailed them together. It was slow, painstaking work. Expensive, too. But when he was finished, the skies parted, the birds sang, and we stood on brown shag carpeting in our fantasy room: a wine room, with its own air-conditioning unit, that held 990 bottles, each in its own individual space. There was a bookcase, too, for our wine books and our books of labels. When the wines were put into the racks, the bottles' caps provided just the dash of color the room needed. The room smelled of pine and wine—heavenly. We put two overstuffed chairs and a table in there. We could drink wine, look at our bottles, and even go to the bathroom. We never had to leave. We put up a little bronze plaque with Tom Miranda's name on it, in honor of his hard work and dedication.

We didn't actually have 990 bottles. In fact, we barely had 100. But this meant we could buy bottles when we saw them, and more than one. We never have believed in collecting for collecting's sake. In fact, we have rarely bought a full case of anything except inexpensive "house wines." The world of wine is so big. We always want to move on to the next, new wine. But with the space, we could at least buy two of everything, so if we liked one, we'd have another.

Our very first bottle in the new wine room brought us full circle. The label said it was Gallo Chablis Blanc. "Many vintners have praised this wine," it said. "It will surprise and delight you." But it wasn't Gallo wine. It was the wine we had made, from that Welch's grape juice kit, on December 7, 1974. It had moved with us from Miami to New York. Now it was home, and it was time to drink it. It was a decade old. It was not Lafite. But it was wine. "Pretty golden-honey-tawny, clear color," we wrote. "Watery nose. Not big at all, but like a somewhat watery Madeira. An aperitif wine." We added later: "We actually drank the whole bottle, and it seemed to have some alcohol."

We'd never met a group of people as passionate about wine as our old Miami tasting group, so we were happy to quickly get back together with them. Eight or ten of us would have a tasting dinner, where we'd all bring a different wine and a different dish. We'd taste California Pinot Noirs against one another, or fine old Bordeaux or Zinfandels.

Bob Hosmon, who coauthored a syndicated wine column for the *Herald,* held an annual tasting at Joe's Stone Crab restaurant to see what white wine went best with stone crabs. Joe's is an institution, and rightly so. Stone crabs are one of God's great gifts, and Joe's is the temple. Stone crabs have coral-colored claws with black tips. By law, only one claw can be harvested from a living crab. To take two would leave it defenseless. So they're quite a rarity. The fresh ones we ate in Florida are fished in the warm waters of the Gulf of Mexico only from late October through May. The juicy meat inside these hard shells is more sought after than lobster, so there's always great excitement surrounding the arrival of their season. The claws are eaten cold, dipped into either butter or mustard sauce or both. Joe's serves them piled high on chilled platters, and you can order from an assortment of remarkable side dishes—cole slaw with relish, creamed spinach, crisp and light hash browns, and "fried sweets," which are thick-cut sweet potatoes fried until they are moist inside and crunchy on the outside. To us, it's the mustard sauce, creamy and piquant, that makes the whole meal come together.

JOE'S MUSTARD SAUCE FOR STONE CRABS

1 tablespoon and ½ teaspoon Colman's dry mustard, or to taste

1 cup mayonnaise

2 tablespoons heavy cream

2 tablespoons milk

2 teaspoons Worcestershire sauce

1 teaspoon A.1. steak sauce

Pinch of salt

Put the dry mustard in a mixing bowl. Add the mayonnaise and, using an electric mixer on low speed, beat for 1 minute. Add the cream, milk, Worcestershire sauce, A.1. steak sauce, and salt. Beat on low until creamy, about 2 minutes. Add an additional ½ teaspoon dry mustard or more to taste, if you prefer a sauce with a little more bite. Put the sauce in a small glass bowl, cover with plastic wrap, and refrigerate until ready to serve.

MAKES 1 CUP SAUCE

New wine stores had opened in Miami in our absence, some of them quite good. Florida has always been a good market for fine wine, so it gets a lot of the good stuff. Also, because it is so international, Florida tends to get wines from all over the world, including Latin America, that other states don't necessarily see. We were always looking for something new. We'd try anything we hadn't had already. One day, we saw a 1982 Cabernet Sauvignon from a brand-new winery we'd never heard of called Kendall-Jackson. It was $7.49. That was the winery's first vintage. It made two thousand cases of Cabernet Sauvignon and fourteen thousand cases of Chardonnay. The Cabernet was so undistinguished that we didn't take any notes on it. Imagine that.

Another time, we were in a wine store called the Wine Warehouse and spied, on the floor, in a basket, some bottles of good-looking old Burgundies. They were marked $1.99. We wondered what was going on. "We just found them," the man behind the counter said. "They were lost in a warehouse for years. Cooked. We're selling them for the labels."

We've always believed that wine is a lot tougher than people give it credit for. One reason people don't keep any wine around the house is that they're sure it will immediately turn to vinegar if not kept in pristine conditions. Hogwash. Storage matters, of course. Any good wine will age more gracefully in a great cellar, while leaving wine on a radiator will ruin it. But there's a whole world of conditions between those two extremes, and we've tasted wine after wine that "should" have been over the hill and was still excellent. In any event, those Burgundies certainly looked fine. So we bought three. We took them home and opened one right away. It was quite good—maybe slightly thin, but still full of Pinot Noir charm. Curious, we opened the second, and then the third. All three were quite good, and worth far more than $1.99. We went back the next week and picked up six more. We opened one right away and it was good, too. We kept the other five. By the time we realized we were being ridiculous and should just go back and buy them all, they were gone.

One day, we found a wild little papaya tree, about six inches tall, picked it up, and replanted it in our yard. Like Jack's beanstalk, it seemed to become a twenty-foot tree, with fruit, in a couple of minutes. We grew our own herbs, and we picked them for dinner. We made pesto from our own basil, and Dottie sometimes got to her strawberries before the squirrels did. We even had our own grapefruit trees. John went out with a big pole, shook some down, and immediately squeezed them. The sweet juice, some from pink grapefruits, some from white ones, would still be warm from the sun. We had a mango tree, too. We'd pick mangoes, make frozen mango daiquiris, and take them to the hot tub, where we'd sit drinking them on hot days.

At night, a couple of Cuban-American friends would often come over, and we'd play dominoes and drink wine late into the night. Dominoes seems like a kid's game to Americans, but we were taught to play by Cubans, and it's no kid's game. It's challenging, tough, and really fun. We played hour after hour while we opened bottle after bottle of whatever was our "house wine" of the moment.

Work was interesting, too. Miami was a great place to be a journalist. The news never stopped. Just when it seemed that nothing more bizarre could happen, something would. Every national story seemed to have a Miami connection, and every Miami story seemed to be one that could happen only in Miami. The newsroom was like a sitcom, with characters like Edna Buchanan, the famous police reporter, who finally won her Pulitzer Prize after John became her boss; Dave Barry, the humorist, who was just as funny in person; and Carl Hiaasen, the great columnist and novelist. The place seemed to attract characters, many of whom were very good writers. As the city editor, John was in the middle of this, trying to get stories done that might change things for the better in such a bizarre and troubled town.

Dottie quickly became something of a local personality. When the plight of Ethiopian Jews became a major story for a while, she wrote a couple of columns that talked about her personal feelings, as a black Jew. In South Florida, home to so many passionate Jews and blacks, this was dramatic stuff. When the first Cuban-American county manager lost his job in disgrace, not long after the first black school superintendent lost his job in disgrace, Dottie wrote about the similar feelings of sadness, disappointment, and anger among blacks and Cubans. She was soon speaking regularly, everywhere, in black Liberty City and Jewish Century Village, and getting calls and letters from Hispanic readers.

She became a regular on local TV talk shows. We were so excited the first time she appeared on one of the taped segments. The show came on, and there she was, looking particularly adorable to John ("Look, the camera adds fifteen pounds to your face!" he said appreciatively). Then it struck us: We hadn't opened a special wine! John ran down the hallway, through the living room, past the dining room, past the kitchen, past the washer and dryer, and into the wine room. He looked around for just a moment and then moved to the right, to the Burgundy area, for one of the $1.99 bottles. Since we wouldn't really have time to appreciate the bottle, there was no reason to open something grand.

John ran back with two glasses and quickly popped the cork. He poured quickly and we clinked. "To your face," said Dottie. "To your bottom," said John, as Dottie spoke on the screen. We then took a sip—and it was like the earth stopped. The wine was magnificent. It was as smooth as velvet, with lots of fruit, yet a richness and a depth that seemed so real we could almost touch it. Unlike most great Burgundies we had had, this one was fully mature, and damn proud of it. There was no tightness left, no pretension. It seemed to almost declare, "I'm just too old to try to impress you. Take me for what I am."

People are always asking us how you know when a wine is at its peak. The answer is that it's impossible to know, since every bottle is different. We sometimes drink wine too young, and sometimes drink wine too old. Part of the fun of the hobby is a sense that you can never be sure what's in the bottle. A few times in our lives, we have tasted a wine and said: This was not as good yesterday, and it wouldn't be as good tomorrow; of all the days of all time, this is the day on which it is perfect. So it was with that wine. The fact that it cost $1.99 made this the greatest wine purchase of our lives.

Usually, when we open wine, John goes to get the notebook, and he talks about where we got it and how much it costs, and gets prepared to write notes. We hadn't had time to do that before we opened this bottle. After the show was over, John went to get the notes. When he did, he realized he had pulled out the wrong bottle. This bottle—a Hospices de Beaune Volnay Cuvée Blondeau, from Alfred de Montigny, 1959—was not one of the $1.99 bottles. We had bought it from a friend for $80.

Expectation has so much to do with a wine's taste. When some wine geek pours stuff that he keeps saying is great, and keeps talking about it, it's awfully hard for the wine to live up to its billing. When a waiter in a French bistro pours a simple glass of Sancerre with no ceremony at all, it's easy to be surprised with its vibrancy and life. The 1959 Volnay was a great bottle of wine. But had we expected it, had we planned it with a special meal, coddled it, talked about it, raised our expectations, it would never have been quite so special. Nevertheless, Dottie thought it worthy of her debut on television.

At the end of October that year, we made a fire in our fireplace for the first time. Our fathers both loved their fireplaces. Until we met each other, we each thought our father was the only person in the world who turned up the air-conditioning so that he could make a fire. When we did that, in Miami that day, we knew our fathers would be proud. Laurenzo's, that North Miami Beach grocery store where the butchers taught Dottie how to cook, was still there, and the wine selection was better than ever. We'd found a 1971 Dom Ruinart Rosé Champagne there for just $35, and that day, in front of our first fire, we opened it.

The next month, during our end-of-year physical checkups, we casually mentioned to our doctor, whom we knew well from our last tour of duty in Miami, that we were trying to get pregnant. He asked how long we'd been trying, and we said about a year. He stopped and looked at us very seriously. "You might have a problem," he said. We were stunned. It had never even crossed our minds.

THIRTEEN

Château d'Yquem 1970

. . .

INFERTILITY WAS A BIG ISSUE IN THE UNITED STATES IN the late eighties and early nineties, the subject of innumerable magazine cover stories and heart-wrenching newspaper features. Older yuppie couples were finally getting around to having children, and they were finding it harder to conceive than they imagined. There were many theories about this. Simply the fact that mothers were older seemed to have something to do with it. A whole industry of fertility specialists and fertility drugs and fertility clinics grew up to deal with the problem, which made sense since so many of the people involved had money to spend.

We were on the leading edge of that curve—after all, the first "test tube" baby was born just a few years earlier, in 1978—and we were clueless. When our doctor asked us if we knew about the fertility cycles, we sheepishly admitted, no, not really. He explained how to figure out the days when Dottie was most fertile, said we should go have a good time, and told us to call him in three or four months if nothing happened. We decided to get through the holidays and start in earnest in January.

For Christmas that year, John commissioned a well-known art forger to make a Dottie present. We never gave much direction to the artists who made our Dottie presents. We just took in John's drawing of Dottie's face and let the artist interpret it. John said he'd like a Dottie in the style of any famous painter. A Dottie Rembrandt? A Dottie Klee? A Dottie Pollock? A week before Christmas, the artist brought it in. It was a Dottie Picasso, three feet high and two feet wide. She was sitting on a chair and it was signed "Picasso." John took it to a place that frames paintings for the local fine arts museum so that it would look even more real. It looked exactly like a Picasso, but also very much like Dottie.

A few weeks later, on January 30, we made our first serious attempt to make Media. We had followed all of the doctor's directions about timing. That night, we made a fire and chilled the Château d'Yquem 1970 Sauternes that we'd bought in 1978 for $30. We'd owned this bottle for years, but we had never tasted an Yquem, which has been one of the world's greatest wines for centuries. In fact, in the Bordeaux Classification of 1855, the top wine wasn't a "first growth" like Lafite-Rothschild. Above them all, as the only "grand premier cru," was Château d'Yquem. Considering how true Sauternes is made, it's amazing that any mere mortal can ever afford it. It's from the Sauternes region of Bordeaux, and it's made primarily from Sauvignon Blanc and Semillon grapes that are attacked by *Botrytis cinerea*—"noble rot." The rot makes the grapes shrivel up, which means they are left with a small amount of concentrated nectar. Grape pickers make regular passes through the vineyard, picking just the grapes that are shriveled enough. Since it's already late in the year when the rot attacks, leaving the grapes on the vine until they're absolutely ready to be picked is risky. The whole crop could be destroyed by insects, birds, or bad weather at any time. It's said that a vine from Château d'Yquem produces a single glass of wine.

Sauternes, unlike most wine, comes in clear bottles, and that's a good thing. As it ages—and it can age just about forever—it gets darker, more golden. It's a little like watching the sun from noon until sunset. It begins bright and clear and then gets darker, more filled with gold and orange, until it finally develops a sunsetlike richness that's so luscious that you can almost taste it before you open it. That's about where our Yquem was when we took it out of the ice in front of our fire. We didn't know what to expect. With our first taste, we were floored. It was indeed sweet and it was indeed mouth-coating. But this was the incredible part: It had very little body. It was so light that it was like a soufflé. It had enough acids to make the wine crisp instead of fat. And when we swallowed, there was a taste of rich, dark earth that seemed incredible in a sweet, white dessert wine. The range of tastes was unbelievable, like nothing we had ever tasted. Rather than being hard to drink, the bottle disappeared quickly. We stayed in the bed we'd made by the fire the whole night. If this was the night we conceived Media, she would be one sweet child.

We spent all of our free time—and there really wasn't that much of it, since we worked long days—shopping for wine, eating at restaurants, and trying to make Media. There was a little land-that-time-forgot store in North Miami called Santino's where a lonely old man stood guard over an amazing collection of old bottles in a store that looked like a junk shop. He'd once run a restaurant with a good wine list. The restaurant went out of business, so he had moved his wine inventory to this shop, but never really got around to taking anything out of boxes or ordering new wines. So there he was, surrounded by great wine, but finding it was like going on a treasure hunt. We went up there and just rooted around. We were always his only customers. He sat there and worked on his art—he was a painter—and we moved around boxes, looking for wine. We ultimately got some great old stuff there, often at remarkable prices. Dottie once complimented one of his paintings and he was so moved that he gave her a 1947 red Burgundy.

We discovered a great Italian restaurant in Coral Gables called La Bussola. It had a fine wine list, and an owner who was passionate about Italian wine. After a while, we asked if we could bring our own wines. A little while after that, we asked if he could just keep some of ours there. So we brought by a mixed case of old Italian wine. We'd go to La Bussola and order one of our own wines, and drink it with the owner. The first of our own wines we had there was an Amarone 1982 from Rizzardi. It's a funny thing about Amarone. It's made from the same grapes, and in the same place, as Valpolicella, the simple, light, quaffable red wine from northeast Italy. But, as the label of that Rizzardi explained, the grapes "are hand selected from the upper bunch called Recie (ears), from which derives the name Recioto della Valpolicella Amarone. The upper bunch is dried in trellises until February, producing a wine which is then aged in oak casks for a minimum of two years before bottling." All of this results in a raisiny, intense, and powerful wine that's relatively high in alcohol. It's perfect for a cold night, which is why we had a 1964 Tommasi Amarone when Miami hit a record low temperature on January 21, 1985 ("less oomph than we expected"). We're glad we drank Amarone when we were young, because just thinking about it now makes us woozy.

We had our kitchen redone. It was such a hassle and so expensive that John almost strangled the contractor. One day, he decided he'd just work on the cabinets himself to get the damn things done. He got up on a ladder, fell, and broke his right arm. That experience ended his home improvement phase.

We cooked for hours in that kitchen, usually late at night when we finally got home. We have never been great cooks, and we aren't great cooks now, but we always enjoy ourselves, and dinner usually turns out fine. There are some exceptions, though, like the time Dottie thought it would be fun to cook a hen. It was so tough that John broke our favorite carving knife trying to slice it.

We conducted tastings with our friends and always learned a lot. We each brought a 1974 California Cabernet Sauvignon to one tasting and found, to our horror, that they were aging faster than we thought they would. When people came over to our Old Spanish house, they'd compete to see who could find the most Dotties, like looking for Ninas in a Hirschfeld. Would they notice the Dottie table? Would they know they were standing on a Dottie rug?

We tried new wines wherever we were. When we went to Dallas for the annual meeting of the National Association of Black Journalists, we had wines from Texas: a Llano Estacado Chardonnay 1984 and a Wimberley Valley "Texas Cabernet (dry)" 1984 from Lubbock County ("Try this wine with broiled, roasted or blackened seafood dishes. It's also excellent with bar-be-que and fajitas," the label said). When we visited Dottie's mother in Tallahassee, we discovered a winery called Lafayette that made several unusual wines, including one called Blanc Du Bois (the label said it had "a spicy flavor with a striking bouquet") and another called Plantation White—"a toast to the Southern Plantation Life Style," it said on the bottle. We tried Maui Blush, from the same winery that made Maui Blanc in Hawaii, and then a sparkling wine from the same producer. We found a 1976 Hungarian white wine on an otherwise pedestrian list at a restaurant in Coral Gables and tried that (it had turned brown). We tried everything we'd never had. We even had a sparkling Johannisberg Riesling from a little winery called Hop Kiln in California and Ingleside Plantation "Virginia Champagne," from Oak Grove, Virginia. We once went to a big tasting of homemade wines on Key Biscayne and tasted a sparkling wine made from garlic. Sure enough, it tasted like garlic.

We conducted a Champagne tasting on our next around-the-country train trip. We boarded the *Silver Meteor* with a picnic basket filled with our first dinner—foie gras pâté with crusty bread, shrimp and crab salad, grilled chicken, steamed asparagus, and pecan pie for dessert—and an ice bucket already filled with ice and a bottle of Taittinger. Our sleeping car attendant greeted us. His name was George Patton. We ended up tasting twenty bubblies on that trip: from France, Ayala Champagne, Krug Grande Cuvée, Laurent-Perrier Blanc de Blancs 1975, Piper-Heidsieck Brut Sauvage (another one of those "no-dosage" Champagnes), Veuve Clicquot 1978, Bollinger Brut, regular Piper-Heidsieck, Louis Roederer, Lanson, Mumm, and Pommery. From California, we had Robert Hunter Blanc de Noirs from Sonoma, Schramsberg Cremant 1980 from Napa, St. Francis Brut from Napa, and Gloria Ferrer. We had Ste. Chapelle from Idaho, and, for old times' sake, the Arterberry Red Hills Brut from Oregon. We had a Henkell Extra Dry Sekt from Germany and Alianca "Classic Rosé" from Portugal. We even had Sutter Home "Sparkler," which called itself "*The* White Zinfandel Champagne of America." We suppose we scandalized the whole train. All people ever saw of us were empty Champagne bottles. Our deluxe bedroom fare included all of our meals, so by tipping Mr. Patton generously, we ensured that he would gladly serve us our breakfasts, lunches, and dinners in bed. He, too, wondered if we were on our honeymoon.

Our first stop on this trip was New York. We spent the night with our old friends the Chirlses and visited our old neighborhood. It was painful. We really missed New York. To be sure, we were having a fine time in Miami. Work was endlessly interesting. But there were some frustrations, too. The publisher had assured us when he flew to New York to offer us jobs that the newspaper was in fine financial shape, but within months of our arrival, he ordered a hiring freeze. Then the *Herald,* under attack from all sides, as usual, decided that it needed to be loved. "Good news" was in; "bad news" was out. It became harder and harder to just report the news and tell it. In the long run, the paper usually did the right thing, but getting there was a daily struggle, and quite wearing.

Dottie had joined an editorial board that for four years had bitterly criticized the Reagan administration. One of the first decisions she participated in was whom the paper would endorse when Reagan ran against Walter Mondale. Even though the majority of the board voted to endorse Mondale, the *Herald*'s publisher, who had served in the Nixon administration, cast the only vote that counted. The paper endorsed Reagan. Dottie thought about quitting, but John convinced her that most people don't care who a newspaper endorses during a presidential race. An editorial board's influence, he said, is primarily on local or statewide issues. On the campaign trail, Mondale commented on the situation, noting that the will of an honest editorial board had been subverted.

We had a chance to move back to New York in 1986. *Newsday*, the Long Island newspaper, was looking for a business editor and a columnist. We came up and talked—we arrived during our beloved Mets' World Series against the Boston Red Sox—but we kept thinking about Norm Pearlstine's advice. We had stayed in touch with the *Journal*'s managing editor, whom we liked and respected so much. In fact, we once took Norm and his wife, the author Nancy Friday, to dinner when they visited Miami and had a fine time at our favorite Miami Beach restaurant. (Just a week later, a kitchen worker killed the chef of the restaurant in the middle of the dining room during dinner. Only in Miami.) John called Norm about the *Newsday* job. Norm, who was always so knowing and so wise, simply said this: "You shouldn't work for a section your boss doesn't read." It was great advice, especially when it turned out, just as he'd guessed, that the *Newsday* bosses seemed to know very little about their own business pages. It also wasn't a good thing that they hadn't paid Dottie the courtesy of contacting her separately about a job. Instead, they had told John that they wanted to talk with her about being a columnist.

But the jobs would take us back to New York. On our way to *Newsday* in Long Island, we drove by Shea Stadium a few hours before a World Series game. What in the world could match that in Miami? We were such big Mets fans that when they clinched their division that year, we opened one of our precious 1974 Cabernet Sauvignons, this one from Clos du Bois, to celebrate ("soft and lovely and so nice").

The job offers turned out to be a good experience for us. It made us think long and hard about why we were in Miami in the first place, and whether we should stay. We felt we'd already done some good work. Dottie was hugely popular across ethnic groups, which was rare in that town. John's staff was doing important work, taking hard looks at "exclusive" private clubs that barred blacks, women, Hispanics, and occasionally Jews; at resegregated public schools; and at how Dade County was really run (the answer: by an unelected behind-the-scenes group called "the Non-Group" whose power derived largely from the fact that it included the top executives of the *Herald* and Knight-Ridder, the Miami-based company that owned the *Herald*). On the editorial board, Dottie was able to cite those stories and call for change, and to ask a few pointed questions of her own—such as, if most of the unwanted pregnancies in Dade County were among blacks and Hispanics, why was the county's only Planned Parenthood clinic tucked away in an all-white suburb about an hour's drive from the inner city? Why hadn't anyone done something about a lake that swallowed several black kids every summer? The day that editorial ran, a fence was erected.

We missed New York and we had frustrations at work, but we decided to stay and plunged into our work, and into Miami, with a renewed sense of purpose.

We celebrated by taking a cruise. Miami had become a huge cruise port, with millions of people taking larger and larger ships. The *Herald*'s offices are beautifully situated on Biscayne Bay, so day after day we saw these huge ships pulling out, with passengers on the sides, waving. Not only that, but once a year there was a charity wine tasting aboard one of the big Carnival Cruise Line ships. We went every year and walked all around the ship, wondering what a cruise would be like. Finally, we booked a bedroom aboard the *Holiday,* one of the new Carnival ships. It was very romantic, but the best day was in Sint Maarten.

Not knowing any better, we simply asked a taxi driver to take us someplace good for lunch. He drove us to the top of a mountain, to a place that looked very much like a tourist trap. They even paid him when he dropped us off. We took one look and decided to leave. We bought two glasses of white wine at the bar—they wouldn't sell us a bottle of wine—and began to walk back down the mountain. Just a few hundred yards down, amazingly, someone had begun building a house that jutted out of the mountain. There was just a concrete foundation and four walls, with no roof, and no one was there. We walked in, sat on the floor, with our legs dangling over the side of the mountain, and looked down on one of those Caribbean views that we'd seen only in travel brochures. We sat there, drank our wine, and then made a guess at which part of the house was supposed to be the bedroom.

When we left, a taxi driver happened to be coming down the mountain, so we hopped in. Dottie finally convinced him to tell us where real people ate lunch, and we soon found ourselves in a shack where we were the only tourists. On each table was an old wine bottle now filled with hot peppers and white vinegar. The special of the day was bluefish and fungee, a dish very much like polenta. The idea was to pour the pepper vinegar on the fish and fungee, to give them some flavor. It was a spectacular dish, which we washed down with cold beer. On the way back to the ship, we found an adorable little restaurant called La Vie Parisienne, and we walked in and made reservations for dinner. At six o'clock, a taxi dropped us off. He asked if we'd like him to pick us up, and we said he should meet us at nine. The restaurant was remarkable, tiny and intimate, and the entire staff appeared to be two women who spoke French. John had chicken in tarragon, thinly sliced breast of chicken in a cream sauce that was then covered entirely with tarragon. There was so much tarragon that we couldn't imagine how it was possible to eat that dish. But with one bite, John pronounced it perfect. Dottie had "Lobster Americaine," which turned out to be sweet and juicy lobster in a creamy brown sauce.

They had a surprisingly good little wine list from which we chose a 1983 Pouilly-Fumé Les Genièvres from Sauvion Fils. Pouilly-Fumé is one of those wines that gets overlooked in the United States, maybe because people confuse it with Pouilly-Fuissé. Pouilly-Fuissé is a white Burgundy, made from the Chardonnay grape, that was briefly popular in the United States in the 1970s, probably because of that very good name. Pouilly-Fumé is a wine from the Loire Valley of France that's made from the Sauvignon Blanc grape. It has a crisp, earthy, grassy, and slightly smoky taste—in other words, a taste that made it perfect with both the chicken and the lobster. The meal was delicious. We even had soufflés for dessert. When we walked outside at nine P.M., the taxi was there, waiting to whisk us back to the ship after a lovely day.

When we returned to Miami, we saw our first fertility specialist. He checked John first, since that was easy, and John was fine. All of the easy tests on Dottie showed there was no problem. The doctor gave us charts and some advice: Stay away from the hot tub near the critical days, and be careful with wine. When that didn't work, he scheduled Dottie for a laparoscopy. With a tiny little scope inserted near her navel, they could have a good look at her tubes to see if there was scarring or some other problem. Nope, her tubes were fine. Everything seemed fine, in fact, and that was the frustrating part. She took pills that made her mucus the right viscosity—ah, a wine term—if only John's sperm could swim straight. She used special suppositories. On days when she had to go in for ultrasounds to see how her eggs were doing, she had to drink prodigious amounts of water, to better see the images. One doctor sent her for unnecessary ultrasounds every week. This went on for a couple of months. As it turned out, he owned part of the ultrasound business. We dropped him and found another.

The new doctor, of course, wanted to do his own laparoscopy exam. So Dottie went under general anesthesia again and, again, everything was fine. Once again, the same lineup of medicines and the same painful minutes in the waiting room with other women there for ultrasounds who sat there silently with their legs tightly pressed together after drinking all that water. A few of those women were on Pergonal, a drug made from urine. One of the nurses said that years ago, nuns someplace in Europe contributed the urine for Pergonal and in that way did their part in the miracle of creation. We don't know if that's true, but it's a neat story. Dottie took her temperature every morning and on days when her temperature spiked—eureka!—we tried to make Media. Sometimes we drove home for lunch and had a go.

One day, we thought we'd hit pay dirt. The doctor told Dottie she had some stellar eggs. This could be it. Smiling all the way, Dottie sped toward the *Herald* to tell John and was pulled over by a highway patrolman. She was so nervous that it didn't occur to her until later that he might have let her go without a ticket if she had explained her rush and thanked him for slowing down a potential mother-to-be. So we left work early and came home and tried to make Media. We had now been trying for four years, and it was tough. What made it even worse was that it seemed that almost every week there was another story in the paper about an abandoned baby or an infant killed at birth, while lots of people like us were knocking ourselves out trying to have a baby.

By 1987, doctors were beginning to get seriously concerned.

We spent a great deal of our time dealing with fertility specialists. We learned more about these things than we ever wanted to know. We learned to ask fertility specialists about their take-home-baby rate, not their pregnancy rate. We learned to be skeptical of fertility doctors, since they'd lose us as patients as soon as they were successful. Our sex life was strictly regulated. Dottie continued to take massive quantities of drugs and she had had yet another laparoscopy, her third. The doctors still had no idea what was wrong.

On April 14 of that year, for our anniversary, we opened our eighth bottle of 1974 Robert Mondavi Cabernet Sauvignon. It was still good, but clearly getting old. The wine room was beginning to fill up. Work was as demanding as ever. In May, a reporter walked into John's office and said, "There's a woman on the phone who says Gary Hart is going to stop campaigning this weekend so he can have a tryst with a friend of hers. What should I do?" The story put the *Herald* in the national spotlight for a few weeks as presidential candidate Gary Hart ultimately dropped out of the race.

In June, the University of California at Berkeley asked us to come out for a week as visiting teachers at a special program for minority journalists. They put us up at a house on a hill loaned to the program by vacationing professors. The restaurants were terrific, and the wine was special. We found a wine we'd never seen before called Clos du Merle ("Sonoma Red Wine, produced from very old vines," according to the label) and drank it on the patio of the house as the sun set one night. Another night, we drank something called Cameron Red Table Wine from Oregon that said this on the label: "Thistlebegoodwine."

During that week, we had an experience that changed our lives. Berkeley is the home of Chez Panisse, which is a famous restaurant now and was pretty well known even then. One day, after teaching class, we called and naively asked if they could take us for dinner that night. "Well, actually," they said, "if you can be

here in ten minutes, we can take you." We ran down to the rental
car and sped down a winding hill to get there on time. This was the
prix fixe dinner ($45):

CHEZ PANISSE

STRAW POTATOES WITH CAVIAR AND CRÈME FRAÎCHE

CARROT AND RED PEPPER SOUPS

GRILLED LOCAL SALMON WITH RED WINE SAUCE AND DILL

AND HERB NOODLES

GARDEN SALAD

FEUILLETÉ OF WARM BERRIES

It looked great, but . . . salmon with red wine sauce? We told
the waiter we were surprised by this, and that we couldn't imagine what wine we'd have with it. We'd always been told that it's
white wine with fish, but how can you have a white wine with a
red-wine sauce? He suggested an Oregon Pinot Noir, specifically a
Sokol Blosser "Hyland Vineyards" from Yamhill County. We were
charmed that Oregon wine had come so far since we first visited
that enthusiastic wine merchant in Portland. Here was one of
California's best restaurants, known for serving locally produced
foods, and it was suggesting a wine from Oregon. Not only that,
but Pinot Noir, the notoriously difficult red grape. With fish even.

Oregon Pinot Noir, which since has become quite fashionable,
tends to be light and a little bit fruity, often with a lively crispness
as opposed to the richness of Burgundy. With the grilled salmon—
light, smoky, and so fresh—it was a pairing made in food heaven.
The next night, when we went to a restaurant called Metropole,

LOVE BY THE GLASS

we ordered salmon and a bottle of Pinot Noir from Carneros
Creek Winery in Napa. To this day, when people ask us about
matching wine with food, we talk about our experience at Chez
Panisse. The point is that it's impossible to know what pairings you
like until you try them. We almost always drink Oregon Pinot
Noir with salmon now, and whenever we do, we're transported
back to Berkeley.

Our life fell into a nice pattern of drinking wine with friends,
eating good restaurant meals, and taking nice vacations. We took
another cruise, kept taking long train trips, and visited Napa and
Sonoma at least once a year. We met new and even more interesting people every time we went. We dropped by De Loach again,
and this time spent a couple of hours with Cecil's son, Michael.
(Michael explained to us, with a mischievous smile, what OFS
means on De Loach's most special bottlings. People assume it
means "Our Finest Selection." But Michael said his father was a
marine and that OFS actually means "Out-fucking-standing." Years
later, at a tasting in Miami, Dottie asked Cecil if that was true. He
grabbed the microphone to state "unequivocally" that OFS actually
meant "Our Finest Selection." But he had an awfully big smile on
his face.)

When we left the winery that day, Michael suggested we eat at
a restaurant in Santa Rosa called Orlando's. On the list was something we'd never seen before, Gary Farrell Pinot Noir. It was full-
flavored and elegant, with an interesting, vibrant taste of berries.
The next day, we dropped into a new winery called Rochioli,
where we tasted its Pinot Noir, which was also outstanding. "It's
funny," John told the woman behind the counter, "but this reminds
me of a wine we had last night called Gary Farrell." That's no surprise, she said; Gary Farrell makes his wine from our fruit and he
works for the winery as a consulting winemaker. She told us his
full-time job was at a winery called Davis Bynum, so we went by
the next day to tell him how much we enjoyed his wine. While we

were there, we dropped into the tasting room. A jovial guy named Manny who looked like an elf in sandals was holding court, telling people that he would pour them a tasting of wines "from the most driest to the least driest."

Within a decade, both Gary Farrell and Rochioli became very famous. Their wines now are hard to find and very expensive. The last time we visited Rochioli, in 1999, a man was in the tasting room whining that he had been on their mailing list longer than a friend of his, yet his friend was able to get the same wines that he could. Why was that?

And, of course, we flew to New York at least once a year, to get our fix of the city, and Cellar in the Sky.

CELLAR IN THE SKY

CHEF'S CANAPÉS
Veuve Clicquot Brut NV
SALAD OF RABBIT, FRENCH LENTILS AND SAVOY CABBAGE
LOBSTER CONSOMMÉ WITH RAVIOLI
SAUTÉED FILLET OF BLACK BASS WITH ZUCCHINI
AND SEA URCHIN
Château St. Jean Chardonnay 1985
ROAST LOIN OF VEAL WITH CRAYFISH
Pommard Gaunoux 1983
MUNSTER CHEESE ON ARUGULA
Château Gruaud-Larose 1979
THREE APPLE DESSERT
Scharzhofberger Riesling Auslese 1983
COLOMBIAN COFFEE
CHOCOLATE TRUFFLES

...

In 1986, per capita wine consumption in the United States peaked at 2.43 gallons a year; 1987 was the high-water mark of our wine experimentation. We only saved labels of wines we'd never had before, and in 1987, we saved 331. We had tried a new wine almost every day of the year. One was particularly notable, in retrospect. It was a 1985 Kendall-Jackson Chardonnay. We hadn't much liked the 1982 Cabernet, but the Chardonnay, which we bought for $6, was different. "Very Good," we wrote. "Plump, well-made. A best buy." How prescient was that? Because K-J was a good buy, the man who invented it, Jess Jackson, became one of the most influential figures in California winemaking.

Jess Jackson was a lawyer who saw a gaping hole in the market: mid-range wine that was good, consistent, and popularly priced. "What I wanted was something that the average person, Mr. and Mrs. Cul-de-Sac, could afford," he told us later. A man who loves history, he enjoys tracing the evolution of the California wine industry, and it helps to do that to fully understand Kendall-Jackson's remarkable rise. In the 1930s and 1940s, "California white wine was not drinkable," he said. In time, some California pioneers made huge strides by perfecting fermentation techniques and beginning to use oak barrels for reds and stainless steel for whites. Jackson had a vision: Using new technology, he could blend grapes from several different vineyards and produce a consistent taste. "Flavor to me is the essence of quality," he said. "My family found out that you could maintain consistent quality and flavors and improve the taste" by blending Chardonnays from different vineyards. "The consumer knows it tastes better." It took them nine years of experimentation to find the taste he was after.

One of the keys to the popularity of Kendall-Jackson Chardonnay is that it is left slightly sweet. Fermentation is halted before it is complete and therefore before all of the grape's sugar is transformed into alcohol. "When I first started, the competition, the inner circle of gatekeepers, stigmatized it," Jackson said. "But they were asleep at the switch. It was just what people wanted." He says there's not really that much sugar in the finished wine, but "the flavor is so intense that you get the impression of sweetness even though it may be below your threshold" to detect sweetness.

Looking back, it's remarkable how far this wine billionaire has come since that first vintage, 1982. "When I started, I couldn't sell a California wine on the East Coast. On my first sales trip to New York, I was turned down by three different distributors. 'Easterners love French,' we were told, 'and we have no room for it.' " Jackson approached a distributor called Winebow. "I said give me your worst salesman and your newest salesman, and my friend and I will take them to the streets of New York. I guarantee that we can sell fifty cases each by the end of the day. If we do, we'll take you to dinner and you'll take our wines." At day's end, Jackson had won the wager. Americans could have a wine that tasted consistently pleasant, was reasonably priced, had the cachet of a known varietal, and even had an easy-to-pronounce name. What could be better?

Kendall-Jackson ushered in the era of the so-called fighting varietals, and its sales went nuts. Jackson made more than two million cases of the Chardonnay alone by the end of the nineties. Others soon stepped into that market, and fighting varietals were all the rage. Jess Jackson was responsible for this—and at least partly responsible for Chardonnay's rise from merely popular to America's sweetheart.

Our infertility problem continued to be a constant source of tension. We thought about it all the time. Our lives were increasingly regulated. Our doctors told us when we could have sex, how we could have sex, when we could use the hot tub, when we could drink wine—and then would always add, "Now, remember, just relax!" We were typical yuppies, spoiled and used to getting what we wanted. We were also both overachievers who believed we could overcome obstacles with hard work and creativity. We were frustrated and angry—with our doctors, with our bodies, and, inevitably, with each other. Conceiving Media had become hard, unpleasant work that neither of us was enjoying.

In early 1988, we called our doctor in New York and asked if he had any advice. "Get yourselves to the nearest teaching hospital that has an in vitro program," he said. Fortunately, Jackson Memorial Hospital, right in Miami, had an in vitro program. We moved our business there. We also decided that if we were going to take another big trip, we should probably do it soon. We decided it was time to go to Italy.

FOURTEEN

Dolcetto d'Alba
"Ristorante Felicin" 1987

. . .

WHEN JOHN'S PARENTS WERE NEWLY MARRIED DURING World War II, they were stationed in Fort Smith, Arkansas. John's mother had never learned how to cook, but their best friends were an Italian-American couple from New York, the Raimondos. When John's father once returned late from a rendezvous with his mother, he was marked AWOL, which would have destroyed his chance to become an officer. Sergeant Raimondo somehow made the paperwork disappear. Later, when John's father became a lieutenant, he liked to warm the troops up in the morning with some jokes. One day, the sergeant rushed into the room first. "The first man who laughs at one of the lieutenant's jokes will get KP for a month," he said. Naturally, no one cracked a smile. Decades later, John's father brought up that story every time he saw a comedian dying onstage.

Everything John's mother learned about cooking, and almost everything John's father knew about food, came from the Raimondos. It was a pleasant coincidence that the Italian-American butchers at Laurenzo's in North Miami Beach had taught Dottie how to cook. As we learned about wine, so many of the best inexpensive wines we had were from Italy, and so many of the most soulful. Not only that, but so many of the winemakers we most admired from California—Martini and Mondavi, not to mention people we'd met like Rafanelli and Pastore—were Italian. There was obviously something very special about Italy and we decided it was the place we next wanted to visit.

We should have bought guidebooks and maps. But we planned the entire trip from wine books, like *The World Atlas of Wine* by Hugh Johnson and *The Simon and Schuster Pocket Guide to Italian Wines* by Burton Anderson. One of them mentioned a place called Giardino da Felicin in Monforte d'Alba, in the Barolo region of Piedmont, so we decided that would be our first stop. Another book mentioned a place called the Villa Le Barone in Panzano in Chianti; that would be our next stop. We'd fly into Milan, spend a night there in a hotel that John's uncle Leroy, a shoe salesman, recommended, and then drive off to Piedmont. The only book we took with us was Burton Anderson's, because it was pocket-size. After all, he said right there in the book: "Piedmont is by far the best-organized Italian region for wine tourism." He said the town of Alba was easily reachable from Milan and that wine roads were "well-marked."

Before we left, we'd received some help from a friend at the *Herald* named Bill Grueskin, who used to live in Italy and spoke fluent Italian. He taught Dottie one sentence—*"Possiamo assaggiare un po' del Suo vino e forse ne compriamo una bottiglia?"*— which means, he said, "May we taste your wine and perhaps buy a bottle?" Bill gave us another piece of advice, too: Italians think that everyone, in their soul, is Italian, so they'll keep speaking Italian to you, figuring that, sooner or later, your inner self will understand it.

Whenever we traveled, we bought bottles of wine and then Dottie packed them into our suitcases. Over the years, she had become quite expert at this. She could pack an entire case of wine into a single suitcase along with everything else. The clothes became the padding for the wine. We had never lost a bottle. But the suitcases got very heavy. This time, we had a better idea. We bought two wine boxes. Outside, they looked like regular cardboard boxes. But inside was Styrofoam designed to fit twelve bottles of wine. These could be checked right onto the plane. We checked two pieces of luggage and two empty wine boxes. When we landed in Milan, we stood in line to go through customs, and the boxes immediately became a matter of concern. Our customs agent looked at our empty boxes and asked us why we were bringing empty boxes into Italy. We explained that we were wine lovers who were going to visit wineries and fill the boxes with wine to bring back. He looked at us and kept asking why we'd carry empty boxes on a plane for thousands of miles. Then, with an almost imperceptible motion, he called over another man. The other man was holding a machine gun. As the man with the machine gun stood right next to us, silently, the first man took apart the boxes. He took the Styrofoam out of the boxes, then separated the top and bottom part of the Styrofoam. He lifted both pieces and shook them. He tapped the sides. He finally told us that we could go, but he and the man with the machine gun watched us all the way to the rental-car counter.

We immediately got lost in northwestern Italy. We both have a bad sense of direction, though Dottie's is astonishingly bad. We kept stopping and asking people how to get to Monforte, and they were as nice as they could be. They leaned into the car and spoke to us forever, in Italian, while pointing up the hills. We had ab-

solutely no idea what they were saying, but they were so nice we
didn't want to let on. We'd drive about a mile and ask someone
else. The one thing that seemed clear was that we should be going
up into the hills, so we did. Higher and higher we climbed. The
roads got narrower and narrower. The good news was that we
began seeing vineyards all around us—below us, to be honest—so
we figured we must be heading the right way. It began to get dark.

The great grape of Piedmont, the one that Barolo and Barbaresco are made from, is called Nebbiolo. There probably isn't
another great grape that's named for a weather condition, but this
one is—because it's derived from the word for fog. It's the fog that
rolls over the hills of Piedmont, playing with the temperatures,
that helps give the wines there such great character. Well, we were
quickly being enveloped in *nebbia,* and we had no idea where we
were.

That was when we saw Harvey. When we were in Miami in the
seventies, the newspaper's food writer was a delightful young man
named Harvey Steiman. We kept in touch with Harvey over the
years as he became a famous wine and food expert for *The Wine
Spectator,* which we had read forever. There he was, walking along
the foggy road somewhere near Monforte d'Alba. It was a miracle. We rolled down the car window. "Harvey?" we said. It turned
out he was on assignment for *The Wine Spectator* and was staying
at Felicin, too, so we gave him a lift. We checked in with the
innkeeper, Giorgio Rocca, and took a walk around Monforte
d'Alba. This is a very small town that doesn't attract a lot of
tourists. Right outside the inn was a little town square, where old
men sat and talked. As we walked by, they stared at us without the
slightest embarrassment, which made it quite charming. When we
walked into a pastry shop, the young man behind the counter
spoke French to us. It was the first time we'd realized this: The
people here weren't used to seeing black Americans, and certainly
not mixed couples. They figured we must be French or maybe

African. So they spoke French to us. That was a break, since Dottie spoke some French, but all she could say in Italian was *"Possiamo assaggiare un po' del Suo vino e forse ne compriamo una bottiglia?"*

A couple of hours later, back at the inn, Harvey knocked on our door and asked if we'd like to have dinner with him and the Cerettos, one of the great winemaking families of Piedmont. Before we knew it, there we were, at Bruno's house being introduced to Bruno and Marcello Ceretto, Bruno's wife, and their various assistants, like Beatrice, a retired American woman who was teaching their children English.

We sat and Bruno poured Krug Champagne. We were surprised he wasn't serving a bubbly from Italy. "Krug?" we asked. He looked at us with surprise. "Of course," was all he said. We hadn't known until then that Krug Grande Cuvée, while not nearly as famous as expensive Champagnes such as Dom Pérignon, is a kind of shared secret among aficionados. Dinner was Beef Barolo, a fillet of beef cooked in the Cerettos' own Barolo wine. Here is the recipe from Emilia, Bruno and Marcello's mother.

BRASATO AL BAROLO

1 kg. (a little more than 2 lbs.) beef fillet, in one piece

5 garlic cloves

1 bottle Barolo Ceretto

Extra-virgin olive oil

Salt

Black pepper

10 fresh sage leaves

1 chopped carrot

1 chopped onion

1 chopped celery rib

1. *Twelve hours before cooking, put the meat into a large glass bowl with the garlic and cover with the Barolo. Turn the meat several times until it becomes almost black from contact with the wine. Remove the meat and dry it thoroughly but reserve the marinade.*

2. *Warm the oil in a large pot over medium heat. Add the meat and brown it on all sides for 10 to 15 minutes. Remove from the pot and season with salt and pepper.*

3. *Meanwhile, add the sage, carrot, onion, and celery to the pot and cook over medium heat until they become tender. Pour the marinade in and bring to a boil. Put the meat into the pot with all the other ingredients and reduce the heat, bringing the liquid to a simmer. Reduce the heat to low, then cover the pan and leave to braise for 2 to 2½ hours. Stir and turn the meat several times.*

4. *You can serve the Brasato with small potatoes, peeled and cut in halves, that should be added to the pan for the last 30 minutes of cooking time.*

Buon appetito!

SERVES 6

This was our very first night in the wine country of Italy. We just couldn't believe it. The Cerettos had simply added two places for us at the last minute and treated us like relatives they'd been expecting for months. When we left, they told us that they'd consider it a privilege if we'd let their assistant Bruna show us around the area the next day.

When we returned to the inn, Giorgio was there, listening to "Moonglow," the theme from the old movie *Picnic* starring William Holden, one of our favorites. He put out his hand and, there in the lobby of the Felicin in Monforte d'Alba, danced with Dottie. Soon Harvey cut in. Then John.

We tasted Barbaresco the next day for the first time. Barolo is the best-known wine of Piedmont. It's a great red, known for its power and its earthiness. Barbaresco is harder to find and less well known. Some people, in fact, think of it as a kind of junior Barolo. When we tasted Ceretto's Barbaresco that day, we understood why some people are passionate about this wine. It had the power of Barolo, the earthiness and the soul, but there was something else. As it "finished"—as it went down our throats and into our memories—it suddenly became elegant and restrained. We'd never had such an experience. Unlike Barolo, which is muscular and big to the end, Barbaresco had an internal elegance, an almost feminine side, that it didn't show until the last possible moment. It seemed incredible to us that any big wine could have such grace.

When we said good-bye to Bruna, she gave us a bottle of grappa, the clear, high-alcohol firewater distilled from grape stems. To this day, on the first snowfall of the year, we go outside and have one small sip of Bruna's grappa. Then we cork it until the following year. We're sure the bottle will last forever.

We dropped in on winemaker after winemaker. Dottie used her one sentence everywhere we went. The winemakers rarely spoke English, but it didn't matter. They all seemed touched by our attention and charmed by our attempt to communicate. One day, someone told us that we had to visit the weekly open-air market down the road, in Dogliani. When we got to the town square, around nine A.M., there was cart after cart of fresh everything— fruits and vegetables and meats and cheeses. We'd never seen such bounty. Then the crowd hushed and a beat-up pickup truck drove up. An old man was driving, and an old woman was in the passenger's seat. In the back of the pickup was a huge whole roast pig. It was just like that scene from *Invasion of the Body Snatchers* when the pickup trucks filled with giant pods drive into town, and everyone turns glassy-eyed and walks to the trucks. Everyone just suddenly got in line. Of course, so did we. As we moved closer to the front, we saw that the old man and the old woman were making sandwiches. The old woman would slice two pieces of bread off a loaf. Then she'd dig into the pig and get out a big piece of garlic. She'd then spread the garlic on the bread. The man, meantime, carved the meat and placed several large slices, gently, onto the bread. By the time we got to the front of the line, we couldn't wait to eat. We got our sandwiches and sat right there, on the curb, and gobbled them down. As we left town, we saw a bottle of wine in the window of a market. It was called Dolcetto di Dogliani. It was too early in the day to think about wine, but we wondered what Dolcetto tasted like.

We were too tired and sated to really think much about lunch, so when we got a little hungry we walked out to the town square of Monforte, passing the old men who stared at us. There was a meat market across the street, so we figured we'd just get some food and eat on our balcony overlooking the hills of Piedmont. We got a little cheese, some olives, a little prosciutto, and a loaf of bread. As we walked back in, Giorgio saw us. We explained that we were tired and were just going to have a picnic in our room. He told us to wait there. A few minutes later, he returned with a plate of cold green beans, a sliced tomato, and a bottle of wine. It was Dolcetto d'Alba, bottled just for the inn. "Drink this," he told us as we took the bottle, "and make love if you can." The Dolcetto was fruity and fun, filled with life, but with some of the earthiness of Piedmont. We sat on our balcony and looked at Italy and ate the greatest green beans we'd ever had, and the best prosciutto, with a wine that seemed to burst with flavors in our mouths. Then we took Giorgio's advice. We spent two weeks in Italy and we ate at some fine restaurants, but this was our greatest meal. Everything tasted just as it should. The green beans were crisp and sweet. The vine-ripened tomatoes were so fleshy and sweet and fragrant that we could have been eating plums, and the salty chewiness of the prosciutto with the creamy, fruity wine was divine. The simplicity of it almost made us weep.

We can't remember how this was possible, but we found our next stop, Panzano in Chianti, without any drama. Maybe the Italians were right—maybe our inner selves really were beginning to understand the language. The Villa Le Barone was so magnificent, so relaxing, that it seemed more like a sanitarium than a hotel. Dottie loved the opulence of it all, the rich tapestries and smart linens, the heavy silver vases filled with roses that grew at the end of each row of grapevines, the glistening crystal. Our room was a converted horse barn, with tall barn doors. Just outside those doors was a view of rolling Tuscan hills, just like we'd always imagined, but even better, even greener. The villa had a lovely, understated restaurant and was altogether perfect except that everybody staying there was an American tourist.

We stopped everywhere we saw a black rooster—the sign of Classico Chianti—and that often meant little houses on the side of the road.

Chianti has a bum rap in the United States because of all those cheap red wines from all over the world called Chianti and because too many people associate Chianti with very cheap wine in straw-covered bottles. In fact, good Chianti, which is made from the Sangiovese grape, is a wonder—earthy and vibrant, with a core of aggressive fruit.

The winemakers we met were mostly rural people, simple farmers, and they couldn't have been nicer, though few spoke any English. At each place, we'd buy a bottle—usually for $3 or $4— and ask the winemaker to sign the label. One time, we walked into a farm that looked like it might have wine. *"Possiamo assaggiare un po' del Suo vino e forse ne compriamo una bottiglia?"* Dottie asked, and they invited us right in. At a table in the barn, they pulled out some nice, rustic wines and began pouring tastes. As we drank, farmhands began coming in for lunch. Soon the barn was filled with Italian men with Tuscan soil all over their clothes. At some point, Dottie nudged John and pointed upward with her eyes. Above us, on a shelf, she had noticed some old bottles covered with dust. She pointed to the bottles and did her best to ask our host what they were. He just laughed and said something in Italian. Dottie persisted. She told him we would like to buy a bottle. Somehow, he understood, but he said no. Dottie said she'd pay him anything for a bottle. He said no. Dottie took out a pen and, on a piece of paper in front of us, wrote this: *$50*.

He said no.

The men at the table were enjoying this. We couldn't believe they would not sell us a bottle of this wine. Then our host looked at us, got a ladder, and got a bottle of the wine. It had no label. He took his big hand and wiped the dust from it. Then he opened the bottle and poured it for us, and for his wife who had joined us, and for all of the men in the room. He saved the last glassful for himself. Then he raised his glass in toast, and we all drank it. It was clearly an old Chianti, deeper and richer and browner than we'd tasted before, but still with the same core of lively Sangiovese fruit. The man would not sell us a bottle, but he would share it with us.

As we were returning, the skies turned black and it poured. We could barely see where we were going. We found Panzano, but the narrow roads, some of them dirt, confused us. At some point, we knew we were on the wrong road, but the dirt road we were on was so narrow that we couldn't turn around. We had to keep going forward, but we couldn't even see the sides of the road. It was pretty scary. Then, suddenly, the road ended and we seemed to be at a mansion. It was spectacular. We made a U-turn in the driveway and figured it had to be a winery. We decided to return first thing in the morning. When we did, it was nice and sunny, a really beautiful day in Tuscany. We drove up to the mansion and a severe-looking woman, dressed all in black, came out. *"Possiamo assaggiare un po' del Suo vino e forse ne compriamo una bottiglia?"* said Dottie.

"JEWS-A!" said the woman. "JEWS-A!"

How could she know? Did we really look Jewish? In any case, what was her problem? *"Possiamo assaggiare un po' del Suo vino e forse ne compriamo una bottiglia?"* said Dottie.

Finally, the woman, exasperated, grabbed our Italian-English dictionary and pointed to *chiusa*—closed. With the help of the dictionary, she explained that we should come back the next day. When we did, a man who looked very much the lord of the manor greeted us. This was no farmer, but clearly a person of some means who was making wine. The man had his young son with him. He was so pleased we were there, he said, because his son was learning English and it would be nice to have someone to speak to. For the next hour, we drank the man's wines, spoke to his son in English, and marveled at the beauty of his estate. This was straight out of *Lifestyles of the Rich and Famous*. As we were leaving, the man said something to his son in Italian. The son returned, carrying a big basket of giant fava beans. "Take these to the restaurant in your hotel," the man told us. "They'll know what to do with them."

When we returned to the Villa Le Barone, we took the beans to the kitchen and made a reservation for dinner. When we sat down, we reminded them about our beans. We had a lovely dinner, with a bottle of local Chianti, but the beans were nowhere in sight. They weren't part of the antipasto. They weren't cooked into the pasta. They weren't a side order for the main course. Well, this was certainly embarrassing. Had they forgotten?

Dinner was over. No beans. What were we going to do? Make a scene? "Goddammit, where are our *beans*?" Then the waitress showed up at our table with a big plate filled with our bean pods. They were exactly as we'd given them to the restaurant. They were raw. She put them in the middle of the table and left. We looked at each other, without a clue what we should do or say. Then she reappeared with some pecorino cheese. We raised our hands to her, indicating that we had no idea what this was about. She smiled and took one of the giant pods. She cracked it open and took out one of the beans. Then she took a little of the cheese and put both of them in her mouth. She explained, as best she could, that the cheese and the bean are meant to be eaten together.

John doesn't much like vegetables of any kind, and certainly not raw. Dottie is not much of a cheese eater. If you'd asked us if we'd like raw beans and cheese for dessert, we would have aggressively declined. But that night, at the Villa Le Barone, the fava beans and pecorino cheese, together with the last glass of a rough local Chianti, were a real treat.

We drove into Siena one day to visit a wine museum, but it was closed. So we made our way to the famous plaza there, where we sat catching the sun and looking at people. When we got hungry, we searched for a place that looked authentic. This has sometimes gotten us in trouble. Years later, in Germany, we went hunting for an authentic-looking place and ended up eating Kurdish food. That day in Siena, what we found was a tiny hole in the wall with a proprietor who knew a little English. When he asked where we were from and we told him Miami, he got a huge smile and, pointing his fingers like guns, said, "Miami! *Miami Vice!* Bang, bang!" Great, we thought, accepting menus from him. He suggested the specialty of the house, a veal dish, so we thought, why not? What arrived was a dish that, ever since, we have made at home, though we've never quite replicated it. It was so simple and rustic: bite-size chunks of veal simmered for hours in a rich broth of onions, garlic, carrots, celery, and herbs, then served with pesto over pasta. The savory meat with the herbaceous basil and Parmesan cheese sauce, together with a fairly rough local red wine, was soul-satisfying.

Everyone always told us that Venice was the most romantic

place in the world. But we'd also heard that aside from sinking into the sea, it was overwhelmed by rude tourists and was one of the world's most overpriced places. In any event, it seemed unlikely that any place billed as the world's most romantic place could ever meet such a lofty expectation. We decided to drop by for a couple of days to see for ourselves, on our way back to Milan to catch our flight. We parked our car in a huge parking lot and then went looking for a taxi.

Okay, we know that Venice is built into the water and that the streets are water. Everybody knows that. But it wasn't until a couple of minutes later, when we saw the boats and realized that those boats *were* the taxis, that it really sank in. My God, this really is Venice, and the streets really are canals. The taxi took us to our very fancy hotel, the Bauer Grünwald, where we paid a fortune for a view of the canal. It was worth every penny. We called down for a bottle of sparkling wine, which turned out to be a delightful Spumante. That night, we ate right on the water, at our hotel's restaurant. We had the Mediterranean mixed grill, a large platter that included fish we'd never heard of, like John Dory, or never seen before, like fresh sardines (John's father ate sardines from a can every day for lunch, but we'd never thought of them as an actual fresh fish). There were odd-looking fish that had been grilled and dusted with herbs and sprinkled with aromatic olive oil and spritzed with lemon, surrounded by odd-looking grilled crustaceans that still had their heads. With these was a bouquet of grilled vegetables, asparagus, squash, and tomatoes, arranged around a timbale of polenta. With it, we had a delightful, crisp white wine. Our waiter, Paolo, thought we were charming, and let us linger forever. He also told Dottie, a lifelong Ferragamo lover, the best place to buy shoes.

When we finished dinner, we ran upstairs to get a bottle of wine—a Merlot from Friuli, a region better known for light whites—and walked a few feet to a gondola. We paid $80 for a one-hour ride, passing on the serenade, which was $20 extra. We sat in the gondola and glided around Venice. It was so quiet. The lights from the buildings made the entire city look like a Rembrandt painting. The only sound we heard was laughter.

Venice *is* the most romantic city in the world.

When we returned to Miami, our wine boxes were filled with bottles, each one signed by the winemaker. The customs agent asked us about this. We explained to him that we'd taken the boxes over empty and had filled them. He was skeptical. He took out every bottle and made us tell him where every one was from, who'd signed it, and how much it had cost. Long after every other person from our flight had cleared customs, we were there, explaining our wine purchases.

At least he didn't have a machine gun.

FIFTEEN

Mirassou Pinot Chardonnay 1969

. . .

*N*OW THAT OUR BIG TRIP WAS OVER, IT WAS TIME TO GO see the fertility specialists at Jackson Memorial Hospital. They did all of the tests over again, including the laparoscopy—Dottie's fourth—with Dottie under general anesthesia. What frustrated us the most was that no one could figure out what the problem was. In our years of struggling to make Media, we'd learned this much: Conception is a miracle. A woman's body is such a complex baby-making machine that even doctors can only understand so much about how all of this happens, or doesn't. Doctors warned us that there are women who are unable to conceive for reasons that are never clear. Dottie, they said, might be one of them. After a while, the doctors gave us a prescription for shots that John had to ad-minister to Dottie every day—Pergonal. Just one pharmacy in Dade County had the drug. It was astonishingly expensive and, like many of the infertility costs, not covered by insurance. Every morning, before work, Dottie drove to the hospital, where they drew blood from her arm, and every evening after analyzing it, the hospital called and told us how much Pergonal she would need. Then John, who hates needles and hates blood even more, filled a hypodermic with the right amount and plunged it into Dottie's hip.

In July, the doctors at Jackson told us that they'd just about given up on conventional treatment. If we didn't get pregnant this month, they told us, we should try in vitro. It was still a fairly new treatment then. Each attempt cost $5,000, and insurance wouldn't pay for that, either. The success rate was low. We sat down with our various ledgers and figured it out. We could put together $60,000. We could try twelve times. But it wasn't just the money. People who had gone through in vitro said it was a terrible procedure, even more invasive than what we'd put up with for the last few years. Hopes got so high, and got dashed so low, and so often. Our doctors urged us not to try in vitro more than three or four times.

We decided we needed to try one more time on our own, so we made reservations for a weekend on South Beach, which was in the midst of a remarkable turnaround. After the bozo community leaders decided to let South Beach go to seed, it just kept going downhill. Natch. Because it was so desolate, it attracted penniless and sometimes violent immigrants from the Mariel boatlift. One bar owner there described his own business as "a bucket of blood." But the Art Deco hotels were spectacular, and a few brave souls were determined to save it. Foremost among these was Barbara Capitman, who literally put her body in front of wrecking balls to save these buildings. A passionate preservationist, she soon enlisted Dottie's help on the *Herald* editorial board to urge officials to preserve the old treasures. South Beach was becoming a cool, trendy place. Even The Famous, the Jewish restaurant where Dottie had first met John's parents, had become a very hot spot called The Strand.

We checked into a loud, vibrant place called the Clevelander, an old Art Deco hotel that was the center of life on Ocean Drive. We got a room in the front, overlooking the Atlantic Ocean, and watched the parade of people below for hours. There are dozens of fashionable restaurants in South Beach now, but back then, finding Lucky's, a glamorous, hip spot in the middle of a still-young renaissance, was remarkable. So was its wine list. Who would have thought? There on the list was a wine we'd heard of, but had never had: a 1986 Sauvignon Blanc from Robert Stemmler Winery. This was a controversial winery, and we immediately found out why. The wine was strange, with as much Riesling character—flowery and a bit sweet with fruit—as Sauvignon Blanc character, grassy and crisp. It was less good than fascinating, and thus perfect with a Miami Beach scene that was odd in its own right. From one end of Ocean Drive to the other was a curious mixture of male and female models and wrinkled retirees.

We had a great time that weekend, but we didn't conceive Media, so it was back to Jackson Memorial Hospital. The doctors said this was it—our last try before in vitro. As a last gasp, an older doctor suggested the "cup method." His younger colleague scoffed. He said this method had been out-of-date for years. John produced some sperm—he was used to this by now—and the doctor put it in a small plastic cup. He inserted the cup into Dottie and told her to leave it in for a while. We'd become used to intrusive procedures, but this was pretty amazing. Still, after the procedure Dottie walked around the office that day feeling quite wonderful, with an almost imperceptible glow deep inside her. What if?

That night, Michael Dukakis accepted the Democratic nomination for president. We drank a Mirassou Vineyards Pinot

Chardonnay 1969 ("Fourth Harvest. #4881 of 5,800. Bottled Sept. 1, 1970"). The truth is, we'd never much liked Mirassou wines, but it was a special treat to have such an old Chardonnay—it was rarely even called "Pinot Chardonnay" anymore—so when a friend offered it to us for $25, we took it. For years, we'd had a great wine every time we tried to make Media, because we wanted fine wine coursing through her veins at the earliest possible moment. But we'd long since given up on that. There was just so much we could do with sweet and romantic gestures to make this whole process more bearable. Every month, for years, we had endured a roller coaster of emotions, from exhilaration and anticipation to disappointment and sadness. So we opened the Mirassou to toast Dukakis. It was still quite good, with some almonds and caramel indicating old age, and there was plenty of fruit and balancing acids remaining. It wasn't going to get any better after nineteen years, but it was still a good wine. We were quite impressed to find it very much alive.

A few days later, our friends Jay and Ronnie dropped by for one of our marathon domino games. John opened a mid-range Bordeaux, a Château Potensac 1982, and poured a glass for all of us. With one sniff, Dottie blanched and said, "This makes me nauseous." It was out of her mouth before she knew what she was saying. Seconds later, we both stopped cold. The smell of wine was making Dottie nauseous? We'd been drinking wine together for fifteen years and that had never happened. Could this just be in her head, or could this be it? We were hopeful enough that, in our notes on that wine, we wrote: "First hint of Media."

A few days later, after Dottie had gone in for her morning blood test, the doctors confirmed it: "Mrs. Brecher, how do you feel about triplets?" Dottie was pregnant. The cup method had worked. There was no doubt about it. We felt fine about triplets. If this was the only time we were going to get pregnant, then we'd have our whole family at one time. We asked if we could have wine to celebrate. The doctors said sure, it was too early for wine to do any harm. That night, we opened a bottle of 1982 Louis Roederer Cristal, the wine John had proposed over. We figured it was the last wine we'd drink for nine months. The next day, the doctors called and asked how we felt about twins. If triplets were fine, twins were better. Finally, they confirmed that there was a single kid in there. There was so much of a certain hormone in Dottie's blood that they had thought there was more than one baby on the way.

We didn't tell anyone about the pregnancy. We'd been through too much already. On August 22, we went to the doctor, who conducted an ultrasound. *Thmmm-THWACK, thmmm-THWACK, thmmm-THWACK.* It was Media's heartbeat! They showed us the baby on the ultrasound and gave us a copy of the picture. They wrote "baby" and pointed an arrow at Media. We'd never been happier.

A few days later, Dottie screamed for John from the upstairs bathroom. When he ran upstairs, he found Dottie slumped over the toilet, screaming in pain. "Call the doctor!" she said. John called and they said to come right over. By the time John returned, Dottie's pain had subsided, but she was holding something in a piece of toilet paper. She had passed something into the toilet. She had miscarried. We both knew what it was, but we couldn't speak. We drove to the doctor in silence. God, we'd been through so much. We just couldn't go through it anymore. We'd talked a little about adopting, but we wanted so much to have our own child, our own little Dottie face running around the house, our own little Media. This was the worst thing that had ever happened to us.

The doctor ushered us in right away, laid Dottie on the table, and put the ultrasound to her stomach. *Thmmm-THWACK, thmmm-THWACK, thmmm-THWACK.* It was Media. She was alive. We were ecstatic. Dottie had simply passed some tissue. But the doctors said we should view this as a threatened miscarriage and said that if it was going to happen there was no way to stop it. There was no use staying in bed. It was nature's way of taking care of tragically flawed fetuses. If it happened, they said, we shouldn't blame ourselves. There's nothing we could have done to cause it. At least for now, Media was still in there. She was a survivor.

We found out in November that our baby was a girl, which, of course, we'd already assumed. She was Media. But we had to come to grips with her name, the only name she'd ever had in our imaginations. Sure, we'd always called her Media, but we're journalists, so people would think they knew why we named her that. We knew a photographer who had named his son Cameron and we just didn't think we wanted to go through the next hundred years explaining that, as best we can recall, Media got her name because it means "between us." So we tried to come up with real names. John's sainted grandmother was Helen, but that wouldn't do for a young kid. Dottie and her mother were both Dorothy, but Dorothy is an old name, too, although it does mean "gift of God," which surely Media would be. We went through one name after another. Then, every night, when we went to bed, John rolled over after he turned out the light, patted Dottie's stomach, and said, "Good night, Media." After a while, we stopped searching for a name.

The third Thursday of every November is "Beaujolais Nouveau" day, when France's first wine of the harvest hits the shelves. It's primarily a marketing gimmick and the Beaujolais, at this point, is more grape juice than wine. Even so, a new vintage is cause for celebration, and we always marked it in some special way, sometimes even with a little party. But that year we weren't drinking wine. People have asked us what it was like to give up wine for nine months, and the truth is that we didn't much notice it. That certainly seems odd, considering our passion, but we were so focused on Media and so busy preparing for—and worrying about—her that wine easily receded to the back of our minds. In any event, one thing that wine has taught us is patience. In a few months, we'd be back to our old ways, and the wines in our cellar would be better for the wait. Still, that year, we bought a single bottle of Nouveau, a Lupe-Cholet, and we each had a sip. In our notes, we called it "Media's first Nouveau."

We'd heard that babies were "viable" at twenty-three weeks, so the day we hit that date—we knew the date exactly, of course—we opened another bottle of wine, a Mercurey 1979, a nice Burgundy. It was pleasant and light, but a bit over the hill. Dottie had a sip. John drank the rest. The next day, we told our parents and everyone else that we were pregnant. For Christmas that year, John had a big flannel nightie made for Dottie with two Dottie faces sewn into the area near the top pocket—a big one and a small one—now that there would be, we assumed, two Dottie faces in the house.

John took up running. We'd always been sedentary—in fact, we laughed at people who wasted their time on things like running—but he decided that he might live longer if he exercised. He decided now that he was going to be a father, he really wanted to live a long time. One day he just put on shorts and went outside and tried to run around the block. He didn't make it halfway. But he kept at it.

Our childbirth classes were specifically geared toward "older parents," which we were. Fathers couldn't be in the delivery room unless they'd gone through the class, so we signed up at Baptist Hospital. The hospital was just putting the finishing touches on a new maternity annex and we figured, given our due date, that Media would be one of the first babies delivered there.

We had a room for Media on the second floor of our house, next to the master bedroom. We'd been using it as a storage area as it waited for her arrival. But as Dottie's due date neared, we still hadn't done anything with it. We hadn't bought a crib or anything else. John had been told that, at some point, Dottie's "nesting instinct" would take over and she'd want to buy all that stuff. Seven years earlier she had bought ten vintage baby gowns and two caps, for a couple dollars each, at a flea market in New York, and they were all we had. She had found the stash before several pregnant women had caught sight of them, and they had all stood around her waiting for her to sort through and hand them her rejects. "How old is your baby?" one of the women had asked. Dottie bought them all.

But now, Dottie's nesting instinct wasn't kicking in, and no matter how much John nagged, Dottie kept telling him that they had plenty of time. John likes to get everything done immediately. Dottie likes to put off everything beyond the last minute. Between the two of us, our timing usually works out just right. But this was getting ridiculous. Media was due in five weeks.

So one morning, to humor John, Dottie said, Okay, let's go shopping. We looked in the Yellow Pages for stores that would have what we wanted, made dinner reservations to reward ourselves after a day of shopping, and jumped in the car. We found a good store and stocked up on everything a yuppie couple could want— a crib, a changing table, two-way radios, bumpers, a super-duper stroller, a bottle warmer, all of that stuff. While we were out, we went to see our old friend Chip Cassidy at Crown Liquors. We've heard that the French have a custom of touching Champagne to the lips of newborn babies as they arrive in this world. We've never checked that out because if it's not true, we don't want to know. We love the idea, and we've adopted it. We told Chip about the custom and told him we were looking for something special. He said, "Wait here." He came back with a bottle of Salon Le Mesnil 1979. This is a very special Champagne. Most top-end Champagnes are made by big Champagne houses that also make less-expensive stuff. Salon makes only this one special wine, and only in great years. It's rare and expensive. The distributor sent just one case—twelve bottles—to the state of Florida that year, Chip told us, and he had gotten only two bottles. Handing us the bottle, he added, "It's on me."

That night, the aurora borealis was visible in Miami's night sky. The *Herald* reported that it was the first display ever of the Northern Lights in Miami. We got dressed up for dinner, John in a coat and tie and Dottie in what we called her "rabbit suit"—an elegant red jumpsuit that showed her stomach to its fullest. We had flown to New York a few months back to buy maternity clothes for professional women because everything in Florida looked like a tent. Anyway, it was a good excuse for a trip. Dottie looked adorable, and particularly lustrous. For some reason, maybe because we were a mixed couple, the maître d' took one look at us and asked, "Are you the entertainment?" Little did he know how close we came to being just that.

We ordered a bottle of wine, a Swan Cellars Chardonnay (we didn't know that it was really Sebastiani, with a new label), and we savored every sip. Dottie had just a little. The food wasn't very good and we were tired from shopping, so we asked for the check and went home.

At 4:10 in the morning, Dottie shook John awake. "My water broke," she said. Still groggy, he asked, "Where is it?" "You're laying in it," she replied. This was it. We called the doctor, who told us the hospital would be waiting for us. John forgot the overnight bag with Dottie's nightclothes, but he remembered the Salon.

The doctor met us there, did some tests, and decided there was no turning back. With Dottie's water gone, Media would have to come out, and Dottie hadn't even gotten into anything that could be called a rhythmic labor. This was not altogether good. Media was five weeks early. Because we knew exactly when she was conceived, there was no possibility of error. Suppose her lungs weren't sufficiently developed? If she were under six pounds, she'd be considered at-risk as a preemie and would have to stay in the hospital, maybe for a long time. Dottie had developed gestational diabetes and this might also cause complications. At six in the morning, something suddenly struck John.

John: *I asked to speak to the doctor in the hallway, privately. He walked out with me, looking concerned. "I just want to make sure I understand this," I said. "When we leave the hospital, we'll have a baby. I mean, this is it. There will be three of us going home. Us and the baby. Three of us. Is that right?" The doctor smiled and said, "That's right," and patted me on the arm. It had taken time to sink in. We'd been together for more than fifteen years. We'd almost given up hope of ever having a baby. And now we had spent our very last night as two.*

Dottie: *I had become increasingly anxious about having a girl and now she was on her way. Would I be a good role model? I'd always been a tomboy and a loner. Would she be a girly girl? Would we be close? Would she like having a mother who worked? Would she think my short Afro was pretty? Would she like me when she was a teenager? All of these thoughts had gone through my head. I was relieved when we learned that we weren't having a boy. I've always thought that raising a healthy black male in this country must be very difficult. When I interviewed Jacqueline Jackson for* The New York Times, *she told me that she was not as worried about someone assassinating Jesse as he campaigned for president as she was about her teenage boys taking the car to go to the movies. "What if they were stopped by police and weren't properly deferential?" she had asked. Scary stuff. I couldn't wait to hold Media and to look into that little face, but it was a bit unnerving that what she would know about being a woman she would learn primarily from me.*

Hospitals were just realizing what a great profit center childbirth could be. They were beginning to compete to see who could attract yuppies with money and good insurance. As it turned out, we were ahead of the new birthing center's construction schedule so we were in the old maternity wing, in a lovely room with a television set. A preseason Mets game was on, a nice distraction as Dottie's labor moved into its eighth hour. The Mets beat the Atlanta Braves, 3–2. With the help of more drugs, the contractions came closer and closer together and, without any special difficulties, Media was born at 1:47 P.M. As she arrived in the world, screaming with great, healthy lungs, John touched Salon Le Mesnil to her lips. "Hello, Media," we both said, sobbing. The doctors let us hold her for only a few seconds before they put her on a scale. She weighed exactly six pounds and she was twenty inches long. She seemed to be fine, but just in case, they put her in an isolation bubble and put an IV in her foot. We could hold her if we suited up in white, anti-germ space suits.

Dottie: *John called our parents with the news. She's beautiful, just perfect, we said. Media was my mother's first grandchild and the first Brecher girl. We decided to hold off on having our parents visit for a few days so that we could have Media to ourselves for a while. We had been waiting for her arrival for so long.*

Dottie stayed in the hospital for an extra day so we could all go home together. Our little Chevrolet was filled with flowers and joy. When we got home, the very first thing John did was tear off the bandage from Media's foot. No more needles, no more pain. "Welcome home, Media," we said. That night, with our very first dinner at home with Media, we opened the 1947 Burgundy that the wine merchant had given Dottie because she complimented his artwork. It was a Vosne-Romanée Les Beaux-Monts from Pierre Ponnelle. Dottie could have only a few sips since she was nursing, but we wanted to bring up our child with wine on the dinner table, and this seemed like a good time to start. The wine was tired, but in a delightfully dusty state of old age.

Dottie took six months off from the paper to be with Media. We did everything by the book, and the book said she shouldn't drink wine while she nursed. Media's pediatrician, on the other hand, said Dottie could have a couple of glasses a week and that it might actually help the nursing. We took Media everywhere in her little carrier. When we went to fancy restaurants, we sat her on the table in it so that we could look at her and talk to her the whole time. When we had romantic weekends on South Beach, Media came with us. In fact, when John took Media out for walks in her stroller while Dottie rested, he found that a newborn baby was a surefire way to attract models. Dottie was not amused.

At home each night, John put Media on his chest and they fell asleep together. Our parents warned us that Media would never learn to sleep by herself if he kept that up, but we couldn't stand to leave her alone. Every night after they fell asleep, Dottie gently lifted Media off John's chest and put her in her crib. In time, John would wake with a start. "Oh, my God, where's Media?" he'd shout, figuring she'd slipped off and fallen on the floor. And every night it would take Media just a few minutes in her crib to notice that her dad's warm, heaving chest was no longer under her and she'd scream until we'd rush in and pick her up. Our parents told us this would create problems, too.

For John's first Father's Day, with Media three months old, we drove down to Key Largo. We loved a restaurant there called Mile Marker 88, so called because it was located at Mile Marker 88 on the way to Key West. Marker 88 was a lovely, romantic place that overlooked the Gulf of Mexico, so we could watch the sunset. It's where we learned that the best preparations of fish are the simplest. We'd have bass and pompano, and they would come gently sautéed in butter, lemon juice, and capers. Over the years, we have had so many remarkable, complex fish dishes. None of them has been as good as those simple preparations of very fresh fish.

In Key Largo, on our first vacation as three, we stayed at an old place called Pop's Motel. Pictures we took show John sound asleep on a lounge chair outside in the shade, with Media sound asleep on his chest. It's funny, but before that trip, we had never taken pictures on any of our vacations together. We saved wine labels instead.

Dottie: *As the end of my maternity leave neared, I began to resent the position I was in. At the time, there were only eleven black editorial writers working at mainstream newspapers in all of America. If I didn't go back, there would be ten. John said we would be okay without my income. I had worked so hard to have Media, and I loved her so much. Each day together promised new adventures and discoveries. I could soothe her with a touch, make her laugh with funny noises. Even our bodies were still in sync. But I felt I had no right to give up my job to stay home with her. Others who had gone before me and opened doors to ease my way had made much greater sacrifices.*

I knew I wasn't indispensable and that I could never hope to represent every viewpoint in the black community. In fact, some blacks disliked me because I challenged the status quo that they were comfortable with, but my voice brought a different perspective to the table. It was unique. As an editorial writer, I expressed my opinions, which sometimes influenced the way people thought and acted and voted. It was the reason I had become a journalist, to move the ball forward, particularly in race matters. But why did Media and I have to pay the price?

Dottie went back to work, and John took a month off.

John: *It turned out to be the most important month of my life, not just the most fun. I'd been a daily journalist forever, and a news-*

room manager for years. Dozens of people relied on me for hundreds of decisions a day. But the paper came out every single day I wasn't there. Not only that, but no one had ever needed me as much, or loved me as much, as Media. Media had the most extraordinary eyes. They were almost black. Even as an infant, she stared at people with those black eyes, and it sometimes made them nervous. We once took Media to a restaurant where, to our horror, a mime was going from table to table. We hate mimes—doesn't everyone?—but we tried to be pleasant. Media, though, in her carrier on the table, stared at the mime so long and so hard that the mime spoke. "Okay, I'm leaving," she said. When Media looked at me, I could almost hear her speaking. Sometimes Dottie would tell me that I was doing something wrong with Media. I finally sat her down and said, "You never have to tell me that. Media will."

Dottie stopped nursing and we told the doctors we were ready to start working on a second child. Dottie was now thirty-nine, and if the next child took another five years, she'd be forty-four. We made an appointment for the following month. In the meantime, though, we could do something we hadn't done in five years: We could have sex for absolutely no reason at all. It was glorious. One afternoon, while Media slept in her crib—and heaven knows that was rare—we had a particularly good time and it was the strangest thing: We both immediately sensed that we had just conceived our next child.

SIXTEEN

Marzemino (Trentino) 1988

. . .

MEDIA WAS ONLY SEVEN MONTHS OLD WHEN DOTTIE told John, "I have that frog-filled-with-eggs feeling again." That's how she'd known she was really pregnant with Media. John took one look at her and said, "I'll go get one of those instant pregnancy tests."

About an hour later Dottie walked down the stairs with a quizzical look on her face. The staircase was in the middle of the house and it creaked when we walked on it. The creaks didn't matter, though. We still felt like movie stars from the 1930s when we glided down those steps. No trip up or down was ever a completely casual exercise. This time, Dottie was frozen on the landing between the two flights of stairs. She looked down at John with a combination of awe, shock, pleasure, and disbelief. "This says I'm pregnant," she said. "Let me look at it," John said, bounding up the steps.

This was too good to be true—probably one of those rare false positives. "I'll call the doctor," Dottie said. We packed Media into the car and made the fifteen-minute drive to the obstetrician's office for a quick test. We sat there, stunned, and then the doctor who delivered Media walked out with a big smile. "Congratulations," he said. "You're going to have another baby."

By the time we returned to our house, we had decided that we definitely needed to move back to New York. We were about to be a family of four. This was it: We were going to be grown-ups after all these years. It was time to settle down for good. Not only that, but we'd always wanted to raise our children—if we ever had any—in New York. They'd be smart, streetwise, tough, and cultured. They also wouldn't stand out, as racially mixed children, in a whole city of diverse people.

There was only one basic question: Would we wait until the baby was born and then move to New York? Or try to move before the baby was born? The latter was clearly problematic. It would mean that we'd have to find jobs, sell the house, move to New York, buy an apartment, set it up, start new jobs, acclimate Media to New York, find a baby-sitter, get new doctors—all while Dottie grew to epic proportions. Waiting had its own problems. We'd be stuck in Miami for another nine months even though we knew we were leaving. Then we would move to New York with a sixteen-month-old and a newborn. Money would be even tighter after the second child was born.

One thing was certain. We had to open a bottle of Champagne to celebrate our second child, and to help us make up our minds about our next move. John went back to the wine room and chose the most romantic bottle he could find: Taittinger Comtes de Champagne Brut Rosé 1982, the same wine we'd had on our very first night in our New York West Seventy-second Street apartment. The wine was elegant yet full-bodied, romantic, and perfect for the occasion. By the time we'd finished it, we had decided: We would try to move to New York before the baby was born. We had something less than nine months. After all, Media was a preemie. Who knew how fast we'd have to do this?

The next day John called Jim Stewart. When John was at the *Journal* before, he and Jim had become close. Jim was a great writer who regarded John as a great editor. We all became friends, spending nights drinking wine together. Jim preferred French, we preferred Californian. After we left New York, we kept in touch, and when Jim became Page One editor of the *Journal,* one of the most prestigious jobs in journalism, he told John he could have a job on his staff anytime he wanted one.

"Sure," Jim had said when John called. "Fly up. I'll set up a lunch." Dottie could worry about a job later, after the baby was born. That would make it tough on us financially, but we'd get by. The important thing was to move fast.

A week later, on a beautiful fall day, John had lunch at a trendy Greenwich Village restaurant with Jim, Norm Pearlstine, and Paul Steiger, Norm's deputy and designated successor. As soon as lunch was over, John found a pay phone a block from the restaurant and called Dottie. "It's done," he said. "I accepted the job."

The next few weeks were a blur. We gave the *Herald* a couple of months' notice, since we didn't want to move over Christmas. We gave away most of the art, antiques, and books that we owned, since we figured they wouldn't fit into a New York City apartment. And we went apartment-hunting in Manhattan. Because we love Central Park, we knew we wanted to live on Central Park West. We also knew that we really couldn't afford it, but surely our house in Coral Gables, now all fixed up, would be worth a fortune, giving us at least the down payment.

The New York City housing market was just beginning to swoon, so it was a pretty good time to be looking. But we needed a two-bedroom that we could move into right away, and the searching was hard, especially on Dottie. As we looked at apartment after apartment, something curious happened: It seemed that, at every other building, our real estate agent moved close to us, looked around, and whispered, "Barbra Streisand lives here." It became a running joke with us. Finally, we thought we understood. Our agent was speaking in code. When New Yorkers buy an apartment in a co-operative building, they have to be approved by a board of residents, which can accept or reject anyone for any reason. Barbra Streisand had once, famously, been rejected by a co-op board on the East Side because she was Jewish. The agent was telling us that despite our possible negatives—an interracial, Jewish journalist couple with one income, one little baby, and another on the way—this co-op board would accept us.

Our real estate agent finally told us that she'd found the perfect apartment for us, but there was one hang-up. It was owned by a famous opera singer named Samuel Ramey, who wouldn't let anyone see it for two days before a performance. That's good shtick, we thought. Build up the anticipation. Welcome to New York. When we finally got into the apartment the day after his next performance, we fell in love with it. It was in a lovely Art Deco building on Central Park West, and if we stood at the windows in the living room and the master bedroom at just the right angle, we could see Central Park. The place was in perfect condition. On the walls leading to the bedrooms were photographs of Sam Ramey as Attila the Hun, Don Giovanni, and in some of his other roles. Just inside the entrance to the apartment was a large closet filled with some of his costumes. When we saw it, we both said at the same time, "Wine cellar!" As we rode down in the elevator after leaving the apartment, the real estate agent lowered her voice, looked at us conspiratorially, and whispered, "Barbra Streisand lives here." We smiled and winked.

We lived in a little, furnished company apartment near the *Journal*'s offices for two months until the various real estate closings could be done. Dottie wasn't just pregnant. It was like she had the entire New York Mets team in her stomach. Almost from the moment of conception, this baby—a girl, we'd learned—had been so aggressive that she seemed more a life force than just a baby. We decided to name her Zoë, Greek for "life."

We were fried, so one night we decided to go out, have a nice dinner, and drink a little wine. We found a baby-sitter for Media and walked over to a nearby restaurant called the Hudson River Club. Its wine list was impressive and we began talking with the wine director, a young man named John Fischer. "Wait, I've got something that's not on the list," he said, and he came back with a Chardonnay we'd never seen. It was called Peter Michael Winery "Mon Plaisir" 1988. The wine was excellent, the latest development in California Chardonnay: the big fruit we associated with American wine, but with some tightness and restraint that was more French. It said on the back: "The soils, exposure and 'clone' of this site give fruit with classical aromas and flavors and an intensity that responds well to traditional Burgundian vinification and elevage: fermentation in Burgundy barrels, malolactic fermentation, and 10 months of original lees contact and stirring. The wine was bottled without sterile filtration. 800 cases were produced." It was signed "Helen M. Turley, Winemaker."

This was a hint of the future. Peter Michael's elegant wines became well known, but Helen Turley became downright famous. She created some of California's "cult wines" in the nineties. It was a sign of a bloated economy then that various impossible-to-find California wines, such as Screaming Eagle, Bryant Family, and Harlan Estate, became whose-cellar-is-bigger status symbols among the newly rich. Their prices rose to incredible levels.

John started work, but he spent most of his time fretting that our house in Coral Gables was still attracting no serious interest. We paid way too much for the opera star's apartment, but it was in move-in condition, and we were desperate. We begged and pleaded for a fast closing, and it was finally scheduled for July 3, just a month before Dottie's due date. The closing was held in a mortgage company's office in midtown. We sat on one side. On the other were Sam Ramey and his wife. By then, we had bought several of his CDs, including Sam Ramey singing Rodgers and Hammerstein. The closing started badly. "You know," the woman from the mortgage company said to Sam, "the girls in my office say you're famous. But personally, I've never heard of you." We all laughed, nervously, and then the woman from the bank went through the list of what everyone had to have. Checks, co-op documents, bank statements, ID.

ID?

"Of course," she said. "You both need to have picture IDs." No one had told us that. Dottie was pregnant in July in New York City. She was wearing tents by then and when she was with John, she didn't carry her purse. She had no ID. And why did she even need it? We told the woman that Dottie had not brought an ID with her. "Well," said the woman, "we'll just have to reschedule the closing." She shuffled her papers and began to close her folder. Our heads were spinning. Reschedule the closing? We were about to have a baby. We had already synchronized the move from Miami. This would ruin everything. "Why do I need ID?" Dottie asked as calmly as she could. "Well," the woman explained, with some irritation, "there are some cases where there's a nasty divorce, and the man tries to sell the house right from under his wife's nose, so he brings along a woman who pretends to be his wife." Then she pushed her chair back and began to stand.

There was a slight pause. The room was totally silent except for the sound of the woman's chair rolling back. Then Dottie, John's ever-mild-mannered wife, began to rise from her seat. She was huge. She was like a killer whale rising from the sea. Slowly, she stood up, her stomach endlessly rising past the table. Finally, she stood straight and—BANG!—she pounded both hands on the table. The room stopped. The woman was frozen in mid-stand, bent at the waist. Nothing was moving. Then Dottie spoke, through tightly clenched teeth.

"Think about it," she said. "If he were going to use a fake wife, do you think he'd bring an *eight-and-a-half-months-pregnant black woman?*"

After what seemed like minutes of silence, the woman from the bank sat down, regained her composure, and simply said, "Let's continue with the closing."

The next day, with Media in tow, Dottie went to our new apartment to wait for the phone guy while John went to work. The Rameys had sold us their apartment and bought a larger one in the front of the building with a spectacular view of Central Park, but they'd kept a studio apartment on our little floor to use as Sam's office.

Dottie: *While I was waiting in our empty apartment for New York Telephone to show up, there was a knock at the door. I opened it and there was Sam Ramey, handsome as all get-out, with his famous megawatt smile and glorious mane. He apologized for not having a shirt on. He had been working in their new apartment in the front of the building, he said. Hell, I didn't care. He had a bottle of Italian wine in his hand, something I had never seen before called Marzemino (Trentino), a 1988 from a producer called Kettmeir. He said Mozart had specifically mentioned this wine in Don Giovanni, one of Sam's greatest roles. In the scene of the grand banquet, just before the climax when he's dragged to hell, Don Giovanni asks for an "excellente Marzemino." Then Sam Ramey—the very handsome, very famous opera singer—held out the bottle and sang that portion of the opera to me, in the richest, deepest voice I'd ever heard, as I stood there just about bursting with Zoë. It was amazing that a human being could produce such a spine-tingling sound, and so effortlessly. I twinkled to my toes. God, I love New York. I had Sam sign the bottle. We have never opened it, and we never will.*

...

A few days later, while Dottie and Media stayed in New York at the company apartment, John flew down to Miami to meet the movers at the still-unsold house. We had shared many bottles of our wine with friends before we left, but there were still five hundred to pack, which took as much time as the rest of the house. John begged the packers to be gentle with the wine, and then flew back to New York to the new apartment. The movers were due to arrive on July 17. Our old friend Charlie Kaiser agreed to help us move in.

On the night of the 16th, our little family spent its first night together in the co-op on a borrowed mattress that we placed in the middle of the living room. In the morning, John heard a loud horn and looked out the window onto Ninety-second Street. It was the moving van, right on schedule. "It's the movers!" he yelled. "Hold on," Dottie said from the living room. "I'm on the phone with the doctor. I feel funny."

We left Charlie with the movers and went to Mount Sinai Hospital, across the park, where Zoë was born at 6:42 P.M. We wanted to touch Champagne to her lips as she was born. This was no problem when Media was born in Miami. The doctors and nurses, who knew what we had gone through to conceive her, thought it was charming. But the people at Mount Sinai weren't terribly pleasant in general, and certainly not about this. When we asked the head nurse if it would be okay for John to take a bottle of Champagne into the delivery room so we could touch it to Zoë's lips, she said, "I wouldn't recommend it," as though we were suggesting pouring the entire bottle down Zoë's little throat with a funnel.

Zoë was two weeks early. With everything else going on, we hadn't bought a bottle of Champagne, and our own wine was with the movers. As Dottie continued with labor, John ran out of the hospital to find a wine shop. He was lucky. There was one just two blocks away. He looked at the chilled offerings and knew right away what he had to get: Taittinger, in a half bottle, because it would be easier to conceal in the delivery room. An hour later, when Zoë arrived, perfectly healthy, John popped the Champagne and touched a drop to her lips as we both said through our tears, "Hello, Zoë."

A month later, John was standing at our front door, waiting for our elevator on his way to work. An exhausted Dottie held Zoë, who was crying. Media was crying, too, grabbing John's pant leg to try to keep him home. When the elevator finally arrived, the door opened and a woman inside, seeing this scene, cooed, "Oh, that is *so* sweet."

It was Barbra Streisand.

SEVENTEEN

Paumanok Vineyards Chardonnay 1989

. . .

ARBRA STREISAND HAD LIVED IN OUR BUILDING WITH Elliott Gould. Long after they divorced, she stayed, and slowly bought every apartment on the floor. Her place ultimately spread to 8,000 square feet, with fifteen rooms, including five bedrooms, five bathrooms, and a 3,000-square-foot terrace with views of Central Park, the New York skyline, and the Hudson River. She lived directly above us, albeit fourteen floors above us. One of the New York tabloids reported the year we moved in that she stiffed the doormen for Christmas because one of them, in the elevator with her, sang "People Who Need People." We doubted that was true. It's a highly professional building, one of the premier Art Deco buildings on Central Park West, designed by the architect Emery Roth in 1929. The building went co-op long ago, and the residents were solid, longtime, older, and mostly Jewish. It was a bit too far north to be cool, although residents included Swoosie Kurtz and other actors.

We really couldn't afford our apartment. Dottie didn't have a job yet, and we hadn't saved any money. Not only that, but we couldn't sell our house in Coral Gables. We'd spent all of our money fixing up that house, and everyone assured us that it was money well spent because we'd get it all back when we sold. We put the house on the market for $225,000—less than we paid for it including the improvements—and still no one was interested. Not only did this create serious financial problems for us, but it was insulting. We loved that house. We couldn't believe no one else did. The real estate agent even told us that the wine room was a negative, because no one would want it and they'd just have to rip it out. Actually, said the real estate agent, there was just one thing about the house that people really loved, and she was worried about it. Day after day, people who came to see the house commented on the big, beautiful Picasso on the living room wall. The agent was sure someone would break in and steal it. We told her to go ahead and hide it. We didn't tell her that it was a fake, and that it was Dottie's face.

When we moved our furniture to New York—including our prized "Picasso"—our house was empty, and pretty forlorn. Inspections pointed out one problem after another, from the foundation to the electric wiring, that our own inspection had somehow missed when we bought it. John's brother Kris, who had become a brilliant stock trader and turned $1,700 into millions, loaned us enough money for our down payment on the co-op. We had two children—one sixteen months old and the other a newborn—one new job between the two of us, and no money in the bank. We were exhausted.

Fortunately, John's bosses at the *Journal* understood. Jim Stewart told him not to even think about work for a few weeks until he felt comfortable. When John edited stories for Page One, which often meant working closely with reporters and rewriting their copy, the reporters were always nice and complimentary. Norm and his deputy, Paul Steiger, welcomed John like a long-lost relative. They said they'd hire Dottie as a reporter whenever she was ready to come back to work, and even wrote a letter to that effect for the bank when we were trying to get a mortgage. New York was every bit as vibrant as we remembered it. We got right back into the habit of having tastings with our old friends, including Jim Stewart, though we found we didn't have nearly as much time, or energy, as we used to.

Our two-bedroom co-op had only five closets, but one of them, Sam Ramey's old costume closet, became the wine room, just as we had envisioned. We found a clever carpenter who managed to make spaces for 770 bottles. It wasn't temperature controlled, but the room was in the middle of the apartment and kept a nice, even temperature. To help keep it even cooler, we added another air-conditioning unit to the apartment. When the wine room was finished, we opened the single most special bottle of wine we had. The label, most of which was typed in capital letters, read "Cabernet d'Anjou. Appellation controllée. Vin Rosé Fruité. 1970." It was from Mellins, France. There was a price sticker on it. "Wine Gallery. Coconut Grove. $3.99."

There was no Vin Rosé Fruité inside that bottle. This was the last bottle of our homemade Welch's wine, from 1974. It had been "aging" for sixteen years. Not only that, but it was the very last bottle we had that at least had the sticker from the Wine Lady of Coconut Grove. We had gone from dating in Miami to a family of four in New York, and this bottle had been with us the whole time. Opening it seemed to close a chapter, and open a new one.

And, surprise: It was still wine. Not good wine. But wine.

That bottle turned out to be a symbol, too, of things to come. For the next two years, we drank primarily the wines we'd brought with us from Miami. We couldn't afford to buy any, so it was a good thing we had a large stash. It was kind of fun and, in truth, many of those wines needed to be drunk. There was a 1979 Ste. Chappelle Chardonnay from Idaho. There was a Meredyth Chardonnay and a Montdomaine Chardonnay from Virginia, made long before Virginia became a hip wine-producing state in the late nineties. There were all sorts of signed bottles from our trips to California and all sorts of weird stuff that we could never stand to open because they were so unusual or even irreplacable—"Sweet Frances" from Soda Rock Winery, a 1972 "Dry Chenin Blanc" from Louis Martini, Habersham "Peach Treat" from Georgia. We drank old Burgundies we'd bought at Santino's in Miami and bottles from wineries that didn't exist anymore. We even drank our last bottle of Maui Blanc, the pineapple wine from Hawaii, and a wine called Welder from Florida Heritage Winery in Anthony, Florida.

When John had worked at *Newsweek,* a friend who visited South Africa brought back a bottle of wine. It was made by KWV, a huge cooperative, and it was Pinotage, South Africa's own wine, a cross between Pinot Noir and Cinsault. South Africa has a very long history of winemaking, a beautiful wine country, and a fine reputation for good stuff, but there was no way we were going to drink a wine from the home of apartheid. So the wine, from the 1977 vintage, sat in the cellar until apartheid was dead. By an accident of history, the wine had been well aged, and it was special—raspberry-cherry fruit, an interesting underlay of soil, and a "finish" that was memorable and almost a little bitter.

We also drank Montinico, "A Vin Santo Wine Exclusively from San Martin Vineyards." Vin Santo is the rustic, dried-grape dessert wine made in Italy. This was a California dessert wine that came in a rectangular bottle with a shiny metal label that said: "This unique wine is produced from a shy-bearing Italian grape brought to California's Santa Clara Valley during the early history of San Martin. As far as known, our 8.4 acres of Montinico vines are the only vines on this continent." This was not very good wine—it was brown and a bit harsh and alcoholic—but it was important to us. John's parents knew nothing about wine and almost never went into wine stores. But every Christmas, his dad went into the wine store and bought a bottle of Montinico for us. Heaven knows why. But every year, it was a bottle we cherished.

When we'd gotten married, we'd bought twelve bottles of 1974 Robert Mondavi Cabernet Sauvignon. We figured we'd have one every year on our anniversary. Twelve years seemed like such a long time then that we couldn't imagine they'd ever be gone. But on our twelfth anniversary, we opened the last one. It was tired, but still showed a great deal of fruit. We wish we had more.

Right before Christmas, we sold the house, after almost a year on the market. A builder offered $180,000 for it and said he'd buy it in "as is" condition. We were desperate, and we sold. We'd lost $5,000 on the house, plus everything we'd put into it. The good news was that we found a great baby-sitter for the kids, Louise Williams, and Dottie started work before the new year, covering minority issues for the *Journal.* After looking for the perfect place for a journalist to work all these years, we'd found it. For the first few months, John worried that he wasn't carrying his weight because he worked only forty hours a week and was never overwhelmed. Then it struck him: He was being paid for his experience and his talent, not his hours. It was a shock. At *The Miami Herald,* hours mattered. From the newest intern to the top editors, people were judged by how long and hard they worked. At the *Journal,* people were judged by their work. It seems simple, but to us, it was a revolutionary concept. Not only that, but the *Journal's* powerful, moneyed, and sophisticated readership meant that we really could help change the world, and our editors believed in that, too.

Any good newspaper should tell people things they don't want to hear. The *Journal* was committed to doing that. At the height of the AIDS epidemic, everyone wrote tons of stories on the subject, many of them important and moving. But we wondered: How do we make our readers, generally male, older, and conservative, care about this on a gut level? They were just the kind of people who needed to join the fight against AIDS, but how? John worked with a reporter named Judy Valente on a lengthy story in which we followed an AIDS patient to his death entirely through the eyes of his father, an older, conservative man from St. Louis. When John was finished editing the story, he gave it to Paul Steiger, then the managing editor (Norm had been promoted to executive editor). The story was so brutally honest, so deeply emotional, that John worried how it would be received by the top editors.

The story ran as written, with the complete support of the top editors, who knew some of the *Journal*'s readers would be deeply offended. Sure enough, some were. But something very important happened with that story. All sorts of conservative, moneyed white men, the kind of people who run America, saw themselves in Paul Henderson's father. AIDS became a very personal epidemic to them all of a sudden. We heard from dozens of important people. That story came within a whisper of winning a Pulitzer Prize, but it won something more important: converts to the cause. (Later, when John was Page One editor, a series of Page One articles on AIDS that he oversaw did win a Pulitzer.)

Dottie was having equally good experiences. She reported that black women were moving ahead in the workplace faster than black men and what this meant in the workplace and in the black community as a whole. This was demonstrably true, but was such a deeply sensitive topic that no other newspaper would touch it. Once, she wrote a story that said that, while fighting racism was still important to blacks, health care, employment, and child care were more important. Her story so offended Rev. Jesse Jackson, the civil rights figure whom Dottie had covered for years and whom she had quoted in the story disagreeing with that thesis, that the day it ran, he called Paul Steiger and said he wanted to fly in from Washington for a meeting.

We'd gone to many meetings like this at the *Herald*. We'd write something that offended someone important. The important person would come to One Herald Plaza for a meeting, where the top editors would apologize and humiliate the reporters and editors involved. We approached this meeting with trepidation. In late afternoon, Reverend Jackson and his entourage walked in. He is a man of great charisma, a national leader who really fills a room, especially a little conference room like the one we crammed into. Across the table, Paul Steiger, always calm and charming, shook Reverend Jackson's hand. As Paul sat down, he said politely, "Reverend Jackson, thank you for coming. We were very proud of Dottie's story when we printed it, and we're still proud of it. So, what can we do for you today?"

We both could have leaped across the table and hugged our boss. He was standing up for the story! Reverend Jackson was as diplomatic as ever and made his points. We had a pleasant meeting and everyone parted friends. On his way out, Reverend Jackson even asked Dottie if she would cover his campaigning on behalf of white Democratic candidates in the Midwest. A few had asked him to help because his speeches about the American worker resonated deeply with people who were being squeezed by cheap labor overseas and factory closings in their towns. We knew that day that we'd be at the *Journal* for a very long time.

A few months later, a liberal think tank in Washington reported the results of a survey in which it found that Dottie's premise was true—fighting racism, while important, was not blacks' number one priority. Dottie was first, and right.

John's work schedule allowed him time for some serious running. One of the reasons we were drawn to our apartment in New York was that it was right next to the Reservoir, the famous 1.5-mile running track in Central Park. John ran around the

Reservoir. He ran across the Brooklyn Bridge at lunchtime. He ran up the Hudson, and he even ran all the way home, from the tip of the island to Ninety-second Street. He ran in races, always finishing near the end but finishing nonetheless. In 1991, he ran more than one thousand miles.

We couldn't afford a vacation in 1990, and we didn't know what kind of vacation we could have with two little kids anyway. But in 1991, we heard about wine country on Long Island. It was just a couple of hours away, there was a beach, there were some wineries, and there was a hotel on the water where we could get a room with a little kitchen for about $100 a night. It sounded perfect.

At its eastern end, Long Island splits in two. The southern fork is where the rich people go, places like the Hamptons. The North Fork has always been rural, mostly filled with potato farms. In 1973, a couple named Alex and Louisa Hargrave decided this would be a nice place for a vineyard. We'd had their first Cabernet Sauvignon, from 1976, all those years before. Slowly, others followed. When we first visited in 1991, there were nine wineries, all fairly closely clustered near our hotel.

We've always been fond of winemakers, of course, but there is something special about a winemaker in an unusual place. Anyone who makes wine in places like Virginia or Rhode Island has to be passionate about it, and, shall we say, nonconformist. The people we met that year on Long Island were both. There was the retired air traffic controller, the retired union organizer, and the retired Sears executive. There were the oddball brothers—the one who ran the place and the one who made the wine and didn't really want to ever sell it. There was the wife in the tasting room who spoke so knowledgeably about her family's wines, but in fact hadn't had a drop of alcohol since she was a teenager and got so drunk with her sister that she vowed never to drink again.

And there were the Massouds.

Charles and Ursula Massoud are owners of Paumanok Vineyards, a very pretty place with good wine for adults to taste and buy and, fortunately, yummy crackers that keep kids happy for a few minutes. The two met in Philadelphia when she was an undergraduate at Chestnut Hill College and he was getting an MBA from the Wharton School at the University of Pennsylvania. On one of their early dates, Charles, a suave Lebanese who had lived in France, took her to a little French restaurant near the university. It had no liquor license, so the owner-chef directed him to a wine store. "So Charles took off and he was gone so long that the waitress asked, 'Are you sure he's coming back?' " Ursula told us later. "I told her that I was quite sure and he came back with a Côtes-du-Rhône. That was my introduction to his passion for wine."

Ursula is from Germany, from a village twenty miles from Alsace, and her family had made wine there going back to the 1700s. Her maternal grandfather owned several vineyards, and although the family no longer owns wineries, it's in her blood. Charles worked for IBM for twenty-two years. In 1971, the company assigned him to Kuwait, an Islamic country where alcoholic beverages are taboo. "It's a dry country and officially you're not allowed to drink alcohol, so there's no market, but many foreigners were brewing beer and making wine and some were even distilling things and they taught us how to do that," Charles recalled. "We tried making beer but we didn't care for it very much. So we started making wine out of necessity."

They bought table grapes and crushed them in the bathtub with their knuckles. "I had such calluses that a friend asked if I was taking karate lessons," Charles recalled, adding, "and we made some very nice wine out of that." Soon the squashing of grapes with their knuckles and their feet got old, so they switched to buying grape juice at the supermarket. But what kept them going, Charles said, was the German connection. Whenever they visited

Ursula's family, they'd immerse themselves in the region's wine culture. At a relative's house, "We'd go down to a barrel in the cellar and fill up a pitcher with wine and bring it to the table for dinner," Charles said. "We mingled a lot with these vintners and it was a great way to really get into it without having to commit to anything."

After seven years in Kuwait, they returned to the United States and, for Charles, to the realization that he was not going to run IBM. "Being overseas was not necessarily relevant experience, and there were others younger than me who were already ahead of me. So I decided very quickly that unless I wanted to get into a nine-to-five job, I might consider doing something else. And in the beginning, it wasn't clear what I was going to do."

They considered going back to Germany and buying vineyards there because they liked the lifestyle so much. But over there, "the winemakers kept discouraging us. They kept telling us that their life is so hard. But then we looked back at how they lived. They had beautiful homes and nice cars, so we thought there just has to be something more to it." In 1978, a year after returning from Kuwait, a map pointing to their future arrived on the doorstep of their home in Connecticut in the form of a newspaper article about Alex and Louisa Hargrave, the pioneers of Long Island winemaking. This was virtually in their backyard. That weekend they met the Hargraves and came back home convinced that they could do it, too.

For the next three years they went to conferences and symposiums on winemaking. They went to Napa Valley and Burgundy. And in 1983, they bought their first property. One of Ursula's uncles traveled from Germany to tour property with them and he liked the land in the North Fork. Ultimately, they figured that at the very least, if their Long Island winery were to go belly-up, they would have property that would be worth quite a bit. "We always believed this place would explode and it's happening now,"

Charles said of the ever-growing value of vineyard property on Long Island. One of the North Fork's last potato farms was sold in 2000 to make room for yet another winery, he said.

Ursula's uncle thought the North Fork had great potential, but he shook his head at how far apart some of the vines were being planted there. In his own humble way, he said they didn't know what they were doing. "He showed us how to do it and we did it exactly like he did," Charles said. And he was right. "It has allowed us to make wines with more fruit intensity," Charles said. Soon, other neighbors followed suit.

Charles was still at IBM, and they were still living in Connecticut with their three boys—Kareem, whose name means "the one who is generous with his heart"; Salim, "the peaceful one"; and Nabeel, "the noble one." They started with fifteen acres in the North Fork, with the whole family working them on weekends, tying the vines. After three years, they owned thirty acres, and in 1991—the year we first visited the North Fork—they sold their first wines, all while Charles continued to work for IBM. The balancing act was crazy. "How we did it, I have no idea, but we did it," he said.

That year, with their first wines on the market, he decided that he had to leave the company, move to the North Fork, and dedicate himself full-time to the vineyard. They now live in a renovated farmhouse next to their tasting room and vineyard.

Looking back, they marvel at how willing they were to take risks. "It shows that it is possible to do different things in life. Going from high-tech to farming is at two extremes, but it has been a rejuvenating experience, like learning to walk again, learning a different trade. You have to dig deeper, have to try harder, and it's amazing what you learn. In that sense, we were both cut from the same cloth," Charles said, nodding at Ursula.

"I have always been a romantic individual. In the nineteenth century, Lebanon became wealthy producing silk. There were beautiful silk factories, almost like cathedrals. My dream was to buy one and restore it and get back into the silk business. Farming also always intrigued me for some reason. It was fulfilling another dream. When you are at the university, you think you can do anything, but most of the major decisions in people's lives they make by the time they are thirty. That always haunted me. It was like an obsession to do something else."

Said Ursula: "It's been so unbelievably satisfying. When I'm in the vineyard, I can spend the whole day there and never look at the clock. It's therapeutic, the whole cycle, and even in the winter it's beautiful." And there's something else. In her family, the relative whom everyone expected to continue the family's wine tradition died in a car accident. The others decided to sell the vineyards. "I am the one who is carrying the tradition on," Ursula said. "I could never have done it without Charles and he says he could never have done it without me." Owning a vineyard and winemaking are like a relationship, she said. "If you don't tend to a relationship, you're not going to be happy. You're not going to get good fruit."

When we first met the Massouds, we were talking with Charles when he suddenly said, "It's sunset!" He took us out to the deck of his tasting room and carried a bottle of his newest Riesling. We stood there drinking the wine and watching the sun set over the Massouds' vineyard. "I love this," he said.

Most new winegrowing areas go through a period of experimentation as they try to figure out the best wines for their region, and we visited Long Island right in the middle of that process. Pindar was selling a "Gamay Beaujolais" and Palmer a "Beaujolais." Pugliese had a Chardonnay Blush. Hargrave had a Pinot Bianco and Lenz had something called "Maiden's Blush." But the strangest was this:

We stopped at a beautiful, modern winery called Gristina. Both girls were still in strollers, and we pushed them, with some difficulty, up the steep sidewalk to the tasting room. Everyone on

Long Island had been charming—friendly, knowledgeable, and pleased to see us, even with the kids. Gristina was different. The young woman behind the counter was indifferent and so were the wines. We tried everything to perk her up, with no luck. Finally, we noticed an unusual wine under the counter. It was a Pinot Noir.

Pinot Noir is the grape that makes the great reds of Burgundy and that California winemakers had so much trouble with for so many years. It seemed incredible that a new winery on Long Island would even attempt to make a Pinot Noir. Hargrave made a small amount, but as far as we knew, no one else had tried it. We asked about it, and the woman behind the counter suddenly grew very animated. "Do you want to try it?" she asked. She opened the bottle and poured. It was excellent—fairly light, but filled with fruit and some taste of the earth that good Pinot Noir needs. It was clearly Gristina's best wine, and we said so. It was probably the best wine we'd tasted on the entire trip, and we told the woman that, too. She leaned over closer to us and lowered her voice. "The winemaker really wanted to make this wine but the owner told him not to," she said. "He made it anyway. The owner told him never to do that again." We asked where the winemaker was, and she pointed downstairs, where the winemaker was working outside with some tanks. We bought a bottle, ran downstairs, and asked him to sign it. "We hear you won't be making this again," we said as he wrote his name. The winemaker just looked up at us and smiled. Gristina's Pinot Noir continued to be its best wine for many years, but in 2001, Gristina told us they'd pulled up their last Pinot Noir vines.

We spent the mornings at wineries, and the afternoons at the pool and the beach. Our very fifties little hotel was right on Long Island Sound, and we had a good-size porch outside. Every day, we visited wineries and bought their youngest and freshest white wines. Then we bought lobsters. Dottie cooked the lobsters and served them on the deck with corn on the cob and potato salad. We sat there drinking wine from local wineries, eating lobster from local fishermen, and watching the girls play in the sand while the sun set behind them.

We visited Long Island every summer after that. More and more wineries were built, and the wines got better all the time. But it changed. The retired FAA flight controller sold. So did the winemaker known as "Mr. Merlot," and so did the Hargraves. They were bought out by big companies, or by rich people, the type that belonged on the South Fork. Truth is, this is probably good for Long Island in the long run. The infusion of capital will mean more wine, better distribution, and more aggressive publicity.

For now, at least, the Massouds are still holding out at Paumanok, watching the sun set from their deck.

EIGHTEEN

Franzia Chablis

. . .

"EXCUSE ME, SIR, DID YOU KNOW OUR BUILDING IS ON fire?"

When we decided to move to New York, we figured it was time for Media to stop sleeping on John's chest. She was thirteen months old and we knew that, sooner or later, she'd have to sleep by herself, and that the transition would be difficult. We knew she'd scream her head off the first few times she was put in her crib awake, and we figured it was better to let her scream in a house in Miami instead of a co-op apartment in Manhattan where our new neighbors might be less than charmed. We'd read all the books that said babies would scream for a little while and then stop. So we put her in the crib and let her cry. It was an amazing thing: Media could scream for three or four hours, effortlessly. Night after night, she beat us. We gave up. Media liked to be near us, all the time. She was a wonderful, bright, beautiful child, but she never slept—our parents had been right, of course—and even when she got older she did not like to be separated from Mommy, Daddy, Zoë, or our sitter, Louise. So when it was time for her to go to preschool in the fall of 1992, we were nervous wrecks.

John was about to run the New York City Marathon. There's a cliché that "the wonder isn't that I finished, but that I even had the nerve to start," and that was surely the case here. John had been running only three years and still moved at a snail's pace. He had never run more than 15 miles in a race, and never more than 20 miles at one time. But he felt he could survive 26.2 miles through New York City's five boroughs.

Dottie continued to write influential stories at the *Journal*. She wrote the first story that fleshed out the deep financial problems within the NAACP under Ben Chavis's leadership. Chavis's predecessor had refused to talk to reporters but told Dottie when she called, "Miss Gaiter, since it's you, I'll talk to you." And he did, saying that he had left the organization with plenty of money in its coffers, not, as he put it, "a Mother Hubbard cupboard," as had been alleged. The paper nominated her for a Pulitzer Prize.

John was having a lovely time taking orders instead of giving them. He had been in management for years and had grown to dislike it. Management is always difficult, but managing newspaper reporters is especially difficult because they believe everything they do is protected by history and the Constitution. You want to change my lead paragraph? The First Amendment says you can't do that. You want to cut my story? Well, what if they'd done that to Woodward and Bernstein? You want to kill my story? I guess "they" got to you. Not only that, but Media and Zoë had changed John's worldview. Work, ambition, and climbing the ladder just didn't seem as important as they once were.

John was also finding, to his delight, that the *Journal* could accomplish any story he could dream up. For Christmas one year during the savings and loan crisis, he thought it would be fun to ask a bunch of S&L experts what they thought of the business practices of George Bailey in *It's a Wonderful Life*. At Jim Stewart's suggestion, John called a reporter in the Boston bureau named Ron Suskind, who understood the concept, got regulators and S&L operators into a room together, and screened the movie. The story was a scream.

We were beginning to dig out of our financial hole and buy a little bit of wine, though we were still drinking mostly what we'd brought to New York. When John's brother Jim came to visit, we pulled out one of our greatest treasures, the 1959 Château Latour. Some wines are legendary because they come from a great vintage and everything seems to fall into place just right. There are the great 1929 Bordeaux, for instance, and the Mouton-Rothschild of 1945. The 1959 Latour was one of those wines. It was a fine year, one of several years of the twentieth century that was declared "the vintage of the century" at the time, and the Latour, which is always the "biggest" of the first growths, was especially huge. Michael Broadbent wrote this about it in *The Great Vintage Wine Book*: "Black/purple when young, still opaque but beginning to show maturity. . . . An enormous wine, dry, full of alcohol, fruit, extract." Then he added, from his notes in 1978: "Quite unready."

This was the bottle Dottie's friend at the *Times* had tipped her off to when we lived in New York in the eighties. Yes, $80 was a lot of money, but it was a steal nonetheless. It spent six years in our Miami wine cellar and now it was back in New York. Jim's visit seemed like a good time to open it.

We had learned that a great Bordeaux, properly aged, is one of life's miracles. The components all come together, the tannins soften, the wine takes on a depth and complexity—almost a profoundness—that isn't possible in youth. But who could afford a famous first-growth Bordeaux that had been appropriately aged? We certainly couldn't. Except for this bottle. We had such high hopes that we thought we would surely be disappointed. Then we opened it. As the cork came out, the bouquet of the wine filled our small dining area. Dottie, across the table, stopped talking to Jim, turned to John, and said, "Oh, my God." The room filled with the smells of chocolate, tobacco, and cherries. When we tasted it, the wine was beyond expression—massive and rich, yet very dry. It had a kind of power we'd never tasted before. It was tough and leathery, with depth and class. As it opened, it became slightly more approachable, with gorgeous tastes that seemed utterly seamless in our mouths—remarkable for a wine with so much taste. We took very small sips, yet it still seemed to explode with taste in our mouths, tastes of cedar and perfect fruit. All of the great tastes of red wine, and all of its history, seemed to be alive in that bottle. It was the greatest Bordeaux of our lives. It even rivaled the great 1968 Beaulieu Georges de Latour Private Reserve we'd had among the vineyards of Napa Valley on our honeymoon—although that Beaulieu, as it turned out, was about to get even better, years after we'd opened it.

The genius who had made that wine, André Tchelistcheff, was coming to the Plaza. He was a legendary figure in the history of California winemaking, someone who proved what California wine could be. We immediately bought two $70 tickets, which even we could afford. It seemed like a great deal, considering that we'd have several old Beaulieu wines and meet André Tchelistcheff. We got there early. Then he walked in. He was a short man, with really big, black eyebrows. He was then almost ninety years old. We could not believe we were in the same room with the great man himself. He was full of life, with bright, somewhat mischievous eyes. He said a few words, and then went table to table, speaking with people. When he got to ours, we handed him the label of the 1968 Georges de Latour Private Reserve that we'd had on our honeymoon. We told him the story of that wine and then we asked him how he knew that 1968 would be such a great year. He looked at us and smiled. "I picked a grape," he said, as he pretended to pick a grape with his hand, "and then I crushed it in my hand"—he lifted his fingers to his nose and he closed his eyes—"and I tasted it. And I knew." For several moments, he seemed to be back in the vineyard, far from the Plaza, and we didn't say a word.

We've always said there is magic in wine, and right there in front of us on that day, we saw the great André Tchelistcheff transported to that magical place. When he returned, he signed our bottle. "André Tchelistcheff," he wrote. "Thank you for"—we never did figure out what the rest of it said. It doesn't matter. We had met him and thanked him for his genius. He died two years later, in April 1994.

In September, the night before Media was set to start preschool, John attended a Marathon training talk at a gym. A longtime marathoner offered tips on the race. At one point he said, "Don't any of you forget this: You are an athlete."

John: *I heard that and thought, Hell, he's right—I am running in the New York City Marathon, after all. It was a heady feeling for someone who had never been athletic. I had played Little League baseball, but my brief career ended when I caught a fly ball in my right eye. When the Marathon talk was over, I walked home through New York. It was a surprisingly chilly night for September, which made the city that much more exciting. Everything was going great. We were both happy at our jobs. I didn't have to manage anybody. We had paid Kris back and we were beginning to dig out of our financial hole. Zoë was adorable and perfect—she even had a Dottie face, the ultimate Dottie present. Media was adorable and perfect except that she never slept. She was starting school the next day and the baby-sitter was great. We were living on Central Park West in Barbra Streisand's building in the greatest city in the world. How did I ever get so lucky?*

As I strode down Columbus Avenue, I passed a woman from our building. I saw her in the building all the time and always said hello, but I had no idea what her name was. "Excuse me, sir," she said, "did you know our building is on fire?"

The fire had started in the basement, from some electrical problem.

Dottie: *The girls and I were at home watching television when the tube suddenly went black. I got up to call the cable company and discovered that the phone was dead. I smelled smoke, peeked out the back door, and shut it quickly. The back stairwell was full of smoke. So the kids wouldn't be frightened, I calmly went out the front door and knocked on a neighbor's door and told them the building was on fire and that there was smoke in the stairwell. Their apartment was clear and they invited us in. I knew that John would be arriving at any moment and would be frantic. So the three of us kept our noses pressed to the window so that when he appeared we could wave and tell him we were okay. From the inside, we could hear the firemen as they searched for people in the building who might need help. When one knocked on our neighbor's door, she opened it. He looked like an alien in his fireproof suit and helmet. When the girls saw him, they started to cry.*

John ran to the building and couldn't believe what he saw. The building was surrounded by flashing fire trucks, police cars, and rescue vehicles. There was even a Red Cross emergency van giving out coffee and doughnuts. He ran to the front door of the building and was blocked by a very large fireman. "My kids are in there!" John shouted. The fireman was concerned. "Alone?" he asked. When John said no, they were with their mother, the fireman said he was sorry, but John couldn't go in. The fire had been contained in the basement, but smoke had filled the building. Worse, the fire had exposed asbestos in the basement. John looked up to the seventh floor, and there, leaning out, were Media, Zoë, and Dottie. "We're fine," they shouted. John spent the night at a friend's apartment. In the morning, we were told that the building would be closed for at least a few weeks and that we'd have to move out. We could come in for a couple of hours to pack some stuff.

This was the first day of preschool for Media, who we thought would have some "separation issues," as they put it at the school, even without being displaced by a fire. Dottie stayed with her for the day while John checked into a residential hotel that many of our neighbors were also using as a temporary haven. It was old, but it was somewhat near our apartment and it had a little kitchen. We couldn't take much with us—we didn't have time to get any wine—but we could get by for a couple of weeks.

Media, as it happened, did fine at school. She has always had an inner toughness and a depth that her teacher at preschool later called "the child equivalent of wisdom." Our temporary quarters were okay, too. Bands that played at the trendy China Club nearby were put up there, so the hotel gave us dozens of tickets that got us into the club cheap. The hotel also had a Chinese restaurant in the lobby. It was just like every other Chinese restaurant in the city, except for one thing: It served unlimited amounts of cheap white wine with dinner. As soon as we sat down, they'd bring a heavy carafe of the wine, and they kept refilling it. It turned out to be Franzia Chablis. In a box.

Franzia, the number one wine-in-a-box brand, is the largest-selling single wine brand in the United States. One of every eight glasses of wine drunk in America outside restaurants is a Franzia boxed wine. The company, which has gone through several incarnations, can trace its roots to 1906, when Giuseppe and Teresa Franzia started a winery in Ripon, California. Their daughter, Amelia, married Ernest Gallo in 1931, and Ernest and his brother

Julio went on to build the country's largest winery. Franzia is part of The Wine Group, a San Francisco company that has grown so large that it is now the nation's third-largest producer of wines. According to Impact Databank, the research arm of the company that publishes *The Wine Spectator,* the wine-in-boxes category has been the fastest-growing segment in the industry in the past ten years.

Wine in a box is incredibly cheap, and closer to some sort of chemical compound than wine. Later, when we became wine writers, we conducted a tasting of boxed wines and they were generally vile. But wine is all about context, as Frank Prial had made us understand so many years before. Right then, in that old hotel with two young children and only a few of our possessions and John just two months from running the Marathon, that deeply chilled Franzia was delicious.

A week after the fire, Jim Stewart called together the Page One staff. Page One of *The Wall Street Journal* isn't like anything else. At other newspapers, reporters and editors run around all day and then, at the end of the day, top editors decide which stories should run on Page One. At the *Journal,* Page One was considered to be a feature page, more a magazine than a newspaper. Every reporter wanted Page One bylines, but they were hard to come by. After all, there were only three of them every day, and just five days a week. Reporters and their own editors discussed a story, then sent a formal proposal to New York. The Page One editor, who reported directly to the managing editor, accepted or rejected the idea. If it was accepted, the reporter worked on it for weeks or months. Then the reporter sent it to Page One, where, if it was accepted, one of a dozen great editors who worked for Page One edited the story, often rewrote it, and sometimes worked with the reporter to totally rethink it. Page One editors often suggested ideas, too, and were then able to get some of the country's best journalists to make them look brilliant. Page One of *The Wall Street Journal* had been one of America's greatest showcases of journalism for years because of the time, effort, talent—and money—that the newspaper put into it.

Norm Pearlstine had recently left the *Journal* to start his own company (he later became editor in chief of Time Inc.). Paul Steiger, the managing editor, was now fully in charge. Jim Stewart had recently written his third book, and his second best-seller, *Den of Thieves.* To a shocked Page One staff, Jim announced that he had decided to take up writing full-time. He was leaving the *Journal.* He would stick around until mid-November, after the presidential election between George Bush and Bill Clinton was over.

John felt sick to his stomach, and not just because he'd miss Jim. John had developed a reputation as a top-notch editor, a good idea man, and a pleasant voice on the phone with nervous reporters. He knew he'd be a top candidate for the job. And he really didn't want it. It was one of the most prestigious jobs in American journalism, but John never wanted to manage again. It was just too bruising, and this was a particularly tough job. Every reporter wanted to be on Page One, and so everybody was always banging on the door of the Page One editor. Every idea that was rejected caused arguments and bad feelings. Being Page One editor was also bound to take a lot more time than being just an editor on the Page One staff.

We talked about this for several nights over carafes of Franzia Chablis. John didn't want the job, and Dottie didn't much want him to do it, since she was still patching him up from all the bruising battles in Miami. But as the days went by, something became clear. John had come to New York to work for Jim Stewart. He didn't want to work for anyone else who would get the job, and where would that leave us? Reluctantly, he applied for the job. A couple of weeks later, John and Paul Steiger shared a taxi home. In the taxi outside of our temporary home, the old hotel, Paul offered John the job. The next day, John accepted it, with very mixed feelings.

That night, we opened a bottle of Krug "Grande Cuvée" Champagne in our old hotel room, but it wasn't much of a celebration. Dottie was very proud of him—it's an important job and one that she knew he would be perfect for—but it was clear that our lives were going to change, and fast. The first thing John did was arrange for a computer at home, so he could be in touch at all times. We'd never had a computer before. Dottie had always resisted one because of the temptation to always work if we had one.

The second thing John did was hire Joanne Lipman as an editor. She was the young reporter who had written about playing the viola on the streets of New York years before. Joanne invented the *Journal*'s advertising column and had become one of the paper's biggest stars. Now coming back from a maternity leave, she was looking for something new to do, and John grabbed her before anyone else did.

We moved back into our apartment right before the Marathon, which is always run on the first Sunday of November. The building still smelled like smoke, the basement—including the laundry room—was closed, the gas was still off so we couldn't use the oven, but at least John would be able to walk to our own home when he finished the race, which ended just down the street in Central Park.

About 28,000 people run the Marathon every year, and most of them are like John—regular people who run slowly. The Marathon is a big challenge for them, maybe the biggest of their lives. The pictures on TV and the newspapers show the elite runners in competition and the runners having fun in costumes and such, but for most runners there is no competition and no fun and games. It's 26.2 miles, and it's scary. John had had knee problems during the year, but he felt strong and was sure he could finish the race, which starts at the Verrazano Narrows Bridge in Staten Island and winds through all five boroughs of the city. We set up a rendezvous point so Dottie could give John some juice and a little food. It was sixteen miles into the race, in front of a wine shop.

John: *Whatever you've read about how great it is to run the New York City Marathon, with thousands of people lining the streets to cheer, it's better than that. For an aging, mediocre runner like me, running through the streets of the city I loved and being cheered by thousands of strangers was one of the best experiences of my life. I was doing fine, too, until I hit the Fifty-ninth Street Bridge. It seems to rise like the Empire State Building, and even experienced runners suffer through it. I suffered a lot, but I knew that Dottie was right near the bottom of the bridge, at the wine store. I pinched her cheek with my sweaty hands and took off again, still at the pace I wanted, about twelve minutes per mile. Just a mile down First Avenue, my knee began to hurt, first with dull pain, then sharp pain. I stopped at one of the medical rest areas and got a massage from a doctor, then took off again. Soon, my knee gave out completely.*

I couldn't run, and could barely walk. I hobbled over a bridge and entered the Bronx. A friend from our Miami days had agreed to meet me at mile 21. By the time I finally got there, it was beginning to get cold, and dark. She gave me her leather coat, which was far too small for me, but it still felt good. I would not have lasted long without it.

I thought if I could get into Central Park, where I'd run hundreds of miles, I would feel like I was home and could make it to the end of the race. The crowds had thinned, but the few people still there cheered the runners as they limped into Central Park. Suddenly the park seemed totally unfamiliar to me, and the hills much steeper. Every few yards, I tried to run a little, to end with a flourish, and found that my right leg wouldn't support my weight. So I kept walking, dragging my right leg behind me.

...

In the Great Lawn of Central Park, where the race ends, Dottie was waiting.

Dottie: *I had gone over to race officials to try to figure out where John was. I thought he must have hurt himself and stopped running. They assured me that, if he had stopped, they'd have a record of it, because the buses that pick up nonfinishers keep a list. So he was out there somewhere, probably in pain.*

Race officials were beginning to take down some of the race banners as John made the last turn in Central Park and saw the finish line. He jogged the final few steps. He finished in five hours, forty-five minutes, and fourteen seconds—26,534th of 27,797 finishers. He walked to the Great Lawn and, of course, right into Dottie. We cried together, and then we walked home. The very next day, John flew to Washington to meet with the powerful Washington bureau for the first time as Page One editor. Busy with his job, he didn't run again for more than a year.

We celebrated Thanksgiving in our apartment with a twelve-pound turkey from a deli, since our oven still didn't work. It seemed like an appropriate time to open one of our greatest treasures, a Heitz Cellar "Martha's Vineyard" Cabernet Sauvignon, from the 1974 vintage. This was one of California's most famous wines—some people have even called it California's first cult wine—and Dottie had paid $125 for it a decade before, far and away the most we ever had paid for a bottle of wine. It was sure to make even a deli turkey special. We popped the cork. The wine smelled of rich, concentrated fruit, almost sweet from ripe grapes. We sipped, and we were transported to Napa Valley, filled with the taste of perfect grapes, just the right amount of oak, perfect aging, and—

The phone rang. It was an old friend from Miami. He was in

town for Thanksgiving and just wanted to say hello. We were happy to hear from him, but one of the greatest wines of our lives was on the table. John finally rushed him off the phone and returned. We sipped. The wine had gone downhill. That marvelous, sweet fruit had lost something, becoming darker, browner, a bit alcoholic. The wine was still very good, but the taste from that very first sip had now been lost forever.

People sometimes ask us whether they should let wines "breathe." We always say no, because we enjoy tasting the whole life cycle of a wine, and you can never be sure whether a wine will lose its most intense fruit immediately after it's opened. We say that because of that experience on Thanksgiving Day 1992.

NINETEEN

Rhône Red

. . .

JUST A FEW WEEKS AFTER THE MARATHON, DOCTORS TOLD US that Dottie had three or four months to live.

Truth is, Dottie always had health problems. As John says, "So perfect on the outside. Such a mess on the inside." Way back in 1975, she had serious pain on her side and in her lower back. We didn't have a regular doctor back then—why would twenty-four-year-olds need them?—so we went to a friend's doctor who immediately put Dottie in the hospital. John stayed with her on a fold-out. The doctor couldn't figure out what was wrong and neither could any of the specialists he called in, so he scheduled exploratory surgery, which is when we fled. We found a good doctor, who took one look at Dottie and said, "Has anyone ever told you that you're crooked?" It turned out that she has a slight curvature of the spine. Because she never knew about it, or did anything about it like exercise regularly, the scoliosis had inflamed various nerves in her back and side and legs, and she had no idea what was going on. It's a chronic condition, but it can be managed.

She has had a pain in her neck her whole life—besides John— that doctors have never quite been able to explain, although one elderly doctor once said it was "Eagle's syndrome." He explained that that's a calcification of some tissue. She's always cold even in August—"It's my African ancestry," she always says—and she seems to have had common colds for decades at a time. She has odd rashes and stomach pains, and a connective tissue disorder that gives her serious pain in her hands, arms, and back. She dislocated her knee as a child and it kept dislocating until she got it fixed when she was in her thirties. When she went in for knee surgery—the New York Jets' surgeon, James Nicholas, operated on her—John brought along our big green stuffed frog, a present he'd bought for Dottie years earlier in Coconut Grove. His name is Jumbo Neil and he wears a bow tie. When Dottie was rolled into the operating room, John put the frog in her bed and covered him up so no one would steal him. Several people had tried to buy him while we waited to be admitted. The next thing John knew, bells were ringing and people were running. A nurse had walked into the room and seen a covered body. She jerked down the sheet and when she saw the bright green frog, she screamed. John sheepishly tried to explain. No one thought it was funny.

While Dottie's right knee was recovering, her left knee dislocated at a small French restaurant where we'd planned to eat before we saw *Porgy and Bess* on Broadway. The paramedics had to move tables of diners out of the way to get her out. When we moved back to New York in 1990, doctors found a suspicious spot on one breast and cut into her to remove it. But they missed it, so other doctors cut into her, too, and did remove it. It was nothing.

So it wasn't particularly surprising that Dottie had some pain in her abdomen right around the time John was running the Marathon. She saw a couple of doctors who said it probably wasn't anything. Then one of them ordered an ultrasound.

Dottie: *The ultrasound operator was scanning, apparently not seeing anything, and then she suddenly stopped and swallowed hard. Being a good reporter, I knew that she'd seen something she wasn't expecting, something that stunned her. Bad news. She told me not to move, that she was going to get her supervisor, and she left me lying there, worried. I had always been troubled with ailments similar to my dad's. He had rotten knees, too. The supervisor introduced herself and passed the device over my body. After a few seconds, she told me to get dressed, that she was going to call the doctor who had referred us, and that we should leave her office and take the films over to his office. That doctor sent us to our old friend, a physician whom we always turn to when we're scared. He told us to hop in a cab and to bring him the films and the records.*

On the way, of course, we read the reports in the backseat. We didn't understand much of it, but we knew enough to understand this: The problem was Dottie's pancreas. It was quite enlarged, and there appeared to be a blockage. It was almost certainly a tumor, and almost certainly cancer, the ultrasound people wrote.

Our doctor sent us to a specialist. The specialist didn't tell us much—you know how doctors always say that "the range of possibilities is so broad that it's far too early to focus on anything"—but he scheduled exploratory surgery for early January, so we decided to go home the next month for Christmas, to visit our families in Tallahassee and Jacksonville. John's present that year was a Dottie watch, which gave new meaning to the term "face of the watch." Dottie told her mother that doctors suspected pancreatic cancer, but we told John's parents just that there was something wrong with Dottie's pancreas. John's mother lived in medical journals and she suspected the truth.

There were other revelations while we were in Jacksonville. Sitting around the dinner table, we were talking about wine when John's mother asked, "What got you two interested in wine in the first place?" We told her that it was a book—*The Signet Book of Wine,* by Alexis Bespaloff—that had appeared mysteriously in John's mailbox one day at Columbia. John's brother Jim stopped dead. "That was from me," he said. "You didn't know?" Jim explained that, when he was in law school at the University of Florida, he couldn't afford real food, so he lived on packaged beef Stroganoff. With each two boxtops, he could get a free wine book. Jim had dozens of boxtops. He sent a book to everyone he knew, including John. He was sure he'd mentioned it, but he never had. The book that began our love affair with wine was a freebie with two boxtops from packaged beef Stroganoff.

Soon after we returned to New York, we left the girls with the sitter and went to the hospital for a biopsy. It was supposed to be outpatient surgery, so we figured we'd be home soon. Dottie went into the operating room and was there for a couple of hours, far longer than planned.

John: *I waited and waited, growing more concerned. At some point, our own doctor, a delightful and calm man we'd come to trust over a decade, rushed in unexpectedly, and didn't even say hello. His face was ashen. "How are things?" I asked. "I'll talk to you later," he said. A few minutes later, the doctor who performed the procedure came out with an X ray and asked me to come over to a lighted board. He put the X ray up on the board. "It appears to be pancreatic cancer," he said. "Let me show you." There it was, clear as day: Even I could see what looked like a little river and then something blocking it. "What does this mean?" I asked. The doctor said the* *course of the disease was usually three to four months. Then he looked at me very seriously and said: "She should put her affairs in order." When Dottie was wheeled out a few minutes later, I tried to hold back my tears, but without success. I gave her the news, which she accepted calmly, as always.*

Dottie: *My first thought was, Okay. I've got to find a way to get through this, to help John and the girls get through this. It really is true that dying is so much worse for the survivors. I'll be gone, but they'll have to carry on. The girls are so young. I don't feel like I'm dying, but I guess I am. What I need to do now, with the time that I have left, is create memories that will be sweet. I need to try and behave as normally as possible, to hold things together. So I guess this is what Daddy went through.*

Our own doctor came over and said he'd already spoken to doctors at Memorial Sloan-Kettering, the famous cancer hospital, and that they expected to see Dottie the next day. The doctors had had difficulty extracting tissue, so they said Dottie should spend the night at the hospital, recuperating. John had always stayed at hospitals with Dottie. But now we had kids, and John really had to leave. So, of all nights, that night we were apart. Dottie spent the night in the hospital, nodding as nurse after nurse told her that her good attitude would help her, that being upbeat can sometimes buy you a few months. John spent the night with Media and Zoë, who were then two and three. John had been in his new job for less than two months.

We told our parents right away. A few days later, John's father called Dottie to say he had been praying for her, to his God and to Jesus, "because you came into the world Christian." That was just like Ben, to cover all his bets. He told her something else, too. He said he'd been praying that God take him instead because his son and granddaughters needed her. They cried together on the phone.

Dottie: *I pray off and on. I thank God for my life and for the lives of my family and friends, but it's not something that I talked about. It surprised me how many supposedly cynical journalists told me that I was in their prayers. One brought in a program from her church, where she had added my name to a list of people who needed special prayers. I was overcome by their caring and I started trying to figure out how this might fit into God's plan for my little family. I wanted to try to put it in a context that I could live with, no pun intended. And this is what I came up with. Maybe my purpose here was to meet John and to give birth to these wonderful children. And maybe there's another woman out there somewhere who would make a better mother and friend to them in adolescence and adulthood, a better lover and friend to John as he grew old.*

I suppose most people want to think of themselves as more than just vessels. Friends have scoffed at me when I've explained my theory to them. Surely, they say, you were put here for a higher purpose than just to have your children and to love John. But my view is that a vessel is not just made special by the quality of what it holds, but that only the most special vessels are entrusted with the most special contents. Every day that I'm with John and the girls, that role, my sense of myself being an incredibly special custodian and helper in their extraordinary lives grows, becomes exalted. Their lives are so sacred to me that I began to see my role in that sense as quite enough. When you're told that you're going, you have to find a way to make it okay. This made it okay for me.

The doctors at Sloan-Kettering were great, but the place itself was depressing, with bald and infirm people everywhere. Most jarring, though, were the people just outside the hospital's doors who were smoking cigarettes. The doctors said they'd do some tests to see what was going on and told us about some treatments that might prolong Dottie's life, like something called the Whipple procedure, whose name made us smile despite the circumstances. The doctors said one other thing: Do not drink. Alcohol, they said, would be toxic to Dottie's pancreas. We would have to face this without wine, which had always been our special thing, the way we celebrated life. It was a terrible thought, but Dottie asked if the alcohol in wine could have somehow contributed to her ailment. The doctor smiled and said no. No one knows why these things happen.

The doctors explained that the pancreas is hard to reach, so it's difficult to do a biopsy that proves or disproves the presence of cancer. They scheduled Dottie for several other tests, then her second biopsy. She was in surgery for a short time, then was wheeled into a recovery room, where John met her. The room was pleasant and the staff was caring, but the experience was terrible. All around us, people were being brought in from their operations and their tests. The room was suddenly filled with screams or sobs or bursts of tears as people got bad news from their doctors. We just sat there silently while there was one explosion of grief after another.

Our news wasn't bad. The doctors hadn't found any cancer. That didn't necessarily mean anything, they warned us, but it certainly wasn't a bad thing. They would need to conduct a few more tests. We would have to come back after they had examined what they found. Test after test followed. We went through weeks just as we always had. We both went to work, when we weren't going to doctors' offices, and then came home to the kids. The medical writers at the *Journal* fed us a constant stream of information on pancreatic cancer. Our boss, Paul Steiger, told John that Dottie's health was the most important concern, but John didn't feel that the new Page One editor could give less than 100 percent to the job. We went to a lawyer and updated our wills. John, who has always handled the money, made sure everything was in order on Dottie's health-care and life-insurance policies.

Week after week passed with no news. Doctors couldn't confirm cancer, so they didn't want to start Dottie on any treatment, but they couldn't rule it out, either. She wasn't suffering rapid loss of weight and she didn't look jaundiced, which are important signs, but her pancreas was so clearly enlarged that anyone could see there was something terribly wrong.

We didn't talk much about this—what was there to say?—but the kids still mention "the time Daddy hurt his foot." John was washing dishes one night after dinner and just started to sob and couldn't stop. He rushed to our bedroom, but not before Media and Zoë had seen him. We explained that John was crying because he'd dropped a plate on his foot. It's amazing what kids remember, because they still remember that. They'd never seen Daddy cry before.

We lived in limbo for four months. Several times each day, to Dottie's ever-increasing irritation, John inspected her like a fresh tuna at the dock, looking for any signs of decay. Finally, during a consultation on the latest tests, the doctor looked across the table at us, smiled, and said, "You don't have cancer." We were thrilled, but skeptical.

"How can you know for sure?" we asked. The doctor paused and replied quietly, "Frankly, because if you did, you'd be dead."

The doctor then explained that all of the pictures of Dottie's pancreas clearly showed a tumor—except that it apparently wasn't a tumor. It was a bizarre congenital abnormality. There was no way to know that from the pictures, he said. Her pancreas was fine, but we still needed to nail down the origin of the pain.

Stunned and weary from the whole ordeal, we left the hospital determined to have a delicious lunch and a bottle of wine at a quiet place where we could take all this in. It was just before three in the afternoon, so most places were closed already. We walked into a famously romantic restaurant called Sign of the Dove, where we asked if they would serve us lunch. They said no, that their kitchen was closing. John explained that we'd just found out that Dottie wasn't dying. They still said no. So we kept walking and found ourselves at a little bistro called Sel et Poivre. They said they'd serve us lunch, and we sat at a window. It was crisp and blustery outside, so John ordered "a glass of big red wine." The French waitress came over with two empty giant goblets and said, "This is the biggest we have. Eees okay?" We smiled and said sure. The giant glasses were filled with some kind of generic Rhône wine—hearty, rustic, life-affirming, and perfect for the occasion. "To your face," Dottie said. "To your bottom," said John.

Dottie: *Friends have asked if roses smell sweeter to me now. It took a while, but, finally, I can say that they do. I know it sounds unappreciative, but the news that I wasn't dying after all didn't make me immediately euphoric. It had taken too long in coming and the emotional damage from the ordeal, from preparing to leave, was tremendous. For the first time I truly understood what my mother meant when she said that Dad would not have wanted us to talk with him about his dying. This dying business is a solitary endeavor, no matter how much you're loved. Your leave-taking is done alone. The ordeal is something that I guess I'll never quite get over. I still pray.*

John: *We've never quite been the same. Having been forced to imagine life without Dottie, I probably became more clingy than ever. And Dottie, having been forced to imagine death, seemed to grow an extra layer of emotional protection. And, even now, I look at her eyes every morning for any hint of jaundice.*

We called our parents with the good news. Dottie's mom said she always knew that the diagnosis was wrong. John's father broke into tears and put John's mother on the phone. It turned out that John's father had been having health problems of his own, but they hadn't wanted to bother us with them. He was having minor strokes—not too serious, but enough that he had to stop driving. This alone was a disaster.

John's parents believed that the second John's father retired, he'd drop dead. They were filled with stories of people they knew who were in perfect health, then retired and immediately just keeled right over and died. So John's father went to the showroom day after day, even after he was sixty-five and the children had grown up and left, and stood there and sold Chevrolets. Meantime, John's mother, with no more children to raise, had taken up pottery and had become quite good at it. They began going to art shows and selling her work. John's father, a natural salesman, loved hawking their wares. They put a sign on the pots that said "Please touch," and that always attracted attention. At some point, they decided that if they traveled around and sold these pots fulltime, John's father wouldn't really be retired, so he wouldn't drop dead. He finally got off the showroom floor and John's parents, for several years, had a marvelous time at art shows. The strokes ended that, since John's father couldn't drive and his mother never felt comfortable behind the wheel.

John's father also always believed in avoiding doctors. He figured that once a doctor found one thing, he'd find another, and another, and next thing you knew you'd be dead. Maybe he was right. After the mini-strokes, doctors seemed to find one thing after another. Finally, Kris called to say that Ben was in the hospital and John should come down. We all went to Jacksonville. When we got there, John's father was in a bed in his hospital room, clearly using all of his energy to sit up. Media and Zoë climbed up to give him a hug, and Dottie told him how much she loved him. A few nights later, Ben fell into a coma. All of us—his wife, his children, his children's wives—sat around glumly. For a man who was so funny and charming, this seemed inappropriate. So we went to a liquor store and bought several chilled bottles of Korbel, the inexpensive California bubbly that he always bought for the holidays. With John's father in a coma, we sat around him, drank bubbly for hours, and took turns telling all of his stories.

John: *When Schenley first sent my family to Jacksonville, my father discovered that he loved lying out in the sun. He had a dark complexion, and he never burned. He just got darker and darker. One of his jobs for Schenley was to introduce bars and barflies to its products, an odd job for someone who didn't drink. One day, my father was at a black bar selling Schenley when a black guy kept staring at him. My father was comfortable everywhere, with everyone, but he grew increasingly nervous. Finally, the man looked at my father and said: "You know, you could almost pass for white."*

For years, my father told us every night at dinner about what really happens on a showroom floor. His stories were funny, but appalling. For instance, he always told us that the salesmen lived for the times a man would talk about buying a car and then say, "But I have to talk to my wife." Then the salesman could say: "That's fine. Bring your wife in and we'll dicker."

We laughed until we cried. He died quietly that night.

Giving his eulogy, John said, "I guess some of you may have wondered how my family received Dottie. Well, she was like the daughter my dad always wanted and never had. He loved her so. Dad was a great salesman and I can just hear him making the sale of his life, convincing God to take him instead of Dottie." Dottie was shocked. She had never told John about the conversation she'd had with his dad.

John's parents had been married for fifty years when his father died, and John couldn't remember their ever spending a night apart. His mother made a valiant effort to live alone, but she never really recovered. Her health slowly failed, and she died three years later. We were in Florida at Walt Disney World when Kris called to say that she was dying, so we sped up the highway and arrived in time to say good-bye. After her funeral, we found a treasure trove of Valentine's Day cards from Ben, one for each of their fifty years together.

Shortly before John's mother died, she had told Dottie that she wanted her to have the Limoges china her own mother had given her for her wedding, the china she had used for Dottie's first visit to Jacksonville. John had asked her to leave him only one thing, and so she'd made a point of it. He got Grandma Helen's brisket pot, the big, black pot in which John's beloved grandma cooked a massive lump of meat for hours while she and John talked. It is a Griswold No. 7 Tite-Top Baster. Patented Feb. 10, 1920. Erie, Pa., U.S.A. On Mother's Day 1996, we made our own brisket in that pot for the first time and served it on Ruth's plates. Brisket is John's signature dish.

John: *I love to make brisket because it always reminds me of the hours I spent talking with Grandma Helen while she cooked her brisket. The key is the pot. I tried to make brisket for years before I got the pot, and it was never quite right. Maybe it's because that pot is magic. But, in any event, it's clear that the pot has to be heavy, with a heavy lid, and should be small enough that the brisket has to be stuffed into it. Otherwise, there is too much surface area and the liquid evaporates, so there's no gravy.*

GRANDMA HELEN'S BRISKET

Get a lean brisket, 2 or 3 pounds. Wash and pat it dry. Put 1 tablespoon of oil in the bottom of the pan and brown 2 or 3 cloves of garlic over medium-high heat. Take the garlic out and put the meat in, fatty side down. Brown until it's browner than you think it should be. Turn it over and brown the other side. Put the meat on its side in the pan and cook 2 or 3 thinly sliced onions with it until they're tender.

Put the onions on top of the brisket, sprinkle in more salt and pepper than you think you need, and then put in 1 table-spoon of your favorite vinegar. Cover tightly and turn the heat way, way down to very low. Turn every hour. On the first turn, add more salt and pepper. The onions should be creating all the liquid you need, but if not, add a little water or red wine.

It should take about 3 hours. You'll know it's done when you put a fork in it and it feels tender. Let it cool for a while and be sure to cut it thinly, and against the grain.

The perfect wine with brisket is a great Bordeaux or a particularly fine Cabernet Sauvignon. That night, with our very first brisket in Grandma Helen's pot, we drank a Christian Brothers 1974 Cabernet Sauvignon, the first wine we'd written into the Cellar Key journal that John's parents had given us for Christmas so many years before. We had collected 1974 California Cabernets our whole lives together. This was the very last one.

Very Good. Big, rich, chewy. Deep and dark. A bit old, but still lovely and fruity, with lots of '74 Cab character, that walk-to-the-table fruit/oak taste.

Robert Keenan Winery
Cabernet Franc 1989

. . .

WE HAD GONE THROUGH A VERY ROUGH TIME. BUT DOT-
tie was alive, the kids were great, and New York was as exciting as
ever. Not surprisingly, John's job turned out to be more enjoyable
than he'd expected. He worked closely with a number of great
journalists. His new job, though, was somewhat awkward for Dottie, who wrote primarily for Page One. She had to send her pro-
posals to his deputies, who rejected some of them. Still, she
continued to write stories about race that rarely had definable
good guys and bad guys, the kinds of stories with depth and context that no one else would write.

One of them took her back to Tallahassee, where her mother
and younger sister Karen and Karen's family still lived. A longtime
white professor at predominately black Florida A&M, where
Dorothy's father once taught, had used the term "nigger mentality" to challenge his black students to shed a mentality of victim-

ization, to go out and make things happen for themselves. During the ensuing brouhaha, he had apologized but argued that the word was used all the time on campus, that even Queen Latifah, the rapper and actress, used it in her recordings. He claimed that had he been black, no one would have batted an eyelash, that the university had a double standard. A journalism professor, he also claimed that his comments were covered by the First Amendment, which protects free speech. In fact, the university's president did tell Dottie, "If he had been black, the reaction wouldn't have been the same. The students would not have complained." Dottie wrote the story for Page One—its first national exposure. The paper nominated her again for a Pulitzer Prize.

John and his assistants were discussing story ideas one day and came up with this one: How do good students succeed at a really bad school? John tried to sell the story without success to a couple of bureaus and finally turned to Ron Suskind, the reporter who had written the story on *It's a Wonderful Life*. Ron reported the story for months and wrote a deeply moving story about Cedric Jennings, a brilliant student at a deeply troubled high school in Washington, D.C. The story won a Pulitzer Prize—one of eight the *Journal* ultimately won for Page One stories while John was in the job, an unprecedented string for the paper. Although the *Journal* has been known as a brilliantly written newspaper for decades, this was the paper's first Pulitzer Prize for feature reporting. The paper won its second soon after.

The school story was more important, though, for the impact it had on the *Journal*'s white, male, conservative readers. Ron and the paper received scores of letters from readers who said they'd never look at a young black male quite the same way again, knowing that each one might be another Cedric, a young man working to overcome obstacles that most of us can't even imagine. It was more proof: The *Journal* really was a place where we could help change the world a little bit at a time.

The editor on the story, and a key part of its brilliance, was Joanne Lipman, John's first hire at Page One, who had turned into a terrific editor and a friend. We occasionally visited Joanne and her husband, Tom Distler, a lawyer, and their two kids at their country home, where our girls could swim, and they came over from time to time for dinner. Joanne and Tom didn't know much about wine, but they always enjoyed our enthusiasm when we shared some with them. One time, after a couple of bottles, Tom said to us: "You know, you two should write a wine column."

At the time, our wine exploration had been severely curtailed by our jobs and our growing girls. On the whole, we continued to drink stuff from our own cellar, old stuff like Sutter Home California Burgundy, which was not vintage-dated but must have been a million years old. We got out from time to time to some of New York's better wine restaurants. Once, we got a baby-sitter—a teenager lived next door, thank heavens—and went to the very hot Gotham Bar and Grill. There on the wine list, we were surprised and pleased to see an Atlas Peak Sangiovese, from California. It was $55—more than we were used to spending on wine, even at a restaurant—but this was a must-have wine.

There was a real irony in this bottle. So much of the California wine industry had been built by Italian immigrants and their children—the Martinis and Mondavis and Rafanellis and so many others whose names have been forgotten. At first, many of them planted Italian grapes that were familiar to them, and they often even gave their wines Italian names like Chianti. But as the years went by, most had turned to what California did best—classic French grapes like Cabernet Sauvignon and Chardonnay. Now the pendulum was swinging back. California winemakers were experimenting with Italian grapes, with some success. Sangiovese is the grape that makes Chianti in Tuscany. Atlas Peak was one of the pioneers of this trend, and its Sangiovese was a very hot wine. But we'd never seen it.

We often tell people that there are no guarantees in wine. Even if you buy a bottle that has been widely praised by wine writers, there's no telling if you will like it. We also always say that the only way to learn anything about wine is to take chances, especially in restaurants, which often offer wines that you can't find anywhere else. Even if you don't like the wine, it's always an experience. The Atlas Peak was a very special experience to us, our first taste of the hot new trend in California wine. We remember it, and we remember the meal because of it. In truth, though, we weren't much impressed by the wine. We found it a bit simple and thin, though with a hint of the lively fruit that makes Chianti so special.

We couldn't afford to go to Cellar in the Sky, and we felt a little funny about going anyway. Alan Lewis had died in 1991, and it couldn't possibly be the same. On the other hand, this was a shame because Cellar was now right across the street. We worked at the World Financial Center, which is part of Battery Park City. When the World Trade Center was being built, the earth that was displaced was used to create new land on the bank of the Hudson River. The idea was to build a whole new little town there, with offices and apartments. That became Battery Park City, and the *Journal* moved there while we were in Miami. John's office looked right across the street at the World Trade Center. In retrospect, we wish we could have gone to Cellar when we had the chance. On February 26, 1993, a huge *bang!* almost threw John out of his office chair. Big noises and even big bangs aren't that unusual in New York. There's always construction, always some sort of gas explosion somewhere, even an occasional building collapse. Soon, though, John saw smoke coming from underground at the World Trade Center. Terrorists had bombed the building. In the aftermath, Windows on the World, including Cellar in the Sky, was closed for renovations. When Windows on the World finally reopened more than three years later, Cellar as we knew it was gone. There was a larger restaurant called Cellar in the Sky, but it wasn't the same. In fact, it closed after a short time and then was replaced by a lovely spot called Wild Blue.

Even if we couldn't afford to buy much wine, we could dream. One day, John was looking at a wine publication and saw a remarkable ad for a wine store. The ad claimed that the store had bought the wine cellar of Martin Ray himself, the curmudgeon who, way back in the early sixties, believed that California could make great wine. This was way too exciting to pass up, especially because the prices seemed ridiculously cheap. Among the wines was a 1962 Pinot Noir. Wow. Way back then, everybody pretty much agreed that California could not make a good Pinot Noir. It was amazing that Martin Ray even tried it. Not only that, but our great old book, *The Signet Encyclopedia of Wine,* said this about the 1962: "QED!" It could have been worse, since the same book said of the 1964 Pinot Noir: "The winery rates this as their very best Pinot Noir. Well, at least nobody's been calling it plain awful. It will be at its best 1975 through 1985. Again, the price will almost certainly make it a poor value." Ouch!

The 1962 was selling for $29.95 a bottle, probably less than Martin Ray charged for it when it was released. We bought a case because this wine was part of history, and it was even from Martin Ray's cellar. We had it delivered and we waited exactly three weeks for the wine to calm down before we opened a bottle.

It's gorgeous. Rich Pinot nose. Sweet with fruit, almost aggressively sweet with just a hint of oak. Classy, with big fruit. Very Pinot, very much like a fine Burgundy. Remarkably, not even a hint of age. Ready to drink, but not a hint of overage. Spectacular. Equivalent of a terrific old Burgundy.

Martin Ray had been vilified during his lifetime for his arrogance, his vision, and even his prices. But as we drank this wine, we got increasingly giddy, and not because of the alcohol. Way back, Martin Ray really was making the greatest wines in California. It's just that they wouldn't really be ready to drink for thirty years. He knew it, and nobody believed him. He once said, in the book *Great Winemakers of California:* "I wish to God that I never had to sell any of my wines, that we could keep all the reds here as long as I live, because I know that *they'll* still be alive." As we drank the very last drops, we raised our glasses in toast. "To Martin Ray," we said. "You were right."

We didn't travel much with the girls, though there was one trip we had to take. The girls had not yet been to Walt Disney World, and the perfect occasion was coming up. The very first night the two of us spent at a hotel together was on Valentine's Day 1974, at Disney World. Disney World was new then, and there wasn't much to it, just two hotels and the Magic Kingdom. But John had been there once during college and thought it was fun, so for our very first Valentine's Day together, we made reservations at the Contemporary Resort ("the monorail runs right through it!"). This was a big step at the time, and we were nervous. It's Disney, after all. What would they think of an unmarried couple sharing a room? Dottie bought a wedding ring for her finger at the Salvation Army, we made the reservations as Mr. and Mrs. Brecher, and we showed up at check-in trying to look very serious and grown-up. We were actually twenty-two years old, looked younger, and were so obviously shaky that anyone who cared would have known we weren't married. But, of course, no one cared, and we got a ground-floor room for our very first night together in a hotel. We ordered room service and stayed in our room a lot. We didn't order wine.

What could be more perfect than to revisit Walt Disney World exactly twenty years later with our children? We made reservations at the Grand Floridian, which didn't even exist back in 1974, and spent weeks showing the girls pictures, buying Mickey autograph books, and shopping for warm-weather clothes in the middle of winter. The day we were set to fly out of La Guardia, there was a terrible snowstorm. When we arrived at the airport, there was a long line outside to check baggage. With Dottie and the girls waiting inside, John—dressed in just a light coat, since we were headed to Florida—stood outside for an hour. Just as he finally got to the front of the line, a voice came over a loudspeaker, announcing that our flight had been canceled. John went inside and explained to the girls that we'd have to go back home. Zoë, then just three, didn't really understand, but Media immediately broke into tears.

We went back home, where John worked the phones to get us on a flight the next day and Dottie peeled off the girls' sweaters and coats. While Dottie was undressing Media, she noticed some red bumps on Media's face and arms. Media said she felt fine. Both girls have sensitive skin, so we didn't panic. Dottie made the girls comfortable, then ran out to buy a chicken to make coq au vin. If we were going to be home for one more night, we might as well enjoy it. We opened a terrific old Burgundy, a 1983 Vougeot Premier Cru Les Cras from Mongeard-Mugneret.

Delicious. Round, rich, sweet and lovely. Just beautiful, some taste of the earth. Perfect right now. Chewy and red. Rich and velvety, every inch a Burgundy.

The next day, Media woke up with chicken pox all over her body. The Lord works in mysterious ways. If we had made it to Orlando, we would have been quarantined in our room at Disney World. We would have been spending hundreds of dollars a day to sit in a room and watch the Disney Channel. Plus, Zoë, who was perfectly well, would wonder why she couldn't go out and have fun, and if we did take her to the Magic Kingdom, Media, understandably, would go crazy. We felt that day that our luck really had changed.

When we finally got to Walt Disney World two months later, for our fifteenth wedding anniversary, we arrived at night at the Contemporary Hotel. Our room was on a high floor overlooking the Magic Kingdom. The girls crawled into bed, and we went out onto the room's patio with a bottle of wine that we'd tucked into our suitcase. As we began to open the bottle on a perfectly clear Florida night, fireworks exploded over the Magic Kingdom, and we poured one of the greatest wines of our lives, a 1979 Château Montrose from Bordeaux.

No one much cared about vintages when we first started drinking wine. Now people are obsessed with them. We always say it's not really something to worry about, that there are so many variables that it's impossible to say anything definitive about every wine from a certain vintage. Here was proof. Nineteen seventy-nine was a so-so year, and the Montrose was said to be a so-so wine. But this wine, which we'd bought for $9.99 in 1983, was a wonder.

Delicious! One of the all-time greats. Ephemeral yet fruity, with incredible class and complexity. Wood, fruit and cream combine for a taste that's perfect yet almost more imagined than real because it's so ephemeral, like soufflé. Long, memorable wood/fruit finish.

Was this at least partly because we were at Walt Disney World with our beautiful young daughters on a kind of twentieth anniversary, on a balcony on a balmy night with fireworks flashing over the Magic Kingdom? Well, as the girls would say, "Duh."

As our fortunes improved, we were able to get out to restaurants more often. There was a little place downtown, in the middle of nowhere, called Alison on Dominick that Joanne Lipman recommended to us. It was an intimate place where half the tables seemed to be filled with furtive couples with a secret. On the list was something we'd never seen before: Sarah's Vineyard Santa Clara County Chardonnay Lot II, 1992. We ordered it. We don't remember anything about the food that night, but we remember the wine. Although it was a Chardonnay, it just about blew our heads off. It was the most concentrated, richest, deepest Chardonnay we'd ever tasted, almost like drinking Chardonnay syrup. It was so unusual that John called the winery the next day to tell them how much we enjoyed it. A woman answered the phone. "Yeah, she produces good fruit," she said. It took John a while to realize "she" was the vineyard. Years later, we looked at the Sarah's Vineyard Web site and this is what it said: "The purpose of Sarah's Vineyard is to listen and allow the essence of the invisible world to be expressed to the highest level in the physical world."

Since we worked together, we could eat lunch together. Usually, we just ran to the cafeteria. But once, we decided to go to a charming place near work called Capsouto Frères. On the list was a wine from Robert Keenan Winery. That was the winery that made the terrific Chardonnay we'd tasted so many years before at the Coach House to celebrate Dottie's job at the *Times,* but we didn't see Keenan much anymore. What's more, the wine was a 1989 Cabernet Franc. Huh? We knew of Cabernet Franc primarily as a red blending grape in the great wines of Bordeaux. We'd never had a wine actually labeled "Cabernet Franc." (In the United States, where most good wines are labeled by grape type, a wine must contain at least 75 percent of a particular grape type to be called by that name.) We ordered it, and we were fascinated by the sharp, aggressive, almost cut-glass tastes of the wine. It was terrific.

When John returned to work, slightly off-kilter after drinking a half bottle of red wine for lunch, he called the winery to order more. The winemaker, a man named Matt, answered the phone. He sent a price list and John sent back a check, along with a note about that great Chardonnay so many years before. A couple of weeks later, our order arrived—along with a gift bottle. It was the 1978 Chardonnay, the very one that we'd had that night at the Coach House, the one that made us realize how truly great California Chardonnay could be. Written on the bottle, in gold pen, was this: "Here's to the memories! Matt & Bob."

Things move slowly at *The Wall Street Journal*—very, very

slowly. The paper is an institution, and it is treated as a kind of national trust by the family that owns it, which is why it's such an oasis of good journalism. Our readers expect to find essentially the same format day after day, year after year, and changing anything is risky. Just look at the name of the paper on the front page. Even *The New York Times* removed the period after its name in 1967. At the *Journal,* it's still there: *"The Wall Street Journal."* Even changing the name of one of our front-page columns, from "Labor Letter" to "Work Week," took months.

The *Journal* had been talking about a weekend section for years. Most other newspapers had weekend sections on Friday. They provided an outlet for all sorts of information people wanted, such as movie reviews and leisure activities, and also made a lot of money. A weekend section made even more sense for the *Journal,* which didn't publish on Saturday or Sunday. But the idea just kind of floated around, and around. By 1994, there seemed to be some energy behind it. Paul Steiger, the managing editor, believed strongly in the concept. But it would be a radical step. The *Journal* hadn't even broken into two sections until 1980, and became a three-section newspaper in 1988. "Weekend" would require a fourth section one day a week. This had all sorts of implications for the layout of the paper, the printing—a complex operation itself for a national newspaper—and for readers. After all, one thing readers liked about the *Journal* was that it was so compact. How would they feel about their *Journal* if it bulked up?

Everyone agreed on this much: If the *Journal* ever started a weekend section, the perfect person to run it would be Joanne Lipman. She had been a fine reporter, an excellent columnist, a great editor, and was close to Paul. Not only that, but she took pride in being a serious shopper, which would come in handy in a section that had to be, at least a bit, about how to spend money wisely.

In 1994, the *Journal* put its toe in the water, printing a page about residential homes, followed by pages about travel and sports. The Weekend section was becoming more real. One day, at Joanne and Tom's country house, Joanne looked at us very seriously and said, "If this Weekend section really gets off the ground and I'm running it, I'd really like you to write a wine column."

Sure, sure, we said, because we were convinced it never would get off the ground and, in any case, it seemed inconceivable to us that we would write a wine column. We'd never written a word about wine, except in our journals, and we really didn't want to. This might seem odd now, but we never talked that much about wine with other people, except our tasting companions. We talked sometimes about wine experiences—visits to wine country, getting lost in Italy, great meals—but we rarely talked about wine in a vacuum, as a discrete thing, because, frankly, that bored us. We've never been interested in talking about the latest vintage in Bordeaux, or whether too many wines are subject to malolactic fermentation, or whether the Santa Barbara area can grow fine wine. Wine, to us, was always just part of another story. Not only that, but it was a highly personal thing, an intimate pleasure.

In any event, most people who aren't passionate about wine don't really want to hear about it. It's a little bit like our children. Everyone knows we have two kids and we certainly talk about them from time to time, but no one wants to hear all of the details about their lives or see pictures. We'd never written about our children, and we never wanted to write about wine, either.

Joanne left Page One in 1996 to become Weekend editor, and John was sorry to see her go. She soon asked us to write some sample wine columns. She didn't say anything about money, and we didn't ask. We're not entirely sure why we went ahead with this. We still really didn't think this would ever get off the ground, so it seemed like it wouldn't hurt to humor Joanne, and we were so fond of her. Even if this did happen, it certainly wouldn't require much time or effort. And we thought maybe it would be a

nice little diversion after focusing on heavyweight, serious journalism for so many years. So we wrote a few practice columns for
Joanne. We explained how to conduct a wine tasting. We gave a
course in Chardonnay 101. We talked about how to prove to yourself that you're an expert.

Joanne was not impressed, and even though she had been
working for John just weeks earlier, she was tough enough to tell
us that. We respected her enough to know she was right. She had a
vision for the column, but it hadn't yet come into focus. One day,
she was looking at our mock columns and said: "Look, all I want
to know is what wine to pick up for dinner on the way home
tonight."

That was it. That was the key. Most of the wine bought
in America—we've heard estimates from 70 to more than 90
percent—is drunk within twenty-four hours of purchase. Joanne,
as a real consumer, had understood before we did that most people didn't want to be "educated" about wine. They didn't want to
become experts. They just wanted to know what wine to buy on
the way home that night or on the way to a dinner party. We realized that, in all the years of people in our offices asking us questions about wine, nobody had ever said, "Hey, tell me about
Chardonnay." They'd asked specific questions, such as "I'm going
to a friend's house for dinner and I'm supposed to bring wine.
What do I take?" Or "My wife just called and said we're having
roast pork for dinner and I should get the wine. What the hell do
I do?"

It was, as the cliché goes, a defining moment. We had one
more. Another of John's editors at the time was Steve Adler, the
special projects/investigative editor. Steve is a Harvard-trained
lawyer. His wife is a successful author. In other words, Steve is, in
many ways, a typical *Wall Street Journal* reader—good education,
good disposable income, worldly, but not a wine expert. This, simply, is what Steve told John: "I'm willing to spend thirty-five dol-

lars on a bottle of wine. I just don't want to get ripped off." Between Joanne and Steve, we now understood just how we should frame our advice.

Those two conversations crystallized our column. We were writing for smart, sophisticated people who just wanted to know enough to get a good wine for dinner. Price was important, but not as important as value.

The first issue of Weekend, including our first column, was scheduled for March 20, 1998—a month before our nineteenth anniversary and eight days after Media's ninth birthday.

TWENTY-ONE

Kunde Estate Winery Merlot 1995

...

ITH NO DISCUSSION, THE TWO OF US HAD DECIDED THAT we'd conduct blind tastings at home among wines we bought right off wine store shelves. It was the obvious thing to do. For years, we'd been frustrated reading reviews of great wines and then seeing, somewhere in agate type, something like: "50 cases made." It seemed to us that if we wrote about wines that were on shelves somewhere, that would be better. Readers might actually be able to buy them.

We bought the first wines for our column on January 30, 1998, at a familiar place. Years before, when we were living on Park Avenue South, we'd discovered an out-of-the-way liquor store called First Avenue Wines & Spirits that had a very nice collection of wine. We spent quite a bit of time there, discovering new things. We lived with the store through the construction of a back room, where the fine wines were going to be. They were always working on that room, and someday, they swore, it really would be open. When we returned to New York after an absence of six years, we walked back into First Avenue and it was like we'd never left. Everyone treated us like we'd been there the day before. The woman behind the counter asked Dottie about the train trip that Dottie had written about for *The New York Times* six years before. It really was as though time had stood still while we were away. The back room still wasn't open, though special customers like us could go back there and, amid all of the boxes, see some remarkable treasures.

We bought fifteen different bottles of American Merlot there, each one for $20 or less. We bought twenty Chardonnays, too, for our second column. That seemed like plenty to us. Our plan wasn't to write a "buying guide"—buy this one, don't buy that one—but simply to taste enough wines to give a general idea of what readers could expect to find at their stores and what they should demand in the way of quality. We conducted our first blind tasting on January 31. The girls put the bottles in brown-paper lunch bags and numbered them. This was going to be fun. We bought a little notebook to keep notes, and we took a page and numbered it 1 through 8, for the eight wines in our first "flight" of wines. Then we tasted them, taking notes just as we always had. "Green, a little off-putting." "More depth than most." "Very young, but with some guts." Of course, we rated them with our twenty-year-old rating scale, from "Yech" to "Delicious!" At the end of the night, we realized that we had eight bottles of wine that we'd barely touched, and we were having seven more the next night. There was just one thing to do with them.

We'd been drinking wines together for almost twenty years, and during that time, as far as we can recall, we'd drunk every sip of every bottle. After all, most good wines changed with each sip, as they got air, as the temperature changed, as our moods changed. We wanted to taste every drop. We once had a wine from

Massachusetts that was awful, but we never gave up on it. We wrote: "Took weeks to drink. Never was good. No fruit." But on January 31, 1998, we did the unthinkable. We poured eight bottles of wine down the sink. John did it while Dottie, unable to watch, left the room. Dottie isn't squeamish about anything. She's the one who picks up after the dog and kills the bugs and once picked up a dead mouse in our house in Coral Gables. But to this day, she cannot watch John pour out the wine.

People often ask us how we write our columns. We have very different strengths when it comes to wine. John has a good memory for wines. He remembers the names and something about the taste of most wines we've ever had. He has read all the wine books, too, and remembers obscure facts. Dottie has a good taste memory and a much more acute palate. She can instantly detect textures and nuances in wines that John misses. Not only that, but she has the charm—anyone who knows us would tell you that—and can talk about wine in a highly personal, understandable way that makes the tastes come alive. It's difficult to describe the way wines taste without referring to other wines—think about trying to describe colors without referring to other colors, or trying to describe the taste of a banana—but we felt that it was important for our audience that we try, and Dottie is able to accomplish that. Both of us are pretty good at picking up the tastes of various grapes that have been blended into wines. We can often identify the component parts.

We've always drunk wines and taken notes the same way: We drink them and talk about them, and as we talk John writes notes. There was no reason to change that now. We talked and John took notes. As an editor for many years, John can also write stories in his head. So by the time we were finished tasting and talking, the column was virtually written. To some extent, John just transcribed it. Dottie then went back and wrote through it, adding warmth, flavor, and charm.

Our first column was 851 words long. We didn't introduce ourselves, but just got right into it. "It's impossible to know how a wine suddenly gets 'hot.' We're old enough to remember the '70s, when everyone was ordering Pouilly-Fuissé from France. Before you knew it, Pouilly-Fuissé was arriving by the boatload, much of it awful and overpriced. And, of course, before long, the boom busted. . . . The current wine on everyone's lips is Merlot." Indeed, it was an amazing thing. All those years California winemakers had been trying to figure out what was the best wine for the United States, what would taste best and what people would buy—and it turned out to be a blending grape from Bordeaux. Some great Bordeaux wines are made primarily from Merlot, but mostly it's used to soften and tone down the Cabernet Sauvignon in great wines like Lafite and Latour. Merlot wasn't even known as a separate "varietal" wine in the United States until the early 1970s and didn't explode on the scene for another twenty years. But when it exploded, it took the United States by storm, turning millions of people into red-wine drinkers.

In that first column, we introduced our little family: "We opened the bottles, put them in brown bags and had our daughters, Media and Zoe, number them behind our backs so we'd have a blind tasting." Zoë's name didn't have the little dots over the *e* because the *Journal*'s antiquated computers couldn't do that.

When we first saw the column on the page, it was exciting. As an editor, John hadn't written under his own name for years, and our only joint bylines together had been a couple of pieces about train travel and our account of that New Year's Eve riot so many years ago in Miami Beach. We had never thought about a name for the column, but when we saw it on the page it was already labeled "Tastings." That was the art editor's idea. He had another idea: It would look better if we had some sort of chart. Since we said in the column that our best of tasting was from Kunde Estate Winery, and the best value was from Bogle Vineyards, why not do a chart with those and a few more? It made sense, so we did a little chart with prices and a few comments. The art director thought it would be funny—a kind of wry self-parody—to call it "The Dow Jones Merlot Index," and so we did.

Wine shops and winery owners told us much later that they felt the impact of our column the very first week, but we certainly weren't aware of it. People have a very close relationship with their *Wall Street Journal*—or, as many longtime readers call it, "the Wall Street." Some just read the front page, some just the editorial page, some just the markets page. They have a specific way of reading it, and they don't change easily. The Weekend section was brand-new, a fourth section in the back, and it seemed like most readers missed it. But it really didn't matter to us. We were just doing this for fun anyway. What we cared about were our "real" jobs, putting out Page One and writing about race issues.

In our second column, about Chardonnay, we mentioned our personal "Yech!" to "Delicious!" rating system and said that we'd rated our favorite a "Very Good/Delicious." When Joanne read that, she suggested that maybe we should include those ratings in the index. And so we did. We had no idea we were creating a monster. Within weeks, wine shop owners were calling to tell us that people—new customers, people who didn't usually go into wine shops—were coming in with the index, ripped out of the newspaper, and asking for "our" wines. The wine shop owners had never seen anything like it, and they wondered what in the world was going on. We received our very first fan letter, from a woman who just signed herself "Carol in Syracuse." She said she loved our approach, our suggestions, and our romantic view of wine. We found out only later that her name was Carol Jung and that she owned three photo-refinishing stores in Syracuse. A longtime reader of the *Journal,* she said she was excited to see Weekend Journal's debut, but was wary of the wine column. "I thought it would be snooty commentary on wine. But it was so down-to-earth, and it wasn't geared toward stockbrokers. It was approachable. I felt like it was speaking to me." As time went on, the letters continued to come in, a few every week, almost all of them charming and supportive.

To be sure, there were a few angry letters, but they were the most charming of all. They were from wine snobs, and they were frankly furious that we were trying to bring wine to the masses. Their tone was clear: "If we would have known you were going to tell everyone about the secret handshake, *we never would have shown you the secret handshake.*" Those letters, even more than the positive ones, convinced us that we were on the right track. Winemakers and winery owners increasingly began offering us "samples" of wine, free trips, and free lunches. We knew—we never even really talked about it—that we wouldn't do any of that. We wanted the wines, the same wines that anyone would buy off retail shelves, to speak for themselves. In any event, after being serious journalists for our whole lives, living with rigorous conflict-of-interest rules, why should wine writing be any different?

For the first few months, letters came to us addressed to Miss Gaiter and Mr. Brecher, but after a while, people wrote to us as "Dottie and John," like people they'd known for a long time. Pretty soon, invitations arrived from readers who wanted us to come to their homes to share their wines. We were so touched and flattered. A couple of businessmen mailed us the wine lists of restaurants where they planned to have corporate dinners, asking us to choose the wines. People started sending in recipes and asking us to choose the wines. For all our years as journalists, we'd rarely heard praise from readers—we were in the business to challenge them, after all—and now letters like this, from Nancy C. Nelson of Olympia, Washington, came every day: "Please know that your column has made a real and positive difference in my life. You have demystified wine for me. I am much more adventuresome now and willing to take a chance on the

262 ∾ *DOROTHY J. GAITER AND JOHN BRECHER*

great unknown. I rejoice in the wines I enjoy, and, just as importantly, no longer consider it a failure if I buy a glass or bottle that I don't particularly care for. It's all just a part of the adventure of life."

At the end of the year, we conducted a tasting of very expensive Champagnes—Dom Pérignon and such. We invited Joanne and Tom over and we dressed in formal attire. John and Tom even wore black tie. We tasted $1,094.89 worth of Champagne that night—the Cristal John proposed over, the Salon we touched to Media's lips, our beloved Taittinger. At the end of the night, the winner was a surprise, the Pol Roger Cuvée Sir Winston Churchill. Joanne had a photographer there that night, and our pictures appeared with our column on December 18, 1998. It was the first time most people learned we were an interracial couple. We didn't hear a word about it.

We were having fun with the column. The feedback we were receiving from our readers indicated that one reason they liked the column was because we were a couple enjoying life, and wine was just part of it. They enjoyed the romance. Dottie often says that most wine columns read like they're written by middle-aged white men who drink alone, and that's what makes our column so different. So John figured he could take a risk. Our twentieth wedding anniversary was coming up, one that called for something special. With the help of our editors, John hatched a plan. He would write Dottie a kind of love letter for our anniversary, and surprise her. The column ran on April 9, 1999, with pictures from our wedding—one of Dottie with her Dottie necklace around her neck, another of Kris, sitting next to the case of Taittinger, reading his "Big Cheeks" poem. People still mention that column. Almost two years later, we went to Wild Blue for the first time. That was the wine-oriented restaurant in the World Trade Center that, at least to some extent, replaced the great Cellar in the Sky. "Oh, my God," said the sommelier. "I know you from *The Wall Street*

Journal. You had pictures of your wedding." She turned to Dottie. "You had that beautiful picture with flowers in your hair."

When Dottie woke up on the morning of April 9, this is what she read:

> On April 14, 1979, in the backyard of Dorothy's family home in Tallahassee, Fla., we were married. There were 17 guests and 18 bottles of Taittinger Champagne, which we think is an appropriate ratio for a wedding. John's brother Jim kept the Champagne chilled in a big, concrete bird feeder. Dorothy's mother kept looking up to heaven, trying to see Dorothy's father looking down.
>
> Next Wednesday, we celebrate our 20th wedding anniversary. We'll probably do the same thing we did last summer, for another anniversary: the day we first met and fell in love 25 years ago. We'll make a reservation at the Marriott across the street, ask for a room with a view, and watch the sun set over New York Harbor while we eat room service and drink the wine we've brought. We'll definitely start with a bottle of Taittinger—not the fancy, expensive stuff, but the simple, nonvintage Champagne, the one from our wedding.
>
> The question is: What wine do we open next?
>
> Our anniversary has always been a time for one very special bottle. Sometimes we've gone to a restaurant and had something remarkable, like the never-to-be-forgotten Domaine Duchet Beaune Cent-Vignes 1969, from Burgundy, that we drank with duck for our first anniversary. Our anniversary bottle can be red or it can be white, but there has to be something special in the bottle. Sometimes, that something special is the wine itself; other times, it's just the memories.
>
> This column is usually a collaboration between us.

People always ask us who actually writes the column, and the answer really is both of us. By the time our tastings are completed, we've discussed the wines so thoroughly that the columns are already written, in our heads. This column, however, is an exception. John is writing it, and Dorothy hasn't been allowed to see it.

This makes sense. John has always chosen the wines for festive occasions. He's the keeper of the cellar and knows better what's in there. And, in any event, if Dottie had to choose among 700 wines, we'd still be deciding what to drink for our 10th wedding anniversary.

As we always say, wine isn't just about good taste and good tastes. It's also about romance and a good life. Every day should be an occasion of some sort, appropriate for a good bottle of wine. But there are some times that are very, very special, and they deserve a wine whose past should be part of your history, and whose present will become part of your future history together. One of the pleasures of knowing something about wine, and certainly one of the pleasures of having a wine collection, is that you can give a great deal of thought to what wine could possibly be appropriate to an event such as a 20th wedding anniversary.

So, with Dorothy at a doctor's appointment (herniated disc), John has spent hours in the wine closet, choosing some possibilities. After a great deal of thought, it has come down to these 10 bottles:

1. Robert Keenan Winery 1978 Chardonnay, from California. We first drank this in 1980 to celebrate Dottie's being hired by the New York Times. The wine was far better than the job, absolutely massive—rich, oaky, complex. Most California Chardonnays have

gone downhill after 21 years, but this is a likely exception. There can't be more than a few bottles of this left in the whole world.

2. Vasse Felix Margaret River 1979 Cabernet Sauvignon, from Australia. Wines from Australia are all the rage now, but back in 1984, when we bought this, we just listed it in our wine records under "Other Countries," such as Romania. Our experience with Australian wines indicates that they're so big and expressive that they just get better with age. We've never seen another bottle of this. And it's from our wedding year.

3. Grace Family Vineyards 1988 Cabernet Sauvignon, from California. Some California wines acquire cult status, which means they're impossible to find. Dorothy spent much of last Christmas season trying to find a bottle of this as a surprise present. It was very expensive—she won't say exactly how expensive—but it's a real treasure. Surely it could age longer, but we're dying to know what all the fuss is about.

4. Schneider Vineyards 1994 Cabernet Franc, from Long Island, N.Y., in magnum. Only 11 barrels of this wine were made, and only 12 magnums. We bought it at a charity auction—the only wine we've ever bought at auction—and asked the Schneiders, a young couple, to sign it. The North Fork of Long Island is one of our favorite spots, and this is one of the best wines ever made there. When we look at it, we think of eating just-caught lobster while our daughters, Media and Zoe, run on the beach.

5. Etrusco Rosso di Panzano 1983 (Cennatoio Winery), from Italy. Lost in a rainstorm in Tuscany, we took a wrong turn and found ourselves at a spectacular win-

ery that was closed. The next day, the elegant owner, who had every right to wonder who had knocked on his door unannounced, instead greeted us like long-lost friends. What followed was one of our most extraordinary winery visits ever, which ended with the owner giving us a basket full of giant fava beans to eat with dinner that night. This wine, which we carried back in our suitcase, was his pride and joy.

6. Sausal Winery 1980 Zinfandel, from California. We love California, and this label always makes us remember our visit there in 1987, for our eighth anniversary. We drank a bottle of this at the winery and were so blown away by it that, right there on the label of this second bottle, we scrawled: "Bought at winery 4/11/87. Tastes of green vines now. Drink 4/11/92 earliest." But we could never stand to open it.

7. Chateau Phelan-Segur 1970, from France. We collected 1970 Bordeaux wines once, and slowly drank them up. It was a fine year, and we tasted them as the wines softened and slowly developed into a majestic later life. We have been drinking them throughout our marriage. This is the last of our 1970s. Sure, for enough money, we could buy some more. But this is ours, one that we've cellared. When we drink it, our 1970 clarets will be gone.

8. Silver Oak 1972 Cabernet Sauvignon, from California. We bought this at the winery, even before we were married. It was the first release from Silver Oak, which later became very famous. The wine is probably way too old. But it once sat in our cellar in Coconut Grove, then in our racks in Manhattan, then in our wine room in Coral Gables and finally in our wine closet on Central Park West. The dust on that bottle is

dust from everywhere we've ever lived. We could never stand to wipe it off.

9. Heinrich Braun Niersteiner Pettenthal 1976 Riesling Trockenbeerenauslese, from Germany. There is nothing quite like a well-aged German wine, and complex, sweet German wines, such as the rare Trockenbeerenauslese, can taste, in time, like nothing else on earth. We wouldn't want to open this too soon, not after saving it all these years; but we wouldn't want to open it too late, either.

10. Monthelie ler Cru 1981, Eric Boussey, from France. This wine was never meant to age much. But we were in Monthelie, in Burgundy, and we walked into this tiny little winery where a young couple made a small amount of wonderful wine. They seemed as much in love as we were. Beatrice signed the bottle, and it's always seemed as if, as long as we kept the bottle, we could return to Burgundy whenever we wanted. On the other hand, if we let it go bad, what would Beatrice think?

Next Wednesday, after we finish the Taittinger, as the sun is setting over the Statue of Liberty and the Staten Island Ferry silently glides across New York Harbor, John wants to pull the second wine out of a bag and have Dottie look at it and, without a word, know everything he's thinking.

So, which one would you choose?

—*The Wall Street Journal,* April 9, 1999

The column was a big hit. It made readers realize, if they had not realized it before, that what we were writing was not really a wine column, but a column about much more than that. Readers called and wrote to ask which wine we'd chosen. But there was an unfortunate kicker to that column, one we couldn't have imagined. Dottie had been troubled for years by a bad disc in her neck. It had gotten to the point that her right hand and arm hurt all the time, and she seemed to have more and more trouble typing. The day that column appeared, the third neurosurgeon we saw agreed with the first two: Dottie needed an operation on her spine, and right away. On April 13, the day before our anniversary, he gave Dottie her latest scar, this one three inches up and down her neck. She came home from the hospital on our twentieth anniversary. We opened the German wine—not because it would have been our first choice, but because, with Dottie heavily medicated, we knew we could only drink a glassful, and we thought it would keep well in the refrigerator. Great German dessert wines can sometimes live forever, but this one, while quite good, was clearly going downhill.

Scotch color with green at the edges. Rich and dark look with minerals and prunes on nose. Dark, rich and very old. Lots of minerals and prunes on taste, with a long, sweet finish, surprisingly easy to drink.

Château Canon 1962

. . .

THE VOLUME OF LETTERS KEPT GROWING. WE DIDN'T have an e-mail address—we were still doing our "real" jobs, and we didn't have enough time to answer all the e-mails we might get—but we still received a steady stream of letters, and we answered every one. The column was generating big impact, attracting plenty of advertisers and giving the *Journal* "buzz" in a whole new area. It was drawing new readers, many of them women, whom the *Journal* had always had trouble pulling in. Weekend was a huge success, and Joanne's star was brighter than ever.

Some of the letters we received asked how long a certain bottle of wine should age, so we thought it would be a good idea to write a column about that. As examples, we decided to open some treasured selections from our own cellar to see how they were doing. Over several weeks, we opened great stuff—a 1980 Zinfandel, a 1976 German wine, a 1989 Château Margaux, a 1979

California Cabernet Sauvignon, a 1971 Amarone from Italy, a 1990 Burgundy, an old Chardonnay, and many more. Our idea was to write about these as examples of how wines age and how to figure out when to open them.

The column was much longer than usual, and our bosses worried that its bulk might scare off readers. But one thing we've learned as journalists is that you can never guess what impact a story will have. Sometimes we've been involved in dramatic stories that we were sure would stop the world, and they disappeared without a trace, as though they'd never run at all. Other times, we've written or edited a story that seemed inconsequential, or ponderous, or irrelevant, and we've been sure that no one would read it—and it got a huge response. It's impossible to tell. The response to our "aging your wines" column was surprising. We received dozens of heartfelt letters from people who had one special bottle of wine. They all wanted to know whether their particular bottle of wine was still good and, if so, when it would be ready to drink. (They also usually added, shyly, "How much is it worth?") We answered all of these letters the same way: Your bottle is priceless. It's impossible to know if it's still good until you open it. Stop waiting for a special occasion to open it and make the wine itself the special occasion. Make a special meal and celebrate the wine itself.

After we'd written this letter dozens of times, it struck us that if so many people wrote to us about this issue, it must be a widespread question. Instead of telling everybody individually about celebrating their bottle, why not just write a column with that advice for everybody? Not only would it be a useful service, but it would be an easy column that required no tasting. It would help to get us through August, too.

August is a dead period at the *Journal*. The assumption is that a great many of our readers are on vacation and not reading the paper, and those who are reading the paper are too tired from the heat to respond much to it. Beyond that, we needed to get some columns in the bag because we were about to spend a month in Napa and Sonoma with Media and Zoë, the first time we had gone there since they were born and the longest plane ride and longest vacation the four of us had ever taken together.

So before we left, we wrote a column in which we told people they should just open that bottle. We decided we'd set a date when we could all make a special dinner and open our bottles together. Saturday seemed like a good bet because people could spend the day preparing. The column introducing that idea would run August 20, and the date of the event was set for September 18. Because we wanted people to open that bottle they'd kept forever, we decided to call it, simply, "Open That Bottle Night." We turned in the column and flew to California.

We'd heard all about how the Napa Valley had been ruined. There was too much money, too many tourists, too many fancy restaurants, too much construction—even a wine train, for God's sake. It was more Disneyland, we had heard, than wine country. So we approached the trip with some trepidation. Would our own special place, our honeymoon paradise, be unrecognizable? The Harvest Inn, that charming little place in St. Helena, certainly was different. It was huge, with two pools, and now very expensive. We were given the Earl of Ecstasy suite, which seemed amusing with two young children in tow. Our patio in the back of the room extended right into a vineyard, where the grapes were green and purple and plump. Workers were pruning the yield—fewer grapes are more flavorful grapes—and they left massive bunches of grapes on the ground. The girls went out among the vines and picked them up and then stacked them on our patio while the sun set behind the mountains, just as it had when we'd had that bottle of Beaulieu Cabernet Sauvignon on our honeymoon. Forget the tourists and the money and the train. Napa was still the place we remembered.

Media and Zoë are very sweet kids, even more delightful than we could have imagined, but they're tired of going to wineries— we've dragged them through vineyards since they were born— so we had to compromise. We visited winery after winery in the morning, then did something fun for the girls in the afternoon. No one knew who we were, and we didn't let on. If people at wineries were going to be nice to us, we wanted them to be nice to us because they're nice people, not because we might do them some good. Some places, indeed, had become large and commercial. The people behind the counter were paid help, and they acted like it. They poured like robots and lacked any intimate knowledge of the wines. But so many of the wineries were just as we remembered, with passionate winemakers and winery owners behind the counter who were thrilled to have someone really want to talk to them about their art.

In both Napa and Sonoma, where we went next, we found people behind the counter who wanted to spend all day tasting with us—much to the girls' horror. It got to the point that the first question we asked at every winery was, "Do you have pets?" If so, that would keep the girls busy for a short while. One morning at ten o'clock, we dropped into a winery near our hotel called Sullivan Vineyards. We had met Mr. Sullivan years before, at a tasting in Miami that featured many wineries, and we still remembered his massive, muscular wines. We'd picked up his wines occasionally since then, but they were rarely available.

There was no sign of life at the winery, and no apparent visitors' entrance. There was something that looked like a barn, so we gingerly opened the door. There were two men inside, working. We asked if we were too early to taste their wines. We had no idea that, right there in the St. Helena phone book, next to Sullivan Vineyards it says, "By appointment only," and they didn't say anything about this. Then we asked if they had any pets. "Sure," they said, and they pointed to a puppy who had just wandered into the tasting room to check out the guests. "This is Zoë," they told the girls. This was a good sign. While Media and Zoë played with Zoë, the winemakers took out a couple of bottles and started pouring wine. We were totally surrounded by barrels, some marked "Minnesota" and some marked "Missouri." John asked what difference it made where the oak came from, and they went into a lengthy explanation of the difference among various kinds of American oak. Then Mr. Sullivan walked in. He was clearly surprised to see visitors, but John told him that we remembered him from that long-ago tasting, and he joined in.

Jim and JoAnna Sullivan met in college and got married in 1959. He was a successful graphic artist in Los Angeles and she was a court interpreter for the hearing-impaired. In the 1960s, they bought a home in Van Nuys that had what JoAnna calls "the most gorgeous arbor." The builder had become ill and never finished the landscaping, but her uncle Charlie, a farmer, visited one day and suggested they plant grapes. Charlie contacted the University of California at Davis, America's top wine school, and soon the Sullivans were inundated with boxes of brochures and a few vines. Intrigued, Jim started haunting the library and doing research and taking winemaking classes. He planted some vines. In 1962, while the vines were maturing, Jim and his best friend, Bob Morris, decided to try their hands at peach wine. The Sullivans had a peach tree that was particularly bountiful. The two men made a thorough mess of JoAnna's kitchen, but the wine they made lasted for ages. "The big debate," JoAnna told us later, "was whether we had enough money to buy a bottle of brandy to fortify it."

The next year, she said, "I put my foot down. I told them we can't do peaches again. The mess was so incredible—all of my pots and strainers were covered in peach pulp for days. They used every utensil I owned. I'm still missing some of them." So Jim went out and bought grapes—table grapes, because he couldn't buy quality wine grapes. They smashed the grapes with their feet—their daughters helped—and served the wine they made at "great big Italian dinners." Every year, JoAnna said, more and more people got involved. "It was a wonderful ritual. The bottles of wines that Jim was making had wonderful characteristics that showed that he could really be a winemaker."

"It started out as a hobby. I just read and read and tasted wine and tasted wine," Jim recalled. "In the early sixties there were not many books about winemaking in America, so I began reading about winemaking in Europe and having a lot of fun with the history.

"I was making fifty to sixty bottles a year. I had tasted better, but what I made was good *vin ordinaire* and I kept saying I could do better if I had better grapes." He read in 1968 that that year marked the first time dry American wines outsold sweet wines and he knew that was an important turning point. "I spent three years looking for the right soil, climate, the right place, and it was in Napa. I searched along the coast from Santa Barbara. Every county had an agricultural adviser, and you'd just talk to him and then you'd talk to real estate people and you'd narrow it down. I'd go up to old farmhouses and talk to the people there about property that might be for sale." That's how he found their first four acres.

Jim was still working as a graphic artist during this time, which had its own stresses and strains. He'd go to Napa once a month to plant the first Cabernet Sauvignon vineyard while JoAnna would go out looking for more property to buy. JoAnna is a gentle soul, intuitive and empathetic, so she was uniquely suited to find the right type of land. "There are some areas that have feeling. Some areas feel depressed, some feel really happy. You know it when you see it. It's magical," Jim explained.

In 1978, they bought a large chunk of land, and Jim began to phase out his design business. He planted, drove his tractor, and worked the soil. He hired help to dig holes and to build trellises.

There was never any question of what they would plant. As Jim sees it, "Even the best bottle of Pinot Noir ever made always wished it was Cabernet Sauvignon," he said. "I enjoy wine, all of it, but when you plant, you're planting something for a long time. I just didn't feel like planting Petite Sirah. I wasn't in it to make a big profit as a farmer. The wine was the goal, and you had to grow the grapes your way in order to make the wine right. It was extremely hard and I would go out every day and say, 'This is too big.' But you'd be surprised. You get it done."

In 1981, they made their first wines to sell. They were selling some grapes to small wineries and making their own, but it was financially hard deep into the 1980s. "It took so much time to go to banks and make presentations. They were putting the money into junk bonds and they weren't lending it out to anybody," Jim said. "I owned the property free and clear and I owned my house, but I had no mortgage and I couldn't get one. I was two or three years ahead of some of the other winemakers. I quit my full-time job and they hadn't. All of these wineries had pretty much the same hump to get over with the banks, but some had more collateral and were slicker talkers. I went to Robert Mondavi and showed him my plans and asked what I was doing wrong, and he said he was having trouble, too, on a different level."

What he and Mondavi and some of the winemakers of their time take pride in is that "we taught the banks how to lend money to wineries. We taught them, 'You *can* get paid back.' " The key was finding bankers who followed their business plans and projections over time and saw that they were right on target.

The Sullivans' winery grew as their family grew. They have five children and are planning to add a new building soon because they want to grow from four thousand cases to around seven thousand a year. They have a loyal following and sell most of their wines to visitors and wine club members. Looking back, Jim said, "I can forget the hard part. The overall experience is really fulfilling. It's unbelievable. You get your feet in the dirt and you don't want to pull them out. There's a passion there."

All month in Napa and Sonoma, we met people like the Sullivans. We did take along a laptop computer and worked when we could. But the best part was being able to spend four weeks talking with Zoë and Media and delighting in their first crush—the Backstreet Boys—and their growing interest in the music of their generation, like Britney Spears, Christina Aguilera, Pearl Jam, Destiny's Child, and Mariah Carey. We listened to pop music the whole time and felt like real Californians driving down the highway all singing together.

In the whole month, we spent just five hours away from the kids. That was the night we went to Thomas Keller's restaurant, the French Laundry. It's renowned as one of America's best restaurants, and we were determined to get there, but it wasn't easy. Calling weeks before our trip, John tried for days to get through to make reservations, but the phone was always busy. He finally sent a pleading letter, offering to come whenever they wanted us there (and not identifying us as writers, of course). They finally called back with a time. We got all dressed up, left the kids with a baby-sitter recommended by the inn, and headed to Yountville—where we could not find the restaurant. We drove up and down the street and couldn't possibly imagine how we could be missing one of America's most famous restaurants. We finally got out and walked. The French Laundry turned out to be a small house on the corner, with no sign and not much evidence of life outside.

Inside was different. When the sommelier came around and asked if he could help us, we said, "Sure, why don't you pair each course with a different wine? Wine is our hobby. We like trying new and different things." Dottie leaned toward him and said, "Just one thing. It can't be boring. This is a rare night out without kids. Surprise us." Then John told him, "You should have fun." The sommelier blinked and said, "No one has ever told *me* to have fun before." He gave us a hard look, then left.

We've given these same instructions to sommeliers at some of America's great restaurants. About half the time, they've brought us middling wines. We don't know if they dumbed down their selections because they're not very adventurous or if they misread us. The greats rise to the occasion. The French Laundry's sommelier took us at our word, bless him. What he brought to us throughout the night was stunning stuff. First, a flute of Champagne with the restaurant's signature starter, a tiny ice cream cone piled high with salmon tartare. What a funny and thoroughly delicious presentation. Then we moved on to "Oysters and Pearls" on tapioca, a plump oyster with osetra caviar on a dollop of tapioca. The egg cup of white truffle–infused custard was a wonder. And as the food progressed in complexity and weight, from lobster to foie gras and from quail to lamb and on to the cheese course, the wines he selected became more complex and heavier. Some he poured from half bottles—the restaurant prides itself on its half-bottle list—and some from full-size bottles.

And then it happened.

When dessert came out, the sommelier appeared with a tall half bottle of something we'd never seen before, a late-harvest Semillon from Swanson Winery. We knew that the winery, which is owned by the heir to Swanson Foods, made good wines, and we knew that Semillon is the grape that goes into some of the greatest dessert wines on the planet. But we'd never seen this wine.

We'd had a magnificent dinner. The wines had been delicious, interesting, and fun, the service excellent. And now, when we tasted this wine, it brought us close to tears. It engaged all of our senses, made us humble before its beauty. It was sweet, yes, but with a certain weight, an enriching taste of the earth, that gave it a kind of comfortable majesty. We're thankful that through all of our years of drinking wine, we have remained open to the wonderment of it, and that we continue to be touched deeply by it. We savor the taste of that wine to this day.

We returned to work just as the first "Open That Bottle Night" column appeared, the one that introduced the idea and told people when and how to open that special bottle. We didn't think much about that column, and none of our editors said anything about it. It was mid-August, after all, but at least the column got us through a week. Soon after it ran, we received our very first letter. It was from Jeff Bloom of Vienna, Virginia. He said he would be out of town for "Open That Bottle Night," so he and his wife, Cindi, celebrated early. Jeff explained that he and Cindi started their cellar in 1985 with three bottles of 1982 Bordeaux, but as their collection grew, they never opened those three seminal bottles. For "Open That Bottle Night," they decided the time had come, and chose the Pichon-Lalande. "The dinner was designed to complement the wine, not overpower it," Jeff wrote. "Cindi found a great recipe for prime rib with a roasted garlic and horseradish crust. The dinner was by candlelight, with well-thought-out music replacing the TV. I'm pleased to report both the wine and the dinner were fantastic. We saved a glass for drinking after cleaning up, and it was better than any dessert we could have had.

"Without going into unnecessary detail, let me conclude by saying romance ensued. Thank you for a wonderful idea."

We couldn't stop laughing. The whole column had been worth it just for that letter. We printed a small excerpt from it just before "Open That Bottle Night," despite our concerns that the top editors of the *Journal,* who have never been very comfortable with sexual references in the paper, might recoil.

For "Open That Bottle Night," we invited over Dottie's cousin Jon Smith and his wife, Wendy. Dottie made her famous roast duck. We opened several vintages of Château Musar, which is one of our favorite little secrets. It's a red wine from Lebanon, and even during the worst of Lebanon's troubles, it was still produced in the Bekaa Valley. We first saw it in a wine shop in New York in 1982. Figuring that $7.45 wasn't too much of a risk for a whole new wine—and from the 1972 vintage, no less—we took a chance. We drank it during an opera in Central Park later that month, and we loved it. It was so very different from anything we'd ever had, with the structure and class of a Bordeaux, but very different tastes. We saw it at outrageous prices from time to time—$5.25 for the 1975, just $2.99 for the 1977. We began to buy them faster than we drank them, and a collection was born. The problem was that, as the years went on, Château Musar became so special to us that we never opened a bottle. It was a classic "Open That Bottle Night" situation.

We had a lovely time that night. We took copious notes about our night so that, if we received no response from readers, we could still write a follow-up column about our own experiences. Over the next few days, we were relieved when five letters arrived with remarkably detailed accounts of the food, the company, and most notably, the special wines. At the end of the week, John told Dottie: "I think we have enough now." He began to rough out a column.

The next week was one of the most extraordinary of our lives. Remember that scene in *Miracle on 34th Street,* in the courtroom, when the mailmen come in with sacks and sacks of mail addressed to Santa Claus? Well, that's what it was like. Kids from the mailroom kept arriving at our desks with stacks of mail. The tops of our desks were filled with envelopes. We took them all home to read. After the girls were in bed, we opened them and read them to each other. Each one was more moving, or funnier, than the last. People from all over the world were sharing what was in their hearts with us, all because of wine. Most of the letters were long.

Many were handwritten. Quite a few included menus and recipes and labels from the bottles. We responded to every one. John sat at the computer and composed letters. Dottie addressed the envelopes until her hand hurt so badly that she had to stop. For almost two weeks, we stayed up until two A.M. every night answering letters. Then we were back at work at nine A.M. at our "real" jobs.

We went from worrying that we wouldn't have enough material to worrying that we had too much. John began leaving a few of the letters on Joanne's desk. With each new delivery, she decided we could have more space—and more and more. By the time the flood ended, we had more than a thousand letters, and Joanne had opened up two entire pages for the column. Still, it was hard to decide which of all of the letters we should include. We did our best. Our follow-up story appeared on October 8. This was it:

> *"I can only express one regret. Had we found an occasion last year to open this great 'gift of the grape,' my bride of over 50 years could have been present to enjoy this event in person rather than in spirit only."*
>
> —JOHN WATSON OF MAPLE GLEN, PA.

> *"As we sipped the wine with its wonderful taste, we suddenly realized that we had been sitting, talking and enjoying the wine, food and each other for over 2½ hours."*
>
> —MICHAEL HUHNDORF OF TUSTIN, CALIF.

> *"Suddenly, the entire house shook, accompanied by a loud noise. Yale ran to the back of the house to discover that a large oak tree had fallen onto the house and deck. 'What are we going to do now?' asked Yale, shaken by the thunderous arrival of Hurricane Floyd. 'We are going to open the wine,' answered Ilene."*
>
> —YALE AND ILENE RICHMOND OF HAMPTON, N.J.

...

That's exactly what thousands of readers, from all over the world, did on the evening of Sept. 18. It was "Open That Bottle Night," when we urged you to open the wine you've been saving for a special occasion, and make the bottle itself the reason for a celebration.

The response was overwhelming. People drank special old wines and special young wines, wines they saved from their weddings 50 years ago and wines they made themselves last year. They drank expensive Bordeaux and Nebraska Chardonnay, and they drank while watching a football game on television and a sunset in Maui. Many of the wines were valuable, but many more were priceless, especially the ones used to toast and remember a departed father, mother-in-law or child.

Many people created an occasion around the event, a time to commune with friends and family—sometimes in person, sometimes by speakerphone and sometimes just by thought. We received nearly 1,000 letters detailing remarkable nights of wine, food and memories. The letters were sometimes funny and often moving, notably rich in romance and notably lacking in cynicism or snobbery. We laughed when we read some, cried when we read others, savored the menus and could almost taste the wine. The message in these bottles was clear: There's more to every wine than an alcoholic beverage. As letter after letter pointed out, wine can conjure up memories in a way that few other things can.

In fact, few readers found the bottle of wine itself to be some transcendent experience. In most cases, it was the story behind the bottle that they wanted to share.

...

"After my father died in 1990, my mother decided to sell the house they had shared for more than 40 years and where they had raised their three children. In the basement she found one bottle of 1962 Chateau Canon in a cabinet next to my father's workbench.

"Why he had purchased a grand cru Bordeaux is a mystery. Such was not his normal fare . . . Knowing him, Dad likely had second thoughts about such a purchase and put the bottle away for some truly special occasion. At some point, I imagine he just forgot about it.

"Last Saturday night, my mother, together with my family, gathered around our kitchen table to 'open that bottle.' I told all not to get their hopes up since I researched the vintage and saw that 1962 was a pretty mediocre year. And then I opened the bottle. We knew in an instant that the wine was still good. It was then that I sensed that there may indeed have been a purpose why my father hadn't opened that bottle all those years before. He had left it for us—in its fading beauty—to remember him by."

—BRUCE ANGIOLILLO OF OLD GREENWICH, CONN.

Some wines brought back recollections of a dear friend, a trip to Provence, a lost love. For Jeffrey Smith, of Atlanta, a special bottle reminded him of the young woman he met a dozen years ago, when they were both just out of college, and both neophyte wine buffs. After a brief romance, he was transferred across the country, but before he left, he gave her a bottle of Burgundy from her birth year, 1964. They drifted apart for more than a decade, while he worked abroad.

Two years ago, he came back to the U.S. He found her, romanced her and, late last year, married her. "Johnna still had that old bottle of wine," he wrote. For Open That Bottle Night, they shared it.

There were all kinds of things to commemorate: weddings, anniversaries, a friend's successful knee replacement, a 77th birthday. Michelle and Alan Morris from Mebane, N.C., drank a bottle of Black Dog semi-dry red wine from Chateau Morrisette Winery in Virginia, in tribute to their "beloved Black Labrador Retriever, Angus," who passed away in July.

Others decided there was no reason to wait for a special occasion. While living in Italy in 1973, Carol Perkin Barsin of Charlotte, N.C., bought 12 cases of Grignolino shortly after the birth of her son, hoping to drink them one day at his wedding. "Now, 26 years and four houses later, I've decided not to wait for my son's wedding," she wrote. "After all, he's not even dating and I'm not getting any younger." (The wine was "superb," she added. "Heck, who cares if my son ever gets married? I could finish all 12 cases on my own.")

Where people drank their wine was almost as interesting as what they drank. David and Kay Walters had a 1993 Nuits St. Georges on their veranda in Thailand. Sunny and Natasha Mahajan drank a 1985 Chateau Meyney— from plastic cups—on a gondola ride in Venice. A surprising number of you drank wine in hot tubs.

Paul Foley of Woodcliff Lake, N.J., set up a conference call with a cousin, Jay Lawrence, of Guthrie, Okla., during which they both drank well-aged German wines and talked about old times. Michael and Renay Fanelli, of San Anselmo, Calif., tipped their glasses after a 25-kilometer trek through the high Sierras. "When not gasping for oxygen, or concentrating on the ability to stay vertical, thoughts constantly drifted to the evening's reward," Mr. Fanelli wrote. The payoff: a Martinelli 1997 Russian River Valley Jackass Hill Zinfandel.

The payoff for Michelle L. Russey was even greater. She and her boyfriend prepared a meal together to go with their bottle. "It was a lovely, crisp evening in Chicago, so we had a fire going in the fireplace, along with candles and fresh flowers. Dinner was wonderful, and the 1996 De Loach Zinfandel was every bit as smooth and flavorful as I hoped it would be.

"Well, the evening turned out to be more special than I had anticipated. After we finished eating, but were still savoring the last drops of our wine, Bob proposed to me." Michelle said yes.

While we love all romantic stories, we felt special empathy for couples who have difficulty finding the time and the energy for romance after having children—or, as William N. Evans of McLean, Va., put it: "A special dinner at home with my wife faces three obstacles—Conor (age 9), Brendan (6) and Patrick (2). Thankfully, Sept. 18 was the first day of the fall soccer season, so our two oldest collapsed early, allowing us to have a peaceful and relaxing dinner."

In the old days, before kids, Bill and Ellen Pullin of Evanston, Ill., used to have special nights when he would buy Brie and she would make "Harvest Grape Loaf, a beautiful and delicious homemade-bread creation, delicately seasoned with cardamom and Grand Marnier, and made in the shape of a bunch of grapes with its leaves." On Open That Bottle Night, they decided to open "our treasured 1970 Chateau Palmer." He surprised Ellen with a wedge of triple-cream Brie—"and Ellen surprised me by making a Harvest Grape Loaf."

As it turned out, food often seemed to play a bigger part in readers' evenings than wine did. We were impressed by the detailed menus readers sent in. Some even enclosed recipes and snapshots of the meals they made.

Readers prepared elaborate meals of caviar, Oysters Rockefeller and filet mignon. Lamb seemed to be a popular choice—lamb stew, rack of lamb, lamb salad and even lamb fries, which Ronald A. White of Tulsa, Okla., informed us "are thinly-sliced sheep testicles, slightly breaded and then sauteed or fried."

One reader started with gator, while another opened his bottle at a wiener roast. ("The wine's label suggested it would go well with roasts, so we continued to roast hot dogs as we drank the wine.") Mario and Marilyn Ruiz, of Miramar, Fla., drank their Chateau Latour 1986 with pizza—fetched from a sentimental-favorite pizzeria, Sir Pizza, after a two-hour-and-15-minute round trip. "The pizza was great," wrote Mr. Ruiz. "The Chateau Latour was good, not great. But it got better toward the end of our meal, and much better as we entered the Jacuzzi with Mr. Barry White in the background."

The special wines readers opened came in all price ranges. Many, like the Ruizes, drank fine "first growths" from Bordeaux. From the U.S., Silver Oak and Jordan Cabernet Sauvignons were a common treat.

Joan and Phil Huff of Louisville, Ky., finally opened a bottle of their homemade "Spanish Red" from 1970. "Yes, it was past its prime (if it ever had one)," they wrote, "but it was still palatable and, most important, it was 1970 once again!"

Some wines turned out to be just too precious: When push came to shove, Robert and Norma Trojan, of Caledonia, Ill., simply couldn't stand to open their 1958 Chateau Haut-Brion. They drank beer instead.

One of the oldest wines we heard about was opened by assistant principal oboe player Alexander Miller and violist Mary Jane Slawinski, of the Grand Rapids Symphony in Grand Rapids, Mich. They were "stuck playing Tchaikovsky's 5th Symphony on Sept. 18," Mr. Miller says, then came home and drank a Madeira from 1827. "It is incomprehensible to us how something 172 years old can still taste so alive, so full of tangy fruit, with aromas of lime blossoms, caramel, coffee . . . and be even a little sassy!"

Kenneth Giniger of New York City opened an 1830 Morgador Port. He and his guests found it "delightful," he wrote, while noting they had no standard of comparison—"none of us having ever tasted a 169-year-old wine of any kind before."

To be sure, there were disappointments. Victor Bonomo of Wilton, Conn., opened a treasured bottle of 1961 Chateau Haut-Brion. "The wine was badly over the hill," he wrote. "The good news is that after 50 years of marriage, the romance is still there." After opening a bottle of 1978 Chateau Margaux, Timothy Paul Brausen of Minneapolis thought it was a letdown. "Like seeing the Rolling Stones in concert these past few years, the myth seemed to exceed reality." Some old wines had turned to vinegar. A special Champagne was flat. Many bottles had crumbling corks, prompting industrious drinkers to decant them using all sorts of devices: a coffee filter, a bandana, a Gatorade bottle.

Readers bore the disasters with exceptional good humor. In Scotland, Humphrey Drummond retrieved a 1932 Chateau Margaux from the cellar of Megginch Castle—and dropped it. "All I could do was to soak as much as I could into my handkerchief and suck away the heavenly juice," he wrote.

Todd Buonocore, of Kennett Square, Pa., saw his plans for a romantic evening smashed. The flowers were arranged, the house was neat, and the flank steak was marinating. Then his date called to say she was running late. When he went to pick her up, he says, he found out why: "She was drunk! Seems she was at Oktoberfest with some of her girlfriends," he explains.

Since he'd already opened his special bottle of 1992 Caymus Cabernet Sauvignon at home to allow it to breathe, he went ahead with his date. "The evening was going well," he wrote, "the wine was vibrant, the mouthfeel luscious," until his woozy dinner companion reached for another glass—and spilled the rest of the red wine onto the floor. "Know anyone who is shopping for peach carpeting with shades of rust?" Mr. Buonocore asked.

Covert Harris of Clifton Park, N.Y., had better luck with his date—if not his bottle.

"I came home from work on Sept. 18 and left my white shirt on—even kept it buttoned at the collar. 1985 Cheval Blanc is nothing to take casually. I snuck into the basement and came up with the hallowed bottle I thought I would never drink. My wife had on her apron and was facing the sink, with her back to me. She had no idea what I was about to do."

But he struggled to open the bottle, causing "a fire-hose blast of wine" to come shooting out. "The amber liquid covered my face, hair, white shirt and about half of the kitchen.

"For a moment I was really angry. But then, this most magnificent bouquet and glow came over the whole kitchen. In its presence, my wife turned to face the source with an expression of wonder and awe. 'It's Cheval Blanc,' I said. My wife instantly perceived the situation and asked only, 'How much is left?'

" 'Enough,' I said, and we sat down at the kitchen table and drank the wondrous bottle."

Why are all of these old wines still sitting around? Some of them evoked such powerful memories that no occasion seemed big enough. Many were like the 1974 Brunello di Montalcino drunk by Elizabeth and Patrick Schirmer of Seattle, as the sun set over the Olympic Mountains. "We received it from a friend when we were married in 1985," they wrote. "He told us to save it for a special night. We immediately became afraid of it, and it has been gathering dust ever since." As Dave Wible and Mary Cusick of Columbus, Ohio, aptly put it about a 1971 Kenwood Cabernet Sauvignon, "We promptly stored the wine in our cellar, which is tantamount to a life sentence in jail."

On Open That Bottle Night, those special wines were freed, and lifted in toasts of all kinds. James W. Kairies, a Vietnam veteran from Dallas, opened a bottle he bought during an emotional visit to World War II battlegrounds in France. "My family and I opened that bottle and toasted the courage of paratroopers everywhere, and especially the incredible heroism of those young boys who dropped into occupied France that cold June night and saved the world."

Thomas McGill, of North Caldwell, N.J., opened a 1927 dessert wine from Cyprus given to him by his mother-in-law, who died on Aug. 23 at the age of 89. "So here's to you, Mom Olson," he wrote. "Thanks for the wine and for the many fond memories."

For Mark and Linda Madsen of Goffstown, N.H., the wine became a reason to celebrate the short life of their son Craig, who died two years ago. They began drinking good wine after he was diagnosed on his first birthday, Nov. 24, 1993, with fatal Tay-Sachs disease.

"To help ease our pain and allow us to enjoy the short time we would have with Craig, we decided we would bring the world to us instead of going out to visit the world. So we started our travels and went around the world trying different wines from every corner of the globe.

"The wine I selected for Open That Bottle Night was a 1994 Conn Creek Anthology from Napa Valley. I selected this wine because it was purchased on the first anniversary of Craig's passing, which was early morning of Easter Sunday, March 30, 1997.

"In Craig's memory, we toasted him and his healthy younger brother, two-year-old Peter Craig (who was toasting with milk), and enjoyed our bottle . . . Thanks for giving us another reason to celebrate our son's short life and remember the good things God has granted each of us."

Peter A. S. Pfeiffer, of Alpharetta, Ga., was also thinking about the important things in life.

"Christmas 1984, my father (who was my best friend) presented to his three sons a bottle of cognac to save for a 'special occasion.' Dad couldn't afford much, but he really wanted us to remember him as we opened these bottles. Well, my two brothers finished the stuff within a week. I decided to wait . . .

"Dad always wanted me to have a son. He never saw the day. You see, we lost several babies. Ten miscarriages and a stillborn. But we persevered through the years. I came close to opening the bottle to have a lonely one with Dad in his spirit many times, but I held off . . . We were blessed with a beautiful girl who we loved dearly and were thankful for.

"[Then on] 3 September we were told to go to the

hospital as our 13th pregnancy looked to be in danger. We had a C-section and out came a healthy baby boy. My 40th birthday was two weeks later, 17 September. I opened the bottle of cognac—finally. After 15 years.

"I can afford some of the finer things in life. I never could share them with Dad; he died before I started to peak. But while my wife was still in the hospital recovering, and my daughter was tucked in to bed, I closed the office door at home, played some soft music, dimmed the lights, put up a framed picture of my Dad and me together at the beach, sat in my leather chair, and had a toast (with this newly opened cognac) to my new son—for Dad. I know he was with me that night in spirit.

"I cried so hard, but I was so happy. That night was one that I'll never forget."

Good times should be savored as often as possible; they heal and help make us whole. "Thanks for the encouragement to make life itself the reason to celebrate!" wrote Joe and Pamela Hodonsky of Stanwood, Wash. And Diane Kopscick of Lewis Center, Ohio, said succinctly, "Drink it, don't revere it! That's what we learned."

The lesson here, then, is pretty simple: What are you waiting for?

Perhaps readers Maryanne and Ray Bunch, of Exton, Pa., said it best: "With our first sip, we realized many things about ourselves. Like the wine, we managed to survive the changing climates and conditions. Although not as vibrant as we once were, we have mellowed and matured with age and our marriage still retains a very special flavor. We toasted a breathtaking sunset, wine lovers everywhere, and, of course, each other."

—*The Wall Street Journal*, October 8, 1999

Our follow-up story brought a whole new raft of letters from people who were moved by the other stories. Dozens of people asked us when the next "Open That Bottle Night" would be. The *Journal* nominated the column for a Pulitzer Prize. To our surprise, we had created a community. People wrote in asking for other readers' recipes and we got them and passed them along, starting friendships. We received the most requests for the recipe for Harvest Grape Loaf. Ellen Pullin says the recipe isn't original—she got it out of a magazine thirty years ago and has fiddled with it over time. It has become a special part of her repertoire.

HARVEST GRAPE LOAF

2½ to 3 cups all-purpose flour

1 package active dry yeast

¼ teaspoon ground cardamom

¼ teaspoon ground nutmeg

¾ cup milk

¼ cup sugar

3 tablespoons butter or margarine

1 teaspoon salt

2 tablespoons orange liqueur or orange juice

2 egg whites, separated

Poppy seeds (for decoration)

Additional sugar (for decoration)

1. *Combine 1¼ cups of the flour, the yeast, cardamom, and nutmeg. Heat together the milk, sugar, butter or margarine, and salt till warm (115°F to 120°F) and butter is almost melted. Add the warm liquid, liqueur or orange juice, and*

one egg white to the dry ingredients. Beat at the low speed of an electric mixer for ½ minute, scraping the sides of the bowl. Beat 3 minutes at high speed. By hand, stir in as much of the remaining flour as possible.

2. Turn out onto a lightly floured surface. Knead in enough of the remaining flour to make a moderately stiff dough that is smooth and elastic (5 to 8 minutes). Place dough in a greased bowl; turn once to grease surface.

3. Cover with plastic wrap, or a damp towel, and let rise in a warm place until doubled (about 1 hour). Punch dough down; let dough rest 10 minutes. Remove one fourth of the dough; cover and set aside. Using the remaining dough, shape it into 30 one-inch balls. Arrange on a greased baking sheet in the shape of a bunch of grapes. Brush with mixture of remaining egg white beaten with 1 tablespoon of water; sprinkle with poppy seeds, if desired. On lightly floured surface, roll the reserved dough to an 8x4-inch rectangle; cut in half crosswise. Cut each square in half diagonally to form grape leaves. Position shaped leaves atop the widest end of the bunch of "grapes." Brush the leaves with the egg white mixture; sprinkle with additional sugar. Cover loosely; let rise in a warm place till nearly doubled (30 to 40 minutes). With a very sharp knife, slash ribs in the leaves.

4. Preheat the oven to 375°F and bake for 20 to 25 minutes or until the bread tests done. Remove from the baking sheet; cool on a wire rack. Serve the bread warm or cool. Let your guests serve themselves by pulling off pieces of bread.

The ripples from "Open That Bottle Night" seemed to last forever. Months later, when we were signing copies of our first book, *The Wall Street Journal Guide to Wine,* at Zachy's, a wine store in Scarsdale, New York, a man and his young son finally reached the front of the line. The man put out his hand and said, "Hello, I'm Bruce Angiolillo." We thought for a minute and remembered—he was the man from "Open That Bottle Night" who had opened the old bottle of Bordeaux left behind by his father. He held out a bottle. "This is my father's bottle," he told us. "I want you to have it." We protested that we couldn't possibly take something so precious. "We have the memories," Mr. Angiolillo replied. "We don't need the bottle."

Hundreds of wine bottles, full and empty, flow through our offices at work. But there is only one on display. It is a Château Canon 1962 and this is written on the label: "To Dorothy and John, Many thanks for a wonderful idea. Bruce Angiolillo."

TWENTY-THREE

Monterra Syrah 1996

. . .

EVERYTHING WENT CRAZY AFTER "OPEN THAT BOTTLE Night." People who had never noticed the column became readers. Joanne's massive display of the column—it started on the front of the Weekend section with a beautiful picture of a huge glass of red wine—had attracted them, and they'd discovered that this was not their father's wine column. Many of them didn't really care about wine. Our most flattering letters, in fact, were from people who said they didn't drink at all but loved reading what we had to say. Our wine guidebook came out the same month. So during the day, John dealt with some of the great news issues of our time as Page One editor, working with and sometimes fighting with great reporters and editors to produce stories that would generate buzz and change the world. At lunchtime, he rushed out of the office to shop for wine. Dottie covered the nexus between race, power, and money, and wrote and rewrote columns about wine in between major interviews.

When we got home, we quickly put six or eight bottles into bags and conducted tastings. Those simple days when we tasted fifteen or twenty wines for each column were over. As our readership increased, we received more and more letters asking if we'd tried this wine or that wine in one of our tastings. We realized that the number of wines we tasted had to grow. We were now tasting about fifty for each column. Do the math. It's a weekly column, so we had to taste fifty wines every week. We never took a week off because we thought the column needed a consistent voice, week after week.

We did homework with the girls, got them to bed, made dinner, and conducted a tasting. Then John poured out the bottles, took detailed notes on the labels of the "losers" and soaked off the labels of the "winners." People all over the country now were rushing to wine shops to look for our recommendations. Our column was posted in stores everywhere. We never intended the index— the list of favorite wines in our blind tastings—to be a buying guide. In fact, we never even intended to have an index. Our intention was for people to use the index only as a kind of road map of tastes and prices. Our more important advice, as we always said, was to look for the kind of wine we recommended. Try a Gewürztraminer, a Malbec, or an inexpensive wine from Chile.

But our readers wanted specificity, so they tore out the index and headed to the wine shop. This was good news—at least it got them excited about wine—but it left some people frustrated because no good wine is made in very large quantities. Many people couldn't find the specific wines we recommended, and a surprising number of wine shop owners, instead of just saying that they didn't have the wine, told people that we must have been mistaken. We must have printed the wrong winery, the wrong vintage, the wrong vineyard, the wrong price. So we decided to save every label of every wine we recommended, both so we could double-check them ourselves and, if necessary, photocopy them for frustrated readers to show them that we were right.

We'd saved labels and taken notes for years, of course, but this was different. We were suddenly cataloguing hundreds of wines and taking off at least a dozen labels a week. Late into the night, and then on weekends, John stood by the sink, soaking some labels off, boiling off others. If they didn't budge, it was Dottie's turn with a sharp knife. Sometimes, when we were finished with that, we'd sit down and answer our mail. We answered every letter. It wasn't just a matter of being polite. The letters we received were so personal, so heartfelt, that it would have been unthinkable not to respond in kind.

The downside to all this is that we stopped drinking our own wine. Our collection in the costume-closet-turned-wine-cellar was up to about five hundred bottles, but we almost never had a free night to drink any of them. We marked wines that were getting old and needed to be drunk with a neck tag. More and more neck tags appeared. We knew some of the wines were going over the hill, but there was nothing we could do about it. We were tasting six to eight wines every night, and we had no time or capacity left for our own stuff.

More and more wine came to the office as "samples." They all went to charity (to a public school's annual auction). Wineries started calling to ask us to lunch or dinner, or to go on a foreign junket.

Then Martha Stewart called. We had heard of Martha, of course. We even bought her sheets at Kmart. The contractor who renovated our apartment used her paints on our walls. But we'd never seen her television show or read her magazine. We knew she was a smart businesswoman, and we'd heard she was really tough. One of her producers called us out of the blue and asked if we'd like to be on the show to talk about wine. This seemed like fun, and certainly good for the book, so we said we'd be happy to. The producer decided we'd do two segments, one on Thanksgiving wines and one on a blind tasting of Syrah, the rough, red grape of the Rhône Valley of France that was becoming hot among U.S. winemakers. The producer sent us scripts for both segments, and we studied them for days. We watched Martha's show. We endlessly debated what clothes would look best on television. Then a car came to take us to Connecticut. We practiced our lines in the backseat.

When we got to the studio, we were amazed how much everything looked just like you'd expect Martha Stewart's studio to look. Everything was in order and marked. The colors were cool and soothing. There wasn't a speck of dirt anywhere. The producer took us into the "kitchen" where our segment would be filmed, and it was so perfect and pristine that we felt out of place. Martha came by, looking just like herself, and told us how happy she was to meet us. Then we went into the greenroom and watched her tape some segments before ours. One thing became clear to us: The woman works hard. She had been taping all day and managing her staff, and her companies, at the same time. This was no prima donna.

We taped the blind tasting segment first. Martha's staff had bought three Syrahs from California, and we'd put them in paper bags so that we wouldn't know what we were tasting. When the segment started, Martha held up a copy of the *Journal* to the camera. "*The Wall Street Journal,* this bastion of financial reporting, is really renowned for that reporting, and news features. But did you know that one of its most popular columns is about wine?" She introduced us and said: "I was immediately guided by 'Tastings,' a new and very interesting approach." She called the column "fabulous" and said, "I was really enamored of your column from Day One."

Geez. This was really fun, and she was sweet. So much for what you read in the papers.

None of us followed one word of the script. Martha numbered the bags as we turned our backs and then we conducted a tasting. She was genuinely interested and had a very good palate, so we just talked. Maybe it made good TV, but it certainly made for a good time. Martha couldn't have been more charming. The winner of our tasting, we all agreed, was wine No. 1, which turned out to be a 1996 from Monterra, a winery in Monterey County. We told viewers that by conducting their own paper-bag blind tastings, they could prove to themselves that they could tell the difference between wines and discover what they like.

We filmed the Thanksgiving segment, too, and it was equally enjoyable. When we left, Martha gave us craft kits to take to Media and Zoë. We must have done okay, because they asked us to be on again soon. When the producer called next, she told us with some excitement: "The Rock is going to be taping the same day!" We had never heard of The Rock. Dottie did some research and discovered that he was a wrestler. The next time the car took us to Martha's studios, we entered the gate right after a very long limousine. As we watched in awe, the door opened and a massive man slowly unfolded from the car. We followed him in the door. "It's The Rock!" said the young women at the reception desk. We followed. "I'm The Pebble," John told them. They looked at him blankly. John and The Rock went into the bathroom to change. The Rock left his shoes behind. They were as big as Cadillacs. He filmed the segment before us. Martha's people thought it would be fun to have The Rock bake cookies with Martha. So there was this massive man standing next to Martha with a mixing spoon. When the cookies were finished, Martha poured two glasses of milk. The Rock said he couldn't drink that. "I'm lactose intolerant," he said.

TV appearances make people known in a way a newspaper never could. For New Year's, a producer at the *Today* show asked if we'd do a blind tasting with Katie Couric and Matt Lauer, and we said sure. We never watched *Today,* but Katie had lived in our building for a few months while her apartment on the East Side was being renovated. We told Matt there wouldn't be a Champagne shortage for the millennium celebration. We'd been saying that for a year, and we were ultimately proved correct. Then Matt called over Katie and Ann Curry and we conducted a blind tasting of three bubblies—Freixenet from Spain, which is always a great buy at about $8; Schramsberg from California, which cost about $25; and Pol Roger Cuvée Sir Winston Churchill, which had won our own tasting of very expensive Champagnes and cost about $100. When we took off the bags, it turned out that Matt liked the most expensive and Katie the cheapest, which gave everybody a good laugh. Matt lifted his arms in celebration of his good taste, and Dottie gave him a high-five.

We were on for six minutes and fifteen seconds at the end of the show. But between the *Today* appearance and Martha, it seemed that everyone in America had seen us. We had been prominent journalists for decades, but those appearances made us into personalities—minor personalities, to be exact, but personalities nonetheless. People actually recognized us. Dottie's mother called. "You high-fived Matt!" she exclaimed. People on the subway and on buses told us they loved our appearances with Martha Stewart. At a school function, a parent we'd known for years grabbed us. "I was just in South Korea on business," he said, "and I was wide awake at three in the morning. Everything was closed, so I just sat in bed going through all of the television channels. They were all in Korean. I was so relieved to finally hear some English, so I stopped flipping—and there you were, talking with Martha Stewart about wine. It was so bizarre I thought I was hallucinating." We also received the first letters we'd ever gotten that mentioned race. Three couples wrote to Dottie to say that they were also in interracial marriages, and they thought what we were doing was great.

The Internet boom was now in full swing. Internet companies were hot, whether they had profits or not. Everybody was going public. The *Journal* itself had started an online effort, wsj.com. The people at Dow Jones thought a wine Web site had potential to make a lot of money. Maybe it could even be part of an Internet spin-off at some point, and we'd all be rich. Not only that, but a company that sold wine over the Internet, flush with cash from venture capitalists, was eager to make a deal with us for sponsorship of the site. The *Journal* wanted us to start a Web site, and to keep it fresh every day.

It was clear that something had to give. We couldn't keep doing our old jobs and our new jobs at the same time. The Web site was pretty much the last straw. Not only that, but our lives were getting increasingly weird, especially Dottie's.

Dottie: *Once I was at a conference on race, and a black woman ran up to me. "I passed the paper-bag test!" she said. I was aghast. I must have looked at her with utter bewilderment. When I was a kid, there was a national black organization that had a pernicious reputation for admitting only light-skinned black people. Some of my friends belonged, but we didn't. To be light enough to join, it was said, black people had to pass the paper-bag test. If they were as light as a brown paper bag, they were acceptable. I'd just spent an entire day immersed in race and there was this lovely black woman standing before me announcing that she'd passed the paper-bag test. I couldn't help it. I just stared at her, speechless. Finally, she looked at me and said, "The paper-bag test. On Martha Stewart. I did my own blind tasting and discovered what I like myself." It was a truly disorienting moment.*

We talked and talked and talked about what to do. Should we give up our real jobs?

We've always been journalists covering serious issues. It was, in many ways, who we are.

But this wine thing is new and fun, and potentially lucrative.

Our real jobs are core to the paper, and therefore secure. Who knows how long the wine gig will last?

But our bosses really do love the column. It's attracting new readers—especially women—who haven't read the paper before. It's attracting non-white male readers, and the paper needs that, too. In any case, if we do the wine column full-time, we would be in a far more entrepreneurial situation, and it's a good time for entrepreneurs.

What does that mean, "entrepreneurial situation"?

But people like us, they really like us, as wine columnists. All we got from readers in our real jobs was grief.

Look, let's get to the bottom line. Would Paul Steiger really be willing to pay us what we already earn just to write a wine column?

We went back and forth. We even sat down with a big piece of paper and wrote down the pluses and minuses of each job. We finally decided. John had been Page One editor for seven years, long enough to be declared legally dead. Dottie had covered race her whole life, and it had grown increasingly difficult. The lines were drawn on race, and everyone in every camp seemed happy just to keep repeating the same tired arguments over and over again. We couldn't do both jobs anymore. We had to make a choice, and we were ready for a change. Nervously, we went to see Paul Steiger.

Paul knew that our column was good for the paper. We were giving a very different, personal face to the *Journal*. Our TV appearances were worth a fortune in advertising. Our column was a fundamental building block of the Weekend section, for which he'd stuck his neck out so far. He didn't say any of this. He just said, "Sure." He said he thought it was a great idea. We could extend the franchise. It would be good for the paper, and for us. To Dottie, who was particularly anguished about her decision, he said that it wasn't a bad thing to have a black woman writing about the good life for the paper.

We set our last day of our real jobs for April 10. That was the day the Pulitzer Prizes were announced. It would be nice if the *Journal* won one more while John was Page One editor.

The *Journal* won the Pulitzer Prize for national reporting, its fourth national Pulitzer in six years, for a Page One series on military spending. John's tenure as Page One editor had coincided almost precisely with the beginning and end of the greatest economic expansion and stock market boom in American history. Later that day, John cleaned out his desk and moved upstairs. Dottie left a message on her voice mail that anyone calling about urban affairs should dial a different number. On that day, we became full-time wine columnists.

Collery Brut Champagne

. . .

*O*UR WEB SITE, WHICH WAS PRODUCED BY THE PEOPLE AT wsj.com, appeared in early July. To celebrate the launch, we conducted a tasting of sparkling wines to see what we could get for under $20 a bottle. On the dusty bottom shelf of a New York wine store, we found a Champagne called Collery, which we had never seen before. It reminded us of all of those small Champagne houses we'd seen so many years before in France, and it was delicious, a perfect start to a whole new enterprise. The Web site was a huge amount of additional work, but it allowed us even more intimate discussion with readers. People could ask us immediate questions—what wine to have with dinner tonight—and, because they were largely anonymous, questions that they'd considered too "stupid" to ask anyone else. We even got a question from a man in the upper reaches of *New York Times* management, who we figured must have been too embarrassed to ask Frank Prial. We got e-mails every day from people who just wanted to thank us for our column and for introducing them to new and different wines. And that's not all. We got notes like this, from Reverend Steven D. Crabtree, then of the Dille Parish, United Church of Christ, in LeRaysville, Pennsylvania:

> *I enjoy your "Tastings" column in the Weekend Journal, and have recently used it religiously . . . Having spent a few too many sermons in a heavy and lugubrious mode, I was looking for something "light," not unlike the tone and uplift I frequently receive after reading your column. Indeed, I have noticed that I don't need to drink a glass of wine at all, I can just imagine it—in a different setting from my Friday evening porch, with the cares of the world pressing on me, squeezing my poor brain, the unwritten sermon fast approaching. "Tastings" is a kind of travel literature, a moment of escape. Perhaps the congregation might like a similar serving themselves, I thought, suddenly. Why can't sermons be more like this wine column?*
>
> *So I just copied a few paragraphs, kept up your spritzy tone, and preached a well-received morning message to my isolated rural parish in northeastern Pennsylvania. "Fun, but not without substance," someone said at the door. I resolved then that my sermons, like any joyful life, could do with a little more variety, and zest, and straight-ahead punch.*

And this, from Claudia Walker, of Mayo, Florida:

> *A couple of weeks ago I wrote to you saying that I wanted an inexpensive wine that was not dry or bitter. You suggested that I try a Riesling.*
>
> *Three years ago I gave my brother a kidney and since then I have not been able to drink red wines, which I adore, because it*

bothers my one remaining kidney. My doctor suggested I try white
if I was going to drink it.

I have no idea how much money I have spent on bottles of
wine where I only had a sip or two. Then I came across the two of
you. Thank you!

I could only find one Riesling where I am. It was very inex-
pensive and very good. I can only imagine how much better an-
other one could be if I happen to find one.

Thank you so much for bringing back the enjoyment of wine
drinking for me. I was about to give up on it.

The Web site was a victim of the dot-com shakeout in early
2001, but it'll be back and, in any case, it was fun while it lasted.
Readers now are accustomed to communicating with us. In the
first three years of the column, we received more than ten thousand letters and e-mails, giving us a unique insight into the questions and concerns that regular people have about wine.

So much of wine, to us, is about history and memories, and
that was brought home to us so dramatically, and so horribly, when
the World Trade Center was destroyed by terrorists on September 11, 2001. We had taken the girls to Windows on the World for
the first time just two weeks earlier, and we'd seen the most magnificent rainbow. Now it was no more. When we wrote a column
reminiscing about our times at Windows and said that "to us, it was
a symbol of everything beautiful and civilized," we received hundreds of notes in response from people all over the world who had
dined there, often only once. One woman wrote of the column: "It
brought life to a building I thought was gone forever." Seventy-six
people who worked at Windows died that day, along with dozens
of businesspeople having breakfast there. Two floors below, our
old wine-drinking buddy Cathy Chirls, so excited about her new
job in the towers, died too. She left behind our friend David and

three young children. We mentioned Cathy's death in that column, and a man wrote to say he was once at a bring-your-own-bottle school function when Cathy suddenly pulled up a chair next to him. "I was going to join them," she told him, motioning to another table, "but I saw what they were drinking, and your Silver Oak Cabernet made me decide that we should get to know each other better." That was Cathy, all right. We loved her, and we will miss her forever, but we have the memories of drinking wine with her, of celebrating life together, and of our friendship, and we'll never lose those.

We always say that if we thought we knew everything about wine, we'd find another hobby, and indeed we have learned a great deal since we started writing about it. We know far more about Malbec from Argentina (the peppery red wine), Pinotage from South Africa (the very distinctive red unique to that country), and Tokaji from Hungary (the great dessert wine that tastes like an orange soufflé) than we could ever have imagined. We know what wine goes best with smoked turkey (a creamy California Pinot Noir). We've even tasted all five great "first growths" against each other every year, which is something we never could afford on our own nickel.

We've tasted more wines in three days as judges at the Los Angeles County Fair—about 250—than we used to try in a year. And we've gone places we'd never been before. The *Journal* invited a bunch of big advertisers to an event in Frankfurt and asked us to conduct a wine tasting. We flew over a couple of days early—to the girls' dismay—to visit the Rhine River and taste some of the wines of the Rheingau region. To actually see the Rhine itself, the source of so much wine history, was thrilling to us. It was like old times. We dropped in unannounced on winemakers, who had no idea who we were, and were greeted warmly everywhere, though we don't speak a word of German. We visited the home of Steinberger, the first fine German wine we ever had, and felt we'd closed a loop in our wine lives.

But the most important things we've learned have little to do with wine. We've learned, above all, that there is still a lot of romance in the world. It didn't take long for readers to understand that our column was less about wine than about loving life and each other, and they responded in kind. So many of the letters we receive are from all kinds of couples who want to share their own stories with us. A couple named Elizabeth and Tom Coulon of Denver read one of our columns about the great white wines of the Loire Valley of France, dropped everything, and visited there. The Coulons are both in their sixties. We finally met them months later, and we've rarely met a couple whose eyes sparkle more brightly at the sight of each other.

At the same time, we've learned that too many people are missing out on the romance wine evokes by just a whisper, and don't even know it. People read our columns and think we're great cooks with lush, trouble-free lives, which is far from the truth. In a column once, we mentioned that we drank a wine with Dottie's mushroom chicken. Several readers wrote to say that it sounded delicious and to ask for the recipe. Dottie wrote them all back to say, Gee, it's just plain skillet-browned chicken smothered in Campbell's mushroom soup, pretty much the same dish we all grew up with. "I use Campbell's mushroom soup in my recipe too," one of the readers told her. "But when I read about your dish it just sounded so special." And maybe it was—not because of the recipe, but because of the wine, and not because the wine tasted good or was a perfect match with the chicken. Wine itself adds a certain elegance, even when accompanied by Campbell's mushroom soup. But, more than that, wine at dinner makes us slow down, and when we slow down, we really talk and listen to each other and we really look at each other, and in that way we get reconnected to the things that we love about each other. And having reached this sweet spot, wine encourages us to linger there, to sip this sweet life, instead of gulping it. Too much of our lives rushes by us. Too few people take the time to savor it, but there's a beautiful sunset somewhere every day, a shorter-than-expected commute, a bonus, a clean bill of health, a triumph of some sort that only you can appreciate. And there's your mate, the enduring love of your life. Maybe we drink wine because we're romantic. Maybe we're romantic because we drink wine.

Unfortunately, though, we've learned that people are even more intimidated by the subject than we had thought. Wall Street players will bet a million dollars on a technology stock but won't take a chance on a $20 bottle of wine. Too many people want to be told what wine they will like, and that's never going to be possible. We tell people what wines we like and why we like them, but tastes are very personal and each bottle is different. The only way to learn anything worth knowing about wine is to drink it.

An irritated wine shop owner once called us because a woman had come into his shop with our index from a column about Barolo, the great red from the Piedmont region of Italy. All Barolo is made in small quantities, and we'd said that in the column. The wine shop didn't have any of our specific recommendations, so she had left. The wine shop owner wanted to know why we'd recommend a wine people couldn't find. We told him that we had urged readers to pick up just any Barolo they came across. We couldn't believe he let her get out of his store without encouraging her to buy one. At least we had gotten her in there. That woman could have had a transcendent experience that night.

People don't always trust wine merchants and they don't trust themselves. They trust us—which is great except that our advice has to be general. We can get you to the ballpark, but you have to find your own seat. Our experience with the Collery Champagne was a good example. We wrote a column about the Collery only to make the point that there are great bargains in Champagne out there on obscure labels. We told readers that any wine from France that says it's "Champagne" has to be real Champagne, under French law, and that means if you see a Champagne for under $20, it could be a steal, as the Collery was. Too many people, though, were determined to find that Collery, surely leaving on the shelves many equally good, unknown Champagnes.

We've learned that Americans are far too California-centric when it comes to wine. It's ironic; just thirty years after Americans were so impressed with foreign labels that American wines were called Chianti or Burgundy or Chablis, it's difficult to get Americans to try real Chianti or Burgundy or Chablis. Maybe it's because California wines taste familiar or the names are pronounceable or the marketing is strong. We've had more than a few readers tell us that we should write only about California wines, because it's all they want to drink. This is unfortunate, not just because it makes the wine world smaller but because most of the great bargains of the world right now are coming from outside the United States.

We've learned that people are as fascinated with the rigmarole surrounding wine as they are with wine itself—maybe more so. We get good response when we write about a kind of wine, but huge response when we write about an issue surrounding wine. We once wrote a column that raised the question: What do you do with the cork when the waiter hands it to you? Our answer: whatever you want. We said there wasn't really any reason to smell the cork, since the wine itself is right in front of you to sniff, but that we smell it because we like the way it smells. Corks sometimes smell like wineries to us, and they take us back to Napa and Tuscany and Piedmont and Burgundy. We received three hundred letters and e-mails in response. Half of them were outraged that we said it doesn't matter, since smell is the most important part of taste. The other half were outraged that we said we smell the cork, since everyone knows the smell of the cork is irrelevant.

Steve Estep of Atlanta wrote: "I long ago gave up sniffing as useless and pretentious, so my ex-girlfriend and I found a fun way to celebrate the awkward moment when the cork is delivered to you like a new infant. Whoever selected the wine gets the cork, and the other person makes a football goal with their hands, thumb tips pointed together, index fingers up (pro), or, for the less skillful, index fingertips together, thumbs pointed up (college). Hold cork gently between thumb and forefinger and flick with middle finger of other hand for field goal attempt. Boy, I almost miss that girl."

When we noted, in three paragraphs, that we'd gone to Charlie Trotter's famous restaurant in Chicago and were surprised that the sommelier tasted our wine before pouring it, we received a ton of angry mail. Half said we were clearly ignorant, because all good restaurants do this. The other half said it was outrageous to have a sommelier help himself to our wine. "I don't think that is any more appropriate than the chef coming out and taking a cut of my steak and tasting it in front of me before the waiter hands me the plate," wrote Dan Murphy, an attorney in San Diego.

When we wrote about the angst of ordering wine in a business setting, business people from all over the United States wrote to us with their own advice, and their own stories of embarrassments. This is how the follow-up story began: "Jim Bahleda, a salesman from Grand Island, N.Y., was trying to be very grown up and very impressive the first time he was in charge of ordering the wine. The waiter opened the bottle, poured a small taste into Mr. Bahleda's glass and then stood by. Finally, Mr. Bahleda turned to the waiter and said, 'I'll be drinking a lot more than *that.*' "

We've learned that there are some real wine jerks out there, people who believe that wine is a drink for the elite and that general consumption cheapens it. There really aren't nearly as many, however, as it seems. It's just that one wine jerk in a room filled with people who are nervous about wine is enough to chill the whole room. We've seen it. Most people are genuinely excited about wine and eager to know more. Given the chance, they will express their curiosity and willingness to learn. One wine jerk is enough to quiet all of them.

We've learned that real wine people—winemakers and people in the business—are just as nice, on the whole, as we always thought. We still don't accept samples or meet privately with winemakers when they visit New York—which they seem to do all the time—and we don't go to any events that aren't open to the public. But we have talked to more people in the business than ever before, because we spend a great deal of time looking for column ideas, interviewing people, and checking our facts. Give them just half a chance and they'll never stop talking about their passion.

We have learned, even more than we knew before, how wine is all about history. When we wrote a column about a great Zinfandel we'd tasted from Ravenswood Winery, one of California's best Zinfandel producers, we mentioned that the grapes were from the Dickerson Vineyard. That brought a letter from Bill Dickerson, who said, basically, If you like what Ravenswood does with my grapes, you should taste what *I* do with my grapes. A while later, we dropped in on the wine class given by Kevin Zraly, whom we met so many years earlier at Cellar in the Sky and who now has become famous as the author of *The Windows on the World Complete Wine Course*. While we were at his class, one of his students told us that we just had to try a restaurant near his home in Westchester County called Crabtree's Kittle House. It has a great wine list, he said.

So we went to Crabtree's Kittle House and there on the list, to our surprise and delight, was one of Mr. Dickerson's wines, a 1989 Ruby Cabernet for just $25. Remember the 1974 Sonoma Vineyards Ruby Cabernet that said on the back that Ruby Cabernet was "an emerging wine that is creating more interest each year"? It never happened. In fact, Bill Dickerson's Ruby Cabernet vineyard is the last in Napa Valley.

The sommelier, to his credit, tried to warn us away from the wine, but we ordered it anyway. We loved it, and we called Dr. Dickerson—it turns out he's a psychiatrist—to tell him so. We also invited him to an event that the *Journal*'s advertising department was putting together in Napa Valley: "Vintners' Open That Bottle Night." Their idea was that even winemakers have that one special bottle they never open and that it would be fun—and good for making advertising contacts—to invite them to dinner. It was held at Greystone in Napa Valley, now the home of the Culinary Institute of America but formerly the home of Christian Brothers Winery. This is where the 1974 Cabernet Sauvignon was made that was the very first entry in our Cellar Key, the wine we drank with John's first brisket in Grandma Helen's pot.

Louis Martini's daughter was there with a bottle of wine that her dad had laid down for her from her birth year. Jamie Davies was there with a special bottle of Schramsberg. Gina Gallo was there with a bottle of the last wine she made with her grandfather Julio. Some readers were there, too, including Carol Jung from Syracuse, our first fan. We both spoke to start off the evening. When John said, "We don't believe wine should be saved for special occasions any more than romance should be saved for special occasions," the whole room broke into applause. Dr. Dickerson brought a very special wine: a bottle of Italian Swiss Colony Zinfandel from 1917—before Prohibition, before Merlot, before Chardonnay, before wine got scary. It was remarkably vibrant and good. So much history—and all about wine.

We have learned, sadly, that wine is still far from becoming an everyday pleasure in the United States, and it may never be. There is too much angst about wine. It still seems like a snobbish pleasure to many people. There are also too many crazy state and local laws. We can't even buy wine at a supermarket in New York State. What kind of message does that send about serving wine with food? Per capita wine consumption is far below its 1986 peak. The United States is now thirty-fourth in the world in per capita consumption, just behind Slovakia and just ahead of Latvia.

Many of us hoped that White Zinfandel would be a kind of entry point for wine drinkers. People might find that they really liked wine and then try, say, Chardonnay, and then maybe Merlot and so on. All evidence, however, points to White Zinfandel drinkers moving away from wine rather than closer to it. The hottest wine at the beginning of the new millennium wasn't wine at all but low-alcohol, fruit-flavored "wine products," such as Canandaigua's Arbor Mist, with names like "Blackberry Merlot." As one official said, tellingly, in the company's annual report: "We identified a potentially large group of drinkers who aspired to the sophistication of varietal wines, but really didn't like the taste."

But ultimately, the greatest lesson we've learned happened on a basketball court.

By the time Zoë was ten, she was fascinated with sports. Her favorite sport is basketball, and she dreamed of watching the New York Knicks play in Madison Square Garden. We figure she gets her prowess from Dottie's mom, who was captain of her basketball team in college. When John, the ever-indulgent dad, called the Garden to order tickets, the woman on the phone laughed at him. You can't just buy tickets, she said. The games are sold out for years. So John asked how to get tickets. "A scalper," she said. We had never bought tickets from scalpers. We're the kind of suckers who would get taken. We'd show up at the gate and hand the tickets to the ticket-taker, who would take a look at them and say, "Hey, George! Look at this! They thought these were real tickets! Can you believe it?" But Zoë was desperate to go to a game, so John found a scalper's Web site that looked honest and ordered four tickets to a game. We could only get them because the Knicks were playing the woeful Washington Wizards, but even so, the tickets were so expensive that John still hasn't told Dottie how much they cost.

The game started at eight o'clock, but Zoë eagerly wanted to get to the Garden early in the afternoon. We compromised on six-thirty. Our seats were at midcourt, about halfway up. A few minutes after we sat down, a man named Doug, ID tags hanging around his neck, walked up to our seats. "Would you girls like to take part in a contest at halftime?" he asked. Media and Zoë, accustomed to bargaining with us, asked about the game and expressed concerns that it was childish. A bunch of kids would take their shoes off at one end of the court, then run to get them, put them on, and then try to make a basket. We told the girls to do it, that being on the court of Madison Square Garden would be exciting all by itself. They continued to haggle. Doug compromised. He asked if they'd take part in the slam-dunk contest. They asked for details and finally agreed. Doug decided that Media was too tall for the lowered basket, and she wasn't really that excited about the prospect anyway. He said he'd be back right before halftime to pick up Zoë.

He returned with about two minutes left in the first half. John went with Zoë while Dottie remained with Media. John and Zoë had to go to the other side of the Garden, so they walked all the way around, past security guards and lower and lower, toward the expensive seats where people like Spike Lee sit. When they got to the runway where the players and the cheerleaders came off the court, Doug explained the rules and Zoë met her competition, two boys, ages eleven and twelve, older and taller.

At halftime, the Garden people dragged a kid-size basket to midcourt. The three contestants each took a practice shot, right there on the floor of Madison Square Garden, while the people in the stands got up to stretch their legs or get a beer. All three of the kids dribbled to the basket and put the ball in nicely. There was a smattering of polite applause.

Now there was one shot each, for victory and a $250 gift certificate to Target. The first boy ran the ball to the basket—he didn't dribble—and stuffed it right in from the front. The second dribbled and dunked the ball hard, but hit the rim. The ball bounced way up, and away.

Then it was Zoë's turn. She started slowly, and began to dribble cross-handed. She dribbled once with her right hand, then her left. The crowd began to watch. She picked up speed, her perfect little Dottie face radiant and her braids dancing in the air. Then she seemed to lose her way. She was far to the right of the basket. She went slightly past the basket on the right. It was so sad—this cute little girl was going to miss the basket altogether—that people in the stands stopped to watch, as if they were watching car crash. What they didn't know was that Zoë is left-handed. Just as she passed the basket, far to the right, she leapt up, turned her body, flew in the air, and stuffed the ball in.

The crowd went wild. A few seconds later, when the judges declared Zoë the winner, she raised her left hand and waved. The crowd began to chant: "Zooooë, Zooooë, Zooooë." Dottie and Media hugged each other in the stands and jumped up and down, pumping their arms and screaming. John and Zoë had to come back the way they had gone, walking the entire half-circle of Madison Square Garden. Everywhere they went, people shouted, "Look, it's Zoë!" and put up their hands for a high-five.

We have had great wines in our lives, and great experiences because of great wines. We hope to have many great wines in the future, and many more great wine experiences. But we will never have a wine that matches what happened at the Garden that night. And that is the important thing: It's just wine. It's not life. It's just a wonderful part of everyday life. Relax and enjoy it.

ACKNOWLEDGMENTS

We owe life debts to many people. You've just met many of them. For help on this book, we're also deeply grateful to our assistant, Shallé McDonald, who aided us at every turn, and to a whole phalanx of doctors who have patched us together so we could complete it, including John Postley, Michael Lavyne, Gary Willner, and Andrew Weiland.

The book is the product of the vision of three extraordinary women. Pamela Cannon, our editor at Random House, challenged us with her ideas, energized us with her enthusiasm, and improved our work throughout. Ann Godoff, editor in chief of Random House, offered rock-solid support from the moment of conception, even when that required pure faith. And Amanda Urban, our agent at ICM—well, Binky is a force of nature that we feel very lucky to have been swept into. They made this book a joy to write.